don't say anything, ever

arthur lugauskas

copyright © 2013 by artūras lugauskas

all rights reserved.

isbn: 1494314681
isbn-13: 978-1494314682

finally on october 9th, 2013 i said it to myself: "don't say anything, ever." i kept repeating that phrase as i drove home. that was all i thought about for hours. that was how i truly felt. the emotions i had were real. my performance almost came to an end. i almost broke down and let go of my character. my strength was tested. my feelings were hurt. then i thought, "how did i get to this point?"

contents

chapter 0 : (pretext)

chapter 1 : (japan plans) 1
chapter 2 : (controversial vma moment) 5
chapter 3 : (japan plans change) 9

chapter 4 : (the nova warm up) 17
chapter 5 : (two year performance) 31

chapter 6 : (disclaimer) 43

chapter 7 : (spring 2012 gmu semester) 49
chapter 8 : (new majors colloquium professor) 55
chapter 9 : (aesthetics professor) 63
chapter 10 : (drawing two professor) 79
chapter 11 : (sculpture one professor) 93
chapter 12 : (sound and vision professor) 99
chapter 13 : (visual voices professor) 107
chapter 14 : (honors seminar professor) 113
chapter 15 : (extras from 1st) 119

chapter 16 : (summertime practice) 133

chapter 17 : (fall 2012 gmu semester) 137
chapter 18 : (art now professor) 139
chapter 19 : (advanced composition english professor) 143
chapter 20 : (fundamentals studio lighting professor) 147
chapter 21 : (sculpture three professor) 159
chapter 22 : (visual voices professor again) 171
chapter 23 : (honors seminar professor again) 177
chapter 24 : (extras from 2nd) 181

chapter 25 : (wintertime warm) 191

chapter 26 : (spring 2013 gmu semester) 201
chapter 27 : (critical theory in the visual arts professor) 205
chapter 28 : (writing for artists professor) 211
chapter 29 : (sculpture four professor) 217
chapter 30 : (sociology professor) 225
chapter 31 : (african dance class professor) 231
chapter 32 : (visual voices professor) 237
chapter 33 : (honors seminar professor) 239
chapter 34 : (extras from 3rd) 241

chapter 35 : (coldest summer) 249

chapter 36 : (fall 2013 gmu semester) 259
chapter 37 : (under the blade) 263
chapter 38 : (stop talking forever) 275
chapter 39 : (unwanted) 285
chapter 40 : (egomaniac) 291
chapter 41 : (calling out bom) 295
chapter 42 : (sounds like a poem) 307
chapter 43 : (point of anything) 311
chapter 44 : (texting truth with finlay) 315
chapter 45 : (no thank you akuna) 323
chapter 46 : (frustration) 329
chapter 47 : (almost dropped out) 335
chapter 48 : (first ever piop art wall) 341
chapter 49 : (calculated) 347
chapter 50 : (undercover genius) 351
chapter 51 : (extras from 4th) 353

chapter 52 : (drop the character) 359
chapter 53 : (stream of consciousness) 365
chapter 54 : (important chapter) 391

take a moment to enjoy these blank pages

and then take a deep breath before you go into my world

::: : ::: ::: : :: :: .... . :: . . .. :: ....
chapter 1 : japan plans
::: :: :: ... :: ..: ... :.:: :::.:: :::.:: :: :: .... ::: ::: ::::::   :::

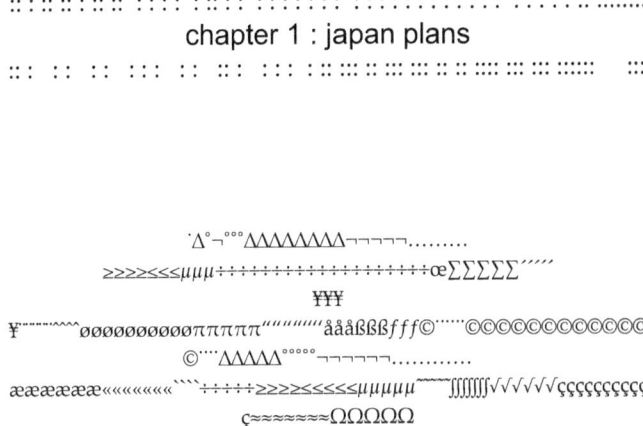

    in 2009, after i finished studying architecture at nova community college for the past two years, i had a debate in my head: either return to nova and get more transferrable credits before a transfer to a university called gmu, or go straight to gmu to study art, or just go to japan. and by just go i mean just go. nothing more to it than buying a plane ticket, going to the airport, flying overseas, arriving to japan, and then questioning, "now what?" and it's not like i was rich or anything. i was thinking of just arriving with around $500 and surviving somehow. and note, i did have a project i wanted to do *if* i went. and that project was write a book. because i like writing and documenting my experiences.

    soon the fall 2009 gmu semester started and i still wasn't enrolled at the university. okay, that option became eliminated. and note, i was already writing during this time period of what was going on in my world. well, then next thing i knew, the fall 2009 nova semester started and i wasn't enrolled. that meant i had one option left from my three options. did i have the balls to just buy a ticket and go? i had around $1,500 saved up during that time. it was from work i did in the summertime and early autumn. it was now towards the end of 2009's october. and i started to check online for tickets to japan for some reason. i mean i know i thought about going, but was i serious about it? nobody really thought i was. i didn't know myself if i was. but, somehow there i was checking for tickets, but not buying.

    then november came along. and this is what i wrote on november 11, 2009 at 4:41pm:

"so, i'm actually in the process of purchasing my ticket to japan! it's kind of 'scary' in a way ... the total is turning out to be $982.35 (1 adult $709.00, taxes and fees $233.40, travel protection plan $39.95). okay, just finished putting in the debit card information and billing address. now time to click the button that says 'complete reservation.' it's now 4:45pm and now it's 4:46pm and here goes ... just clicked it ... wow, i'm about to go to japan!"

my departure date was for november 18, 2009. i was ready to experience a new culture, see what happens, and write about the ups and downs to come.

don't say anything, ever

arthur lugauskas

don't say anything, ever

chapter 2 : controversial vma moment

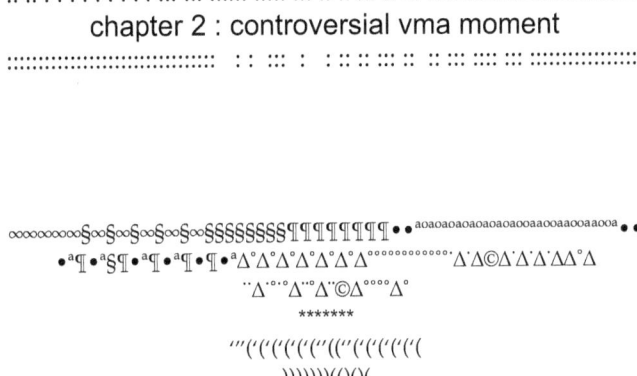

now in japan i reflected on the last months i spent in america. much had happened. from good times with friends, to playing more and more poker, to almost developing a new relationship with a new girl, to this controversial vma moment that happened on september 13, 2009. it was the most talked about thing and i was curious about it. i tried to ignore it, but i wanted to figure it out for some reason. i wanted to know the whys and reasonings in regards to what happened. why did people react the way they did?

the moment i'm talking about is the kanye and taylor moment. why did he do what he did? what were the thoughts in his head before he went on stage? why did almost everyone react so harshly against him? these were all questions i didn't know the answers to upon first inspection. but, one thing about me was that i didn't automatically hate the man. i wanted to understand. i was maybe one of the few. how do i put this, kanye basically became the most hated person on the earth during that period in time. and people wanted him to die. what!? die!? for an award show!? and what did he *actually* do!? give it some thought if you know what i'm talking about. he literally said "i'm really happy for you" to taylor! and yes, then he said, "beyonce had one of the best videos of all time." but note, he didn't say that taylor had a bad video or that she was a bad artist or that he didn't like her for that matter. now, i'm not saying what he said was necessarily the right thing to say. i'm not saying his timing could have been better. but, i'm also not saying what he said was necessarily the wrong thing to say during that exact time. honestly, i didn't know. but, i did think that what he did didn't deserve to generate an overload of hate from almost everyone for years to come and i didn't think people should want him to die because of that one moment that happened in the public eye. i kept thinking about this moment and analyzing the situation from a point of view of trying to understand different perspectives. my conclusion in regards to kanye was that he basically spoke his honest opinion from his heart. my conclusion in regards to taylor was that i'm not sure what she should have done at that moment. i don't know what i would have done if i was kanye or taylor during that time. one thing i do know is that i'm not kanye. another thing i do know is that i'm not taylor. but, it's so crazy how something that might be so small in some ways can be so overwhelmingly big in other ways. like the actions and the words were so quick and simple, but the thoughts and peoples new points of view and explosions in peoples minds were so huge and crazy. and then i understood this controversial vma scenario as kanye saying something you're "not supposed to say" out loud in the public to an audience. but, according to who? society? traditional thinking? or who? he chose to be an individual. he put himself under the blade and the repercussions were what they were. i became really curious about all this and decided to do something i never thought i'd do.

arthur lugauskas

don't say anything, ever

chapter 3 : japan plans change

$$%%$%$%%$$$$$$$###############
'&'&&'&'&'''&'&'&'
)))))0000000000000%%%%%%%%%%%%%%%%%%%%%%%%
%00000000000000000000000000000000(((((((~~~~
|~|~~|~|~~|~|~~|~|||~|||~~~~|~|~
~~~~~
0==0

my brain activity was going 100mph. what do i do? i have all these ideas! i want to know this! i want to know that! i'm in japan! i have plans! and the biggest plan is that i have no particular plan! how could i be more creative!? that's what i care about - creativity! what's my life about? what do i do with it? where do i go now? i'm purposely doing things i want! no one told me to go to japan! i just went! it was my decision! i wanted to go! and who else would do such a thing like just go?! i'm sure a lot of people would, but do they actually go through with what they say they would do? some do. some don't.

    so, in japan i was busy writing and experiencing this place i've never been to before. i was also busy skateboarding, walking, interacting, getting a job basically talking to people in english and having conversations with them, going on dates with girls i was interested in, quickly learning about deception first hand (for instance, i met this one girl, we went out and about, we got to know each other, then she told me that she's married to an architect, but since he was out of town she felt too lonely being home alone, so she liked to go out and try to get her way with guys, etc.), developing as a person, struggling (my most memorable meals were eating bread with a topping for breakfast, lunch, and dinner most of the time), surviving somehow, living super simple, building friendships, going to acting auditions, having different meetings, testing my strength, growing creatively, and so much more.

    with all this noise in my head, there was one noise that was too loud and made me come up with something that i didn't know if i was ever going to achieve. there was a plan developing in my head, secretly, without even myself (the owner of my own brain) really understanding what it was or its existence for that matter. so, i was thinking back to that vma moment and if all kanye did was be honest out loud, then what if i try to do something like that? if all kanye did was speak his opinion and put his life and career on the line in the process, why don't i do something like that? how do i understand how he felt and what made him do what he did? i guess i have to live with speaking absolute truth out loud. i have to be doing what's real from my heart. and without being afraid of people hating me for speaking *my* opinion.

growing up i was a happy, humble, and shy kid. when i'd make friends i'd be outgoing with them. i enjoyed playing and being active. i had dreams. i wanted to do things. my travels during my younger years made me be different from other kids in school. there was a certain individuality that came out of me anywhere i went. i always did well in school. usually i was quite, though. i did what i was told to do when it came to assignments. i did my homework on time. basically i was a good kid. i never wanted anything wrong or bad for anyone. but, there was something more. i wanted a lot. but, i never asked for too much. i appreciated a simple toy or just a basketball to play with. i was never demanding or requiring luxury. i was happy just being alive. no worries in the world. time with family, playing with friends, and having fun; that was life. but, in my head, as i got older and older, i started dreaming bigger and bigger. i was believing in my dreams and what i wanted to do. as i kid i did anything because i was allowed to do and be anything. as long as i did good at school, my mom supported my other endeavors and activities. once in high school i started questioning why i wasn't "allowed" to be a "professional" in five or eight fields instead of just one. because of my travels and going to different schools in north america, europe, and south america i never had childhood friends that i grew old with at school and went to college with. i would make friends in these different cultures i was living in and then move again and again. and i was dealing with having to learn and study in three different languages. north america was one language, europe was another, and south america was another. i think all these experiences helped me be a full blown individual. an individual that doesn't want to follow. an individual who questions what traditional or contemporary society believes one should and should not do. though i never overly vividly showed my individuality, it was in me. i didn't know how strong it was until high school. i questioned colleges and how people are expected to live their life according to society. my biggest strength was creativity. that comes with individuality. and i was a curious kid. very curious. i wanted to know what was going on. i wanted to know the this and thats. and i liked excitement and spontaneity. but, i'm a juxtaposition because my liking of structure was a prominent feature in me also. it's thanks to my biological parents. one was all about school, following the rules, and structure. the other was all about not school, taking chances, and seeing what happens. and then you have me, a combination of the two. wow, right? how do i survive? there was a constant balancing act with my genes. it's been interesting living. life is interesting. where am i going with all of this? well, let me tell you. so, in high school i'm questioning this concept of going to college and thinking about life. i almost knew how my life would be if i went to college. like, i could do school, get my degree, get a job, live life in one place, get a girlfriend and kids, and that's my life, right? go on vacations sometimes and get older. beautiful, right? at one point i was on track with that, you know, i got a girlfriend, things went good for a year, but, then she didn't want me anymore, i got busy crying, then my other genes kicked in, and my life course changed, and blah, blah, blah. where am i going with this? okay, what i'm trying to say is that even though i was shy and quite and humble and nice, i did have big dreams and desires to do things maybe no one has done before. i didn't speak up about all that too much. sometimes i'd mention what i want to friends, but often times i'd forget about the other twelve things i wanted to do in addition to the seven things i just stated. yeah, ideas on ideas, and professions on professions. i thought i could do it all. why not, right? when you're 4 or 5 years old you could be anything and many things every day, right? why can't i do that as an adult? well, you know what, i can if i want to. from a pretty young age i believed anything was possible. even what people thought was impossible i believed was possible. so, me wanting to be whatever i wanted to be i thought was completely possible. i just had a hard time telling everyone exactly what i wanted to do out loud. maybe i was embarrassed, shy, or scared at the responses i'd get from what i say. i don't know. i kept a lot to myself and kind of just put forth some things i wanted to do. like when it came to school, if i had to choose a major, well, i was interested in architecture and/or art. but, i've had a big problem with the concept of school because it's so limiting in what one could become. as a child you could be anything, remember? but, when it comes to school, there is this list, right? this list of majors in regards to what you could choose to be. and the list is limited! there are only, what, one hundred, one thousand, three thousand fifty nine majors you could choose from? or whatever that number is for different colleges or universities. when you were a kid, there was limitless and infinite options. now, why do you have to be limited eighteen years or so later? i know you don't have to be limited if you don't want to, but school is structured around limitation. and i understand the reasonings could be "it's a business" or "you have to narrow down the options for kids" or whatever. but, i question why isn't there a degree in imagination? or is there and i just don't know about it? why isn't there a degree in creativity? maybe there is. is there? i don't know. i haven't seen those exact words as degrees. yeah, you could say imagination and creativity can fall into, i don't know, psychology and this or that. but, no, what about solely being an expert in that field and doing the most creative things possible? no, that's not emphasized! people don't like change like that. people only like change in theory, not in practice. okay, i know i'm going off on these tangents, but, okay, so, what i'm saying, for like the third time or so, is that after my two years of architecture studies i decided to go to japan simply because i wanted to and i didn't have any particular plan because i didn't feel i needed one (even though society thinks that's wrong, that's unconventional, you're "not supposed" to do that, that's crazy, blah, blah, blah) and once i was there i remembered the kanye and taylor vma incident and i thought, "what if i told people exactly what i wanted to do and was honest and true with my work and with what i'm interested in doing? what if i questioned 'common' thinking when i wasn't 'supposed' to? what if i was a complete individual out loud and overcame my shyness barrier?" then i thought, "how would i do all this? i'm really am a pretty shy guy. i'm overly humble. i'm nice. i'm weak. i'm scared. but, i am interested in acting and i've studied that during the time i studied architecture. hmm. i like art and art has been an interest of mine. i'm mostly interested in being the most creative i could be. how do i connect all these dots? when i was thinking about going to gmu i thought about studying art there since they didn't have architecture. my stay in japan is expected to be two months and three weeks. i'm thinking about going to korea for a bit and then back to japan, but what if i change that thought and return to america? and what if i come back with a plan (this is probably the structure side of my genetics talking)? and what if that plan is to do a performance on a major scale? like, what if i act out a role as someone else? and what if this someone else is the 'honest out loud with certain thoughts and with saying what he feels from his heart and heavily going for what he wants to go for in life' version of me? what if this someone else is like an 'ego' i develop? and what if this 'ego' is outspoken and honest out loud when he's 'not supposed' to be honest out loud? what if this 'ego' just speaks that truth that no one wants to hear? what if this 'ego' does exactly what he wants to do? what if this persona is me as a complete individual not conforming to societal norms? how do i approach doing all of this? and why do i want to do this? i think it's all about me being creative in life, but maybe something more will come out of it. how do i do this at a level where no one will notice and i could keep my character in full effect at all times? school is probably my best bet. and studying something that encourages creativity is probably my best option for studies. hmm. okay, i think i got it. my unplanned kind of planned japan plans have changed into something else that is kind of planned, but explosive and curious about what the outcome will be. after my two months and three weeks of japan living ends i'll return to america as akuna lunersks."

arthur lugauskas

don't say anything, ever

chapter 4 : the nova warm up

i tend to be late to a lot of things. and i was no different when it came to catching my plane back to america. yes, i missed my flight. but, technically i didn't because my flight was at 5:00pm and i arrived to the airport around 4:56pm. i had time. i wanted to make my flight. but, i guess the reason they didn't let me run to the plane was because they thought it was going to take longer than 4 minutes for me to go through security and all that stuff. well, i lived in narita airport for another 24hours or more before i made it to another flight. that was an interesting experience. i write about it in a book i was working on while in japan. but, this book you are reading right now is about something other than japan.

so, after i was back in america i knew what i was up to. or at least i pretended to know. my plan was to start speaking my opinion and truth out loud. but, i had training and practicing to do. we were now in 2010. and i was in my early twenties. and by early twenties i mean i just turned twenty last year. okay, well, i thought about where the best place would be for me to start training. or with whom should i be extra expressive first. yes, with my friends. i mean, they were excited to see me return from asia. did i change? how was my experience? you know, they had their questions. and i had answers. so, soon enough i started being very shyly extra outspoken with them. and it was relatively easy because they thought i was joking about my big goals and dreams that had to do with a variety of things. and that was okay for the time being. but, i wasn't joking when i said what i said about certain things. and listen, i do joke a lot, don't get me wrong, but, there are some things i truly believe to be true and i don't say them lightly.

my first stop was to be at another place where i'd be looked at as a peer, not know anyone, and be surrounded by strangers. and i found school to be the best option. well, i decided to go work on being an individual out loud at nova first. just as a warm up you could say. and the idea was to get my "general studies" degree and then receive a guaranteed admission into gmu. and then once in gmu, akuna would be built enough to do some sort of two year performance that i was thinking about. so, yeah, this initial build was estimated to take about a year i thought.

at nova i have a summer and fall semester to do. and i realized i'd have credit overload in each semester if i wanted to be on time for my possible some sort of two year performance at gmu. and if i did well or pushed myself to do really well at school and cram so much in such a short time then that could raise my "ego" and/or help me develop an "ego". i'm not even sure what "ego" really is actually, hence the quotation marks on "ego", but having this idea of me having an "ego" of some sort was i guess what i was aiming for, in a way. because i guess that's what it's called when you have a certain level of confidence and you think you are that good and believe that you are able to achieve all that you set out to achieve. that's societies definition to "ego", right? i don't know.

okay, so after speaking to a counselor at nova about the classes i'm supposed to take in the time frame i had given myself, she got concerned about my aspirations. but, since what i wanted to do from her point of view seemed undoable i felt like she just went with the flow of my wishes. in her head she had already decided that i'm not going to complete the classes i had to complete and get the credits i had to get for a "general studies" degree in a short summer semester and a full fall semester. but, that didn't matter to me, because i thought if i knew about the dots i had to connect, then i'd figure out something. and note, i had already missed the spring 2010, summer 2010, fall 2010, and the spring 2011 nova semester. why? umm, yeah, i started dating this girl, she became my girlfriend, and then i was working a lot and getting my money up, and i was building akuna through conversations with people i knew who were around my age before i started building further with people i didn't know who were of all ages, and blah blah blah excuses. but, don't worry, i have great writing material and short stories that are in development in regards to some stuff that was happening during those times.

okay, so, back to the past and this school thing. after figuring out all the necessary requirements for getting this "general studies" degree and what i have to do in order to have a guaranteed admission into gmu i was looking at taking 41 credits and 12 classes. and that should test my endurance for sure, right? if i could endure the beating of classes and homework and assignments coming at me full force at all times of the day, i should be one step closer to being able to handle the same kind of shots from human beings once i'm expressing myself more and more.

then i realized that this would be tougher than i thought because i was broke, so i thought i should work in the summer. then wow, i really got to a point where i wasn't sure if i was going to actually pull this off. this was what my summer 2011 nova semester looked like:

-art 101, history and appreciation of art one, 3 credits
-eng 125, introduction to literature, 3 credits
-his 102, history of western civilization two, 3 credits
-ite 115, introduction to computer applications and concepts, 3 credits
-phy 201, general college physics one, 4 credits
-phy 202, general college physics two, 4 credits

okay, do you think a 20 credit load summer semester is crazy? not too crazy, right? okay, well, to make matters at a whole nother level, 16 of those credits were expected to be taken in 6 weeks. yeah, that's how i connect dots sometimes. and i didn't fully realize this at the time, but that is unheard of! i honestly don't know anyone who is stupid enough, or smart enough, to do such a thing. am i crazy? 16 credits in 6 weeks! really!? yes, really! i'm being honest with you here. 16 credits in 6 weeks. and listen, i never even really got into credits and stuff. i just looked at classes and i never was worried about, "oh, i'm taking 12 credits this semester" or "i'm at 18 credits, this is crazy." i just looked at it as, "okay, what do i have to do in a certain amount of time to achieve this?" it was no different here. but, since people know about credits and are concerned with them, i'm here to emphasize what i went through at a certain time in my life. what is 16 credits in 6 weeks? how many weeks is a fall or spring college semester? something like 15 or so, right? okay, so 6 times 2 is 12. and 16 times 2 is 32. that would mean taking 32 credits in 12 weeks. whatever. something like that, right? actually, do you want to calculate and or do ratios or find the question mark here: 6weeks/16credits = 15weeks/?credits. does the number seem crazy? well, this was my first step. achieve something so out of reach of achievability. or maybe many have done this and it's not big deal. i don't know. this was a big deal for me. so, i'm writing as if it's a big deal. i did do it and it was certainly not easy. i remember going to school around 8 or 9am and sitting in up to three classes for around three hours each and then going home around 9 or 10pm and then doing homework until maybe 1 or 2am and then doing it all over later on that morning. and my weekends, yeah, catching up on homework. i did that for the 6 weeks. how did i do it? i had to hustle. and i'm not talking about anything to do with drugs or such. i'm talking about being smart and school hustling. learning about things you can and can't do. how to get the grades. what you have to do. what options you have. using peers to help you. and i don't mean cheating either. i'm not interested in cheating or lying. i haven't been into those things growing up. but, i have been interested in being creative and smart with things. that's what i used, my biggest weapon - my brain and thoughts and creativity - to make it through those 6 weeks. it was tough, but i did it and now i could be proud of what i achieved. and yes, it helped build this character of akuna with raising this concept of "ego" he is supposed to have. and at the time of doing those crazy 6 weeks of classes i thought, "okay, this is hard, but doable." then i realized how incredibly insane doing such a thing is, apparently. but, the reason i thought it wasn't the biggest of deals at the time was because i wasn't interested in what societal norms thought in regards to the number of credits per semester that are doable are. i just had a goal and went for it. i ended up getting a's in all my classes except for phy 201. in that class i got a b. and i think that was the hardest class i've ever taken in my school life. like ridiculously hard! i spent the most time on that class and got the lower grade as opposed to what i got in all the other classes. it was crazy! the way i passed that class was because i had a smart girl who helped me by studying and working on homework with me during late nights/ early mornings, i hustled big time in that class with using my brain in figuring things out, and i tried doing all the bits and pieces and extra credits that counted towards my grade in the most efficient and thorough manner i could with my time. and i had such small amounts of sleep during that period of time in my life.

    then came the second 6 weeks of this summer semester. i took only phy 202 this time. yeah, 4 credits in 6 weeks! a big, huge change. but, i was now working a lot during that time. and i realized, whether i have physics with four other classes or physics alone for a semester, it doesn't matter because it's super hard and time consuming for me! physics is amazing, but really extremely hard for me. i did get an a for physics this time around, but it was so extremely difficult.

these summer semesters really helped me confirm further that anything is possible. and i was kind of secretly building akuna and preparing for what i wanted to do and be when i got to gmu.

then the fall 2011 semester at nova came along. this time i had 21 credits lined up. the classes were as follows:

-art 102, history and appreciation of art two, 3 credits
-art 121, drawing one, 4 credits
-art 131, fundamentals of design one, 4 credits
-art 132 fundamentals of design two, 4 credits
-mth 152, math for liberal arts two, 3 credits
-pht 101, photography one, 3 credits

this was a much different load. there were a lot of art classes and i took this as an opportunity to test a few things out.

for art 102, well, there's not much to say about that. i don't see myself as being good at history of any sort and i got a b for that class.

for art 121, well, i wasn't good at drawing. or well, i was not too bad at perspectives because i learned a bit about how to do them during my architecture studies. but, when it came to the human figure and drawing still life and stuff i was so bad at it i think. still though, i did do all the drawings and work and assignments for the most part. my professor thought i had an imagination and a certain style. i actually surprised myself with this cross hatching drawing i did of this "robot" looking figure. yeah, i thought that was one of the better drawings i did. other than that, i did some drawings that helped me get better maybe. i don't know. i usually rely on creativity. do i? i don't know about that either. but, yeah, probably. and maybe my curiosity helps with my observation skills. because i remember getting so curious about how simple lines can create an image. sounds so obvious, right? but, for me that was an amazing discovery. well, i ended up getting an a for that class.

    for art 131, well, that was a good class for me to voice out some things. the professors name was fundofdne. he was cool. i learned that he wakeboarded. and he learned that i skateboarded. he gave a certain freedom with his assignments and one day i took that opportunity to say that i wanted to do something which involved me taking photographs and collaging them for my project. it was something along those lines. and he said, "that's a pretty narcissistic thing to do." i didn't know the meaning of the word "narcissistic" at the time, but later on that day i looked it up and understood what he meant a bit more then at the time of his vocal projections towards me. don't get me wrong now, he said what he said in this smiling joking sort of fashion, but maybe there was some truth in that sentence. i thought later on, "good, good, what i'm doing is working." i was trying to build akuna in a certain way so right off the bat there would be a certain idea of him upon meeting him. but, for that to happen it had to be natural. it had to be real. this character had to be me, inside me, all over me. because that's how you pull off a role at its maximum level - when you *are* the role. so, me being called a narcissist in this case maybe wasn't necessarily a bad thing. i was doing something right maybe. because i knew i wasn't a narcissist, but i also knew that certain society is trained to look at certain behavior as narcissistic, even though it could have nothing to do with narcissism. well, that comment was one of the first jabs i had to take. and understand that what fundofdne said to me certainly affected me. but, the way he said it and the quickness of the truth told was what made me be able to take it. i slowly felt my humble character of me fading away. i was choosing to do this. i understood that. and i was ready to see how much more i could take. also, note, that for this class i did plenty of work. and i did end up getting an a. but, i was doing assignments at this time. i wasn't doing completely whatever i wanted. i was still in this bubble of structure and doing assignments relatively quickly. i wasn't quite trying to make work that is truly amazing and moving. i wanted to get the grade. my care for art wasn't at it peak. but, it was growing. and something else interesting about fundofdne was that he taught not only at nova, but at gmu too.

     for art 132, well, that was a wonderful class for my career as an artist and creative. even though this class was a design class, it ended up being where i kind of learned how to paint. or a little bit at least. the professor was a painter and he emphasized on small painting projects. it was during this class i started to bring more care for what i did. especially because after my first assignments i felt embarrassed. i did them relatively quickly and they looked pretty bad. actually they looked horrible and awful. and after those i started getting into painting more. well, not that much. but, i did start putting more and more time into my projects. eventually i'd lose sleep just to do a painting i cared about. i was curious. i enjoyed creating. and i was beginning to be creative and free with what i did in school. my professor noticed and appreciated the work i was doing. and by the end of his class, i received an a and compliments like, "very creative. very original. very imaginative."

for mth 152, umm, yeah, it was just something i had to take. i didn't give this class much time. it was simple math. and math was one of the subjects i was more comfortable with. but, in this class there were times when the math was so simple that it was complicated. it was strange. it's like i overlooked the simplest things. maybe in part that had to do with me caring more about this beautiful girl in class than actual class. we sat next to each other and i'd help her sometimes. and this person was a stranger i could start to show off this "ego" that i'm supposed to have. i think i was still too nice. but, at times i was extra confident. my actions fluctuated. but, yeah, i was disappointed to be in this class because in high school i took some calculus and this was just like basic math. it was fine though, i got an a, i didn't get the girl. kind of. that's another story.

for pht 101, well, this was another class i built akuna in. one day we had an assignment and it was about your alter ego. cha ching, right!? bingo! yes! the place to let akuna out in assignment form! i basically started hinting at something. and revealing myself. but, really, who cared to notice? this was where i was, in a way, giving out clues to what i'm doing right here, right now writing this. for this alter ego assignment i basically had an image of me: this kind, shy, genuinely good person, who was a bit reserved and delicate and not really loud. and then an image of my alter ego, akuna: this cocky artist, who is loud, outspoken, honest, and still a genuinely good person who wants good, but of course his persona overshadows his good intentions at times and when that happens people only see his "ego" instead of his true-from-the-heart good intentions.

and that's basically what i did and said for that assignment. but, the students and professor just looked at it as an assignment. they didn't really take it as something true. and i actually had a big issue in that class one day. there were these girls, right, i'm a happy person, smiling, being outgoing when i begin knowing people, being funny at the right times, and enjoying creating, and i don't know, maybe they weren't used to that or something, but in the darkroom these girls hinted and quietly said to me, "wow, i'm surprised you're not falling over. are you okay?" i thought, "huh, what?" and then they said whatever else they said basically implying that i was on drugs. i got overly offended at that. seriously!? i can't just be me!? to be this active and alive i have to be on drugs!? that caused such anger in my head because i was seriously annoyed at them for genuinely thinking that i'm "on" something. reason being is because i've never done drugs, never tried drugs, never smoked, never been drunk, i'm not into any of that stuff, i never got into any of that stuff, and i don't feel the need to do any of that stuff. why? because i'm too busy being creative, i'm too busy working on my projects, i'm too busy enjoying life, etc. and i just really got offended that such thoughts came out when i was just being a happy version of me and trying to make people smile. i felt so disrespected from their assumption. i had no interest in laughing with them or doing anything near them anymore after that moment. but, i guess i have to understand that people assume things. i'm guilty of assuming things. maybe wrong things about people. and if that's how they felt at that time, then that's how they felt. we move on and go our separate ways, right? so, yeah, i had an incident like that. but, other than that class went well and i got an a.

so, i know i just kind of described a few things that went on in this class and that class. maybe i didn't give you enough insight as to what else i was doing. well, let me tell you in the next chapter what else i was doing in order to do one of the most mind blowing, you never saw this coming, creative things i could think of. brace yourself.

don't say anything, ever

arthur lugauskas

don't say anything, ever

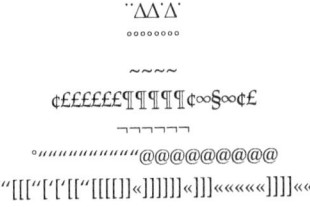
chapter 5 : two year performance

¨ΔΛ˙Δ˙
ooooooo

~~~~
¢£££££££¶¶¶¶¶¢∞§∞¢£
ㄱㄱㄱㄱㄱㄱ
°″″″″″″″″″″″@@@@@@@@
‴[[[″[′[[″[[[[]]«]]]]]«]]]««««]]]««

okay, we are here. the fifth chapter already. it feels like the other ones just flew by. if you haven't, maybe take a quick break before you keep reading. or just drink a glass of water. i'm actually about to drink some water. literally i actually am about to go drink water before i start the next sentence (author drinks water). wow, that was some good filtered water. did *you* drink filtered water just now? and yeah, i actually drank from a wine glass. what did i suggest for you to drink out of? oh yeah, a glass. well, was it a wine glass?

i should have said, "go drink some filtered water from a wine glass." lets try this again, shall we? i'm about to go drink another wine glass of filtered water before i start my next sentence and you should too (yes, literally i'm about to drink water on this november 2013 9:09pm evening) (author drinks water). yes! that was some great water! maybe you're asking me, "why do you drink water out of a wine glass?" well, i don't know. wine glasses are attractive and sexy. water is beautiful and vibrant. i think the two go together well. and i like clean water. and drinking from a wine glass is fancy, right? okay, back to the story. wait, let me say something else. the fun things about writing how you want to write and having fun with what you write and enjoying being fully creative with writing and not following any "rules" you don't feel like following are that you could write whatever, whenever. i'm here to be real with you. i'm writing and you're reading. i'm here to give you friendly and readable writing. fun writing. writing you could just read. i'm like bringing this human aspect to writing and speaking directly to you. pretend we're having a conversation. i like stories. do you? i like thinking. do you? i like ideas and inspiration and possibilities and conversations. do you? sometimes i like going off on tangents to new galaxies and wait, wait. where am i going with this? wow me. not wow me, but wow to me. you know? sometimes when i converse with certain friends we start on ground on earth and then minutes later end up in this crazy imaginary world in another universe talking about these thoughts that make sense to us (but, may not make sense to anyone entering into our conversation cold handed) and we imagine and shape reality to what we want it to be at that given moment and then we study it and question stuff and bring things in and neglect things that don't need to be thought of and blah, blah, blah. okay, really, next paragraph we begin what this chapter is about.

    i'm smiling now and almost want to get into more tangents, but stop, lets talk about what this two year performance was thought to be. okay, so while i was in my fall semester at nova i built this akuna character outside of school also. like i've stated before, i'm outgoing with friends, right? and there are certain friends i connect with quite strongly because we have similar thoughts and ideas on life. with these friends i'm able to be me and give them that truth on what i think about anything and then them not automatically criticizing what i say or bashing on my opinion. so, during this time period i started telling these friends more about these "invisible dreams" i had. more about these goals i want to reach. i started testing how far i could go before they thought i was crazy for having such thoughts. but, i never told them about akuna and this upcoming two year performance i had in mind. but, i was working on being fully honest with what i simply believed i can do in life. because it's this honesty that i'm going to have to consistently give to strangers when i get to gmu. i had to train my open mouth of unlimited truth to be second nature to me. i had to *become* akuna in order to do the greatest performance of my life during this point in time in my life.

    one friend i started to connect more with was finlay. he's a writer and has made some short films. the more i spoke truth to him about my fantasies, the more i learned that he had similar thoughts to mine. i didn't know this about him. i thought of him as this humble, shy, nice guy. i thought he was harmless. and i do believe he is a genuinely nice guy, but the more i spoke with him the more i realized he had ideas similar to mine when it came to society, rules, expected norms, and life itself. during this time i was becoming more of an artist. maybe i've always been an artist? i don't know. i considered myself a creative and an individual. no need for labels. i'm everything and anything i want to be. and you know what, maybe that's what an artist is. if an artist is a creative individual who is everything and anything, then that was and is me. i didn't realize finlay has already considered himself an artist for the past couple of years. maybe i was blinded by my own interpretations of him. whatever the case, i never knew he wanted to be great. i never knew that he wanted to impact the world with creativity. i never knew he was as confident in his work and ideas as i was. because listen, i also wanted to be great. and i also wanted to impact the world on a major scale with unbelievable creativity. so, the more we learned about each others similarities the more open we got. we started talking about society and "typical thinking" and all these thoughts that a lot of people don't talk about. so, this was helping my confidence in a way where it allowed me to get closer to saying what i "shouldn't say" to others according to societal norms. i now knew i had someone who thought like me and someone who understood where i was coming from when i said what i said. and that was good and helpful for me because if i got bashed by people judging me without thinking about what i actually said i could analyze that scenario with finaly if i wanted to after the fact. and i liked my conversations with finlay because we enforced each others ideas and supported one anothers dreams, no matter how far out of reach they may have appeared to the untrained mind.

      then i got this idea. well, i ended up doing a lot of art during my fall 2011 nova semester. but, i hadn't really documented it. and that's when some dots connected. in order for me to be akuna i had to know who he was. he was me unmasked. he was the truth beneath the truth. he was what you don't say out loud. akuna was a creative genius. he was a genius thinker. he was a creative superstar. he was one of the greatest living artists today. he was unbelievable and undeniable, but denied by society because of politics. he was that rose that grew from concrete. he was at that duchamp level of thought. he was at that van gogh level of passion. he was at that magritte level of wit. he was at that da vinci level of busy with ideas on top of ideas. he was at that michelangelo level of amazing. he was at that warhol level of persona. but, more than anything he was an individual with an individual mind. he was all of that and he had to prove it. to start things up before the full dive into the two year performance he had to get his ammo up. why am i still saying "he"? *i* had to build in order to go into gmu as akuna - me unmasked. so, if i was to portray this superstar artist i had to do something to line me up with superstar artists. and if i'm to be this creative genius i have to something creatively genius. right? so, i thought. thinking is like my drug. i think a lot sometimes. i thought and i thought and then i thought this, "okay, i've done a lot of art lately. from these design classes and drawing class and photography class i've produced a lot of work. and i still have my architecture drawings and models that i haven't documented yet. and i still have childhood works of art that i don't remember doing (but these works of art have my name on them and my mom saved them for years and years and said that they are my works). and at this time i don't have any documentation of them. most big time game changing artists have documentaries about their life and works of art. instead of me just photographing my works for documentation, why don't i do a full-length documentary about me and my artworks? right? that's unheard of, right? a full-length documentary film coming from an artist who is twenty-two years old is something new, right? the documentary will be about my career as an artist so far. what career? i just told you, my career! but, no, maybe not that. something more creative. well, okay, the documentary can document my thoughts and my art, but, okay, i got it, it will be my introduction to the art world! yes, who has ever introduced themselves to the art world through a full-length feature documentary!? okay, umm, i have to make it though. i don't have money. what do i do? i do what i'm best at: be creative. okay. hmm. finlay does short films. hmm. but, i shouldn't approach him with this documentary idea just yet. he might get scared. what do i do? okay, i know. i'll tell finlay that i want to do this interview where i speak about some views i have on life and then talk about some of my most recent artworks and what they are about. that should be vague, but understandable enough for him to not question too heavily if there is something more to it than that. yes! that should work!"

    and it did work. finlay came over and we started filming. he'd ask questions and i'd answer them. but, he did give me some stumpers. he had a lot of knowledge. he didn't let me off the hook that easy. he made me think. we had a few filming days here and there during late 2011. that footage was expected to be 1/3rd of my documentary that was to come. finlay wasn't aware of this at the time. but, during our filming there was a particular creative way in which the documentation of me and my art was done. i'm happy about that. thank you finlay!

    and now note, if you feel like you have work that is good enough or thoughts that are important enough to make a film or movie or documentary on then you should do it. if you think your life and the experiences you've had are worth talking about and expressing and showcasing to the world then do it. i obviously think i have things to say and that my art is worth documentation and that i'm great enough as a person, individual, creative, and artist to have a documentary film done about me and my art. why not think that? i know why. because according to popular thinking you are "not allowed" to have a documentary about you and your art at age 22. you're not established enough. you're not old enough. blah, blah, blah. blup that! it's your life. do what you want to do. you don't need to follow what others think you shouldn't do. be creative. be weird. speak your mind. be an individual.

    the next creatively genius superstar thing for me to do was plan this two year performance. i was going to try to fully be akuna for my two years at gmu. and to let you know, there's an akuna in everyone. i know i've described akuna in a certain way earlier in this book. and by earlier i mean really recently. but, i want you to know that akuna is that character that is childhood truth and honesty. akuna is that person saying what he wants to be instead of being to embarrassed to say it because of the backlash he might get or the uncoolness from others he might feel. akuna is that believer that anything is possible. akuna is that person who challenges thoughts and questions what's real. akuna is that truth. when you're a child and you say what you want you're not crazy. you're a child or a dreamer. but, when you're an adult and you say what you want you're crazy. you're arrogant. you're dumb. you're stupid. you're hated. you're discriminated against. you're judged. you're "not allowed" to dream anymore. akuna is that rejection to all that negativity! akuna is that nail that is sticking out and saying, "i feel like being real for a change!" akuna isn't about arrogance! akuna is about dreams! akuna is about possibilities! akuna is about knowing you could achieve anything! with all that said, now you should have a good grasp about who akuna is and who i'm about to "play" in the real world. well, actually in the school world. i have this theory that school is a fantasy world, but i don't want to get into that right now. maybe in another piece of writing or something. i don't know. but, okay, akuna and his two year performance. what is all this about. well basically it's kind of simple. once i knew i was getting a guaranteed admission into gmu i have started getting things loosely planned out. are you ready to know what this plan is? are you sure?

    the two year performance plan: before i go on, time for another wine glass of filtered water (author drinks water). wow, the filtered water was so good that i had a round two right after round one (this is true and just happened). to the reading audience out there, don't worry, you're not reading alone. i'm reading with you as i type? am i? or am i thinking what i'm typing? i don't want to lie to you, so that's why i have question marks. hmm, okay, so if i'm thinking and typing what i think am i also reading what i think as i type? wow, that was an interesting sentence to write. do you get what i'm saying at all? maybe i've lost you. i don't know. are you as curious as me? okay, right, the two year performance plan. so, i've been building and training to become this akuna lunersks persona, character, "ego", whatever you want to call it. i wanted to fully immerse myself in this role. i didn't want anyone to discover my overly nice, quite, shy, humble persona. i knew gmu has this thing called senior project. it's a class that combines what you've learned and gives you the opportunity to showcase your creativity and artistic ability to an audience during this thing called "senior show." and since i knew about this, my plan was to do a performance piece. or actually the greatest most creative most dedicated senior project i could think of. and i planed to do this in the place where it should be welcomed the most - in the school of art building. so, i planed to study art and get a bachelors in fine art. during my two years at gmu i wanted to be akuna. i was to be performing and no one was to know. everything i did in this performance was to be research for this book that i'm writing right now. but, i had to live and breath as akuna to be the most successful. and i wanted to succeed. i knew i was shy and that's why i had to look at this as a performance piece. i had to look at this as a piece of art. and i wasn't going to be out there to attack anyone. if anything i was probably going to be the one who got attacked. and i hoped i was ready enough to handle everything and not break down. and to be fully successful with being akuna for four semesters, which is equivalent to two years, i have to make sure no one knew *for real*. right now no one knows i'm even thinking about this. that's good. i have to hide akuna from everyone. that's another challenge for me because i'm actually a really open person. i'm not really secretive. once i'm comfortable with you, and even sometimes if i just met you and feel good vibes, i'm open like i've known you for a long time. i like being honest and friendly. those are some things i'm good at. i do have my timid moments, but they don't show so much when i know you. so, for me to of kept this performance a secret and unrevealed until my senior show in 2013 i had to take on this character and fully immerse myself in him and forget i was even this character at all. like mr. ledger and his role as the joker. he was the best joker. he

became the joker and forgot he was the joker. he took
that role like none other. i'm here to be akuna like none
other. i'm here to forget about my shyness for two years.
i'm here to not be overly nice for two years. because to
be this character i have to *be* this character. that's the
only way people wouldn't notice my performance. to be
successful i really had to forget that akuna is a persona
who i didn't grow up as (in a way kind of sort of) and
act like i've been akuna my whole life. and if i was very
successful i knew that the reactions from people would
be real. maybe too real. and the feelings i would feel
would also be real. and for everything to work in
harmony i can't tell friends, family, or anyone. and i was
thinking that sometime in october or november 2013 i'll
have this alarm go off to remind me that i'm doing a
performance and that i should finish it by writing my
most vivid experiences of my research from my
performance in book form for my senior show. but, until
then i just had to be and play out my role. never break
character. take the hits. take the shots. go through the
ups and downs. make it through everything without
dying at the end. like barbara in *nickel and dimed* i had to
live it to get the proper information and research for my
book and story. okay, now, get ready to come into akuna
lunersks' world. i am now akuna lunersks. you are in
my world. i'm in control and you don't know it. you
think you know me, but you have no idea. trust me.
you didn't see any of this coming. don't act like you did.
akuna is here.

don't say anything, ever

arthur lugauskas

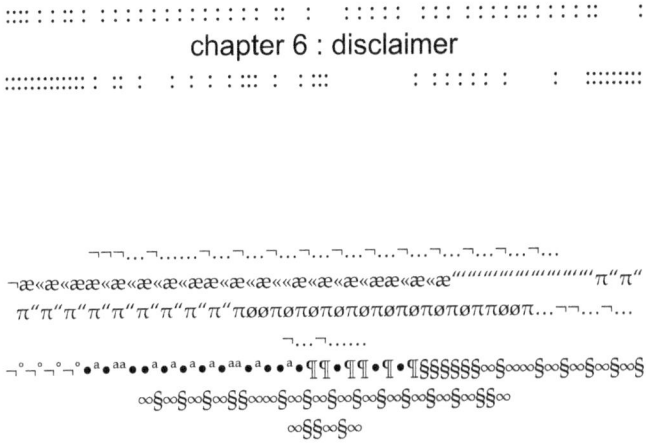

chapter 6 : disclaimer

    wait. before i go any further i have a disclaimer. or at least i think what i have to say in this chapter is considered a "disclaimer." in the forthcoming pages i'm about to be real with you and i'm talking about full-blown-honesty-realness. i'm about to write some truth. this isn't a game for me. a lot has happened in the last two years. my feelings have been hurt severely. people have tried to make me feel like i wasn't going to be what i wanted to be. i've been hated. my creativity and honesty hasn't been appreciated by some. my thoughts on what *my* life is about have been tested. people have tried to make me feel less of myself. people have tried to make me be a follower and not a leader. trash talking has occurred behind my back. i've been underestimated and laughed at. there have been a lot of dreamkillers trying to kill *my* dreams. i've dealt with a lot of negativity and nonbelievers. but, with all that came some positivity. i certainly have had people appreciate who i am as a human. there are people who love what i do. these people appreciated my aspirations and dreams. they supported me and pushed me to go further. they believed in me and encouraged me. so, yes, i have had ugly and amazing people whom i've come across.

    let me tell you something else. some people "can't" handle the truth. i'm sure some people are going to hate this book. i'm sure others are going to be so selfish and think what i write is all about them and then they'll probably think i'm trying to bad-mouth them or talk trash about them or something else stupid like that. that's not my intent! and that's pretty selfish, right? a book about so many stories and all you think about is this character that might resemble you in some way maybe. like all you care about is yourself and what i write about "you" and depending what i write about "you" determines if you like the book or not. please. this book isn't about you or "you" or *you*. and please, read the whole book from front to back before you start criticizing it. take what i write as an experience. i'm here to bring excitement in writing and take you on an up and down and all over and around roller coaster. honestly, i don't think some people are ready to read what's next just yet. some people are too closed minded and aren't educated enough about individuality and being expressive and saying what's true. so, if you're one of those people and plan to get mad at me for expressing *my* feeling then don't bother reading any further. it's ridiculous if you think you can hurt me and then tell me that i'm "not allowed" to express myself creatively. and anyway, all that exists in the pages that proceed are words and more words. it's like if i or you or someone does a certain drawing, right? what is it really at it's surface? lines on paper maybe? and that's it. if you make more out of it, if you get stories, if your mind is stimulated, then that's amazing. but listen, since some people already have a negative view towards me, well, they are probably going to go into this book in a hateful negative manner. and those people will probably completely disregard what i *actually* say because their mind is too blurred by this idea of already simply not liking me. and i just think it's sad that those people are missing out on some fresh water from replenishment island.

    and now that we maybe filtered the people who aren't ready to read this book just yet, pay attention. first off, i want to thank those of you still reading right now. i really appreciate you giving me your time. and with this book i want you to have the best time of your life reading it. so, back to this disclaimer business. in the upcoming chapters i'm about to write about things *i've* been through. i'm not here to lie. i'm not here to "call out" anyone. i'm not here for bad intentions. i don't want bad for anyone. i'm not here to hate anyone. i'm not here to hurt anyones feelings or talk bad about them. but, what i am here to do is give you a level of honesty that is scary to give. i'm about to tell you truth that i "shouldn't" be telling you. i'm about to bring out a level of realness that i'm "not supposed" to bring out. i'm about to put myself under the blade while i release *my* frustrations, *my* pain, *my* truth. this isn't about ego.

this isn't about arrogance. this isn't about bringing anybody down. this is about creativity. this is about having fun with life and being whoever you want to be. this is about believing that anything is possible. this is about remembering what it was like to be a kid and have parents and anyone who came across you tell you, "yes, you could be anything in life. follow your dreams. don't give up." i'm here to tell you exactly how i felt at certain points in time during the past two years. and note, feelings are the only facts!

don't say anything, ever

arthur lugauskas

chapter 7 : spring 2012 gmu semester

fffɔfɔfɔfɔɔfɔɔfɔɔfɔfɔ
ΣΣ´Σ´Σ´Σ´´´´´´´Σ´Σ´´
¨¥¥ππππ π´´´´\\\\\\\
«æ«««ææææææææ«««æ«ææ«æ«
æææ`÷÷≥÷÷≥÷≥÷≥÷≥
÷÷÷÷÷÷÷÷÷÷÷÷æ
<><<<>><<><<><<><<><<><<><

we made it baby! we're studying at the school of art (soa) at gmu! it's january 2012! time for art, creativity, and pushing limits! wait, i didn't mention this before, but i did have a portfolio review a couple months back (prior to the start of my spring 2012 gmu semester) that determined if i was "good enough" or "allowed" to go for some sort of art degree at gmu. i guess i basically had to know what i was doing when it came to art if i wanted to further my development in art or something like that. and if my review didn't go well, i guess that would have meant no art school because i don't know how to make good art or something? i don't know. well, in any case, for the review day i brought a lot of works i did during my fall 2011 nova semester and also a couple of my architecture models i did years before. overall the things went well and i got accepted to be on the bachelors of arts (ba) track. that was cool, but now that i was here i started looking more into what ba and bfa (bachelors of fine arts) differences were.

     as i did my research, my knowledge on degrees in universities expanded. the ba is basically a safe route in a way and you have the opportunity to minor in something other than art. the bfa is more about art and studio classes and taking a variety of different art classes and art, art, art. after learning this, my structured "be safe" genes contemplated on continuing the ba and finding a minor. but, then my "take risks and don't worry" genes kicked in and told me to just go for a bfa because you are here to be creative and do amazing things with art. it was weird having these two options. i didn't know what to do at that time. like, "which do i choose?" but, after looking through different minors and seeing possibilities like film, dance, psychology, and a few others, i thought, "no, why do i want to spend time doing these when i have this performance to do?" and then i kept thinking, "you're not doing a performance, this is real, be real, you are akuna, forget the performance, be the character, be akuna, you are akuna..." slowly i was forgetting about performance and just being who i've trained to be - myself at full honesty. and, i did think that if all failed and everyone hated me and if i couldn't handle it anymore it won't matter because it's done in school and ofter times students are overlooked because they come by the dozens and hundreds and thousands and who'd remember little me with the biggest dreams of them all, and after you're done with school, what you did in school in a way doesn't matter, what matters when it comes to school in a way is just having a degree and i understood things like this in order to have this "back up" plan if stuff got too crazy and out of hand with emotions, and because i had this "back up" plan i allowed myself to be fully emerged as akuna sooner than i thought. but, so, yeah, this ba/ bfa business. i thought and thought and came to this conclusion, "if i'm here to study art and be the most creative possible i might as well go all the way and do art things and go big or go home." i decided to take the bfa route, but since i was on the ba track i had to switch. and i learned that apparently you have to get into the bfa program via another portfolio review if you are currently doing the ba program. but, when it came to my case, apparently i had the option to just switch to the bfa because after my first portfolio review the ba track was simply recommended and there was nothing preventing me to choose the bfa route later on. it was just a matter of me asking my counselor to switch my major. so, i went about doing that and stuff got funky. the ba track wasn't just recommended to me because my portfolio didn't contain the best art, but also because my transferred credits made the ba option more appealing. and then i learned that for me to do a bfa it might take over two years. and that meant more than my four expected semesters! already some nonbelieving was taking place. i said, "what do i have to do to get the bfa in two years?" once i got the paper telling me which classes i had to complete for the bfa i started putting puzzle pieces together. and next thing i knew, ba da bing, ba da boom! all figured out! all i'd have to do was have four 16-18 credit semesters. sounded good to me! i went to my counselor and she switched me to the bfa program. no problem baby!

don't say anything, ever

arthur lugauskas

chapter 8 : new majors colloquium professor

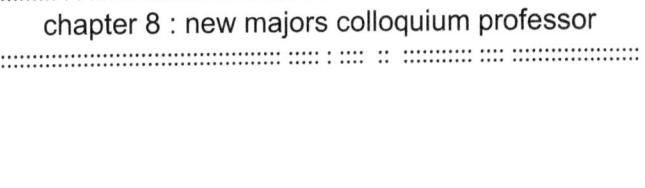

interesting enough, my counselor ended up being my new majors colloquium professor. her name was newsy. she was an active, nice, young woman. when she was in school she studied dance. and now she was working as a counselor. but, i felt like she really enjoyed her job because she was always positive and smiling. i liked who she was. and being in her class was fun. but, her class was one of the weirder ones. it didn't meet every week and it was a 1 credit course. it took place in an auditorium and was primarily for new art students. nothing too crazy went on in this class. but, when newsy was getting a feel for who was studying what when it came to art, i found out most people were studying graphic design. and most people were doing a ba. i was one of the few doing a bfa and even one of the lesser few with my concentration in sculpture. yes, sculpture was my concentration if i didn't tell you that earlier. are people too scared to be fine artists? i don't know. all this information was an interesting eye opener for me.

soon enough newsy told the class about a particular assignment that was going to be a huge bulk of our grade. and that assignment was to do a lot of research on a living artist of our choice and then either turn in a huge binder on the artist with all this printed material or do a blog with all our gathered information. but, for the time being, the first step was for us to pick three artists and write three sentences about why you want to research them.

to help pick our artist newsy gave us a piece of paper with suggestions. i started looking up briefly all these artists names from the page i had on my desk one night and i remember filtering almost too quickly through artists i thought weren't that interesting or creative or eye catching or whatever. and note, this list was around 40 artists and we had to just pick three. and of course, this list had plenty of famous and popular names, but too much. and newsy knew that a lot of people might just go with a favorite artist that they've liked for a while now. and she thought if that happened then not be as much learning and research would happen. that's why newsy wanted us to write three sentences about three artists. that forced some people to do at least a little research on an artist they may not know anything about. newsy was interested in simply broadening our perspectives on living artists today. she had good intentions. and the idea was, after we'd pick our three artists, she'd choose which one she thought best suited us to research. and she didn't want anyone to research the same artist as another classmate. yeah, basically no overlaps.

    so, one evening as i was researching these artists from the list of suggestions newsy gave i came to this particular thought, "hmm. what if i just pick myself? i'm a living artist. and newsy did say we could go off the list, but if we did that then she would have to approve of the 'off the list' artist. i'm off the list. and i'm guessing no one else is suggesting researching themselves. and i don't think there would be an overlap because i'm pretty sure no one is choosing to research me. that's a good idea. i should choose me. i find me interesting. and if i research me maybe i could learn more about me and that could help me. that's like a win win win situation. yeah, i think i'll propose that to newsy."

    so, the next time i saw newsy i went up to her and told her that i had a creative take on doing the assignment. as she listened asked me to keep going with my speech. and then i went on with saying that i was thinking about doing myself as the topic and artist of research she gave me this smile, but didn't automatically reject the idea. instead she told me to still do the three sentences assignment and that it was okay to have myself as on of the three possible artists of research, but that i had to have at least two other living artists that i was interested in researching. then excited with that news i went home and looked up these artists from the list again and found four that appealed to me. and them my "be safe" genes kicked in and i decided to write about three of those four artists. but, what about myself? don't worry, i wrote about me too. i think i just wanted to have three artists other than myself in consideration just in case whatever or to show newsy i would work hard or something. i'm really not sure.

next thing i knew, next class rolled around and it was time to turn in our three sentences assignment. i was happy to of done mine the way i did. and note, in this class i usually sat next to a friend named dan. i actually had him in my art 132 class at nova. we met there because we both sat in the back of the class. and now we both made it to gmu and sat in the middle of this auditorium. he's known me for a little while now and knew i had ambitions and that i was interested in pushing the limits. so, on this day when we were turning in our assignment of the three artists i asked him which artists he liked. he told me and then asked the same question back at me. and i fearlessly and jokingly told him that i was my first choice. he saw that as humor. it seemed like he wasn't too surprised that i would do something like that. wow, that class period was a good one. especially when i turned my paper in because i did so with a smile.

newsy gave our papers back a couple weeks later. she said she circled the artist she thinks we should do. i was excited to see my results. when i received my paper newsy didn't circle any single artist, but she wrote this on the bottom of my page, "you could do 1/2 research on yourself and 1/2 research on any of your other three chosen artists." i thought, "okay, fair enough." i really appreciated that my creativity wasn't neglected and turned down. and i appreciated the opportunity to be an individual. i was sure no one else in that class chose themselves. but, they could have! why didn't they!? it could be really fun and interesting to research yourself, right? or do you think you know you? i don't know if you know you as much as you think you know you. or, at least i'm not sure you're aware of views others have about you. especially the ones they don't tell you. and it makes sense for you to not know because how would you know if you're not told and you're not the one out looking in?

    you know what, it really was amazing that newsy allowed me to be myself and take this assignment where i wanted to take it. why? because my creativity lead to greater creativity. that's what happens when you allow individualism. great things can happen. great things can be invented. invented? yes, invented. i invented something. so, my project was not to basically do this huge research assignment, but divide it in two. half the project about me, half the project about my artist of choice, anish. and i had the freedom to do a combined blog or one blog for each artist or a combined huge binder of pages or two medium binders. well, i decided to go the blog route. and not a combined blog. instead, one for solely me and one for anish information. but, of course, i was excited and i started with wanting to learn more about myself. and i was thinking about how to go about researching me. i thought and thought and. thought contemplation went down i tell you! then boom! i realized that i didn't remember my super young child years. or i should say i didn't remember the day i was born until age 5 or something like that. so, to learn about me, why don't i start from the beginning? then i decide to do just that. so, i began to "interview" my mom and ask her how i was growing up during my youngest years. i took notes. pages and pages of notes began to happen as my mom was telling me about me. and i was fascinated to learn more. i was proud of my kid self. i was proud of myself as a baby. because my mom said i was a good baby. that i didn't really cause problems. and i was a happy child. and she said so much more. then my inventiveness came in. i decided to go beyond a blog. and i came up with this word and invention. drum roll could start now. keep the drums going. yeah, keep them hitting (author just did a mini drum roll in a hotel in pa at 3:31am). i invented autobioblogphy. now time for claps. yeah, more claps. some screams. yeah! yeah! next paragraph time.

    so, what is an autobioblogphy? well, young grasshoppers, here is the definition i would like the dictionary to have one day: autobioblogphy - an autobiography of a persons life that turns in to a blog in that same persons life. and another definition for it should be - a live book. so, to reiterate, what i planned to do was write my autobioblogphy, which would be an autobiography of my life that turned into a blog in my life. and this would be a live book being written before your eyes. i would be in control on how fast you could read this live book once you got to a point where you were waiting for my next post. and i choose when to post and that would have control of you're pace of reading. no skipping pages if i was in the beginning of the book. you want to know more about me right now? well, if we aren't on that next page, please just wait. patience. and then once my autobioblogphy idea came to fruition i realized what i was doing was no longer an assignment. instead it was something i actually cared about and was excited to do. this was something special, new, fresh. i was just trying to be creative and i think i found a beautiful integration of combining interactivity and writing and reading and storytelling and blogging and the internet and self-awareness.

    i kept having conversations with my mom about tiny me and working on my autobioblogphy more and more. i learned a lot about me. soon the class was coming to an end, but i hadn't even started on the anish blog. newsy liked my autobioblogphy and read some of my posts because i emailed her my progress. but, class was coming down to the wire and newsy warned us to not leave our research until last minute. sometimes i'm a heavy last minute guy. my anish blog was left for last minute. and newsy was right about how ridiculous it would be to leave a project that is supposed to take 2/3rds of a semester for the last week or two before classes ended. very bad idea. my research on anish was weak. i think horrible actually. i found some stuff, hustled my way in putting together a blog that looked better than it actually was, and somehow made my anish research look substantial enough. but, in my head i saw what i did as something really weak because of my procrastination and lack of care. but, in any regard, it's great newsy was open enough to allow me to learn about me because look what she allowed me to give to the world. new terminology! and a new way of combining an autobiography and a blog! so, thank you newsy for your positive energy and good vibes!

arthur lugauskas

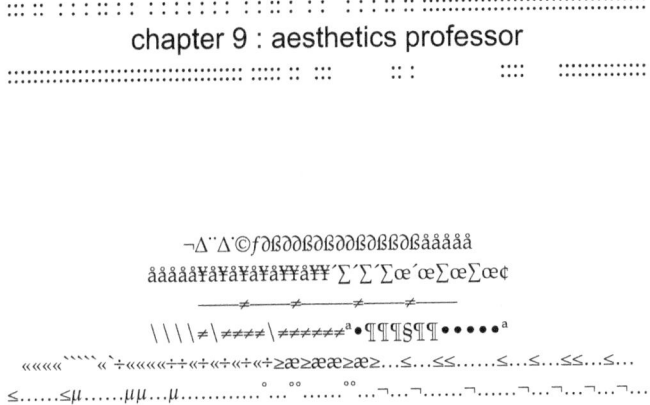

chapter 9 : aesthetics professor

time for beauty! i walked in this class like a star. and i was full of confidence after day one for some reason. aestan was the professor. during the first day she wanted to get to know a little bit about all of those who were taking her aesthetics class. we went around the room as students introduced themselves. some students didn't really know what to say. many just relied on the stock, asked for, answer, which was what their major was, what year they expect to graduate, and what kind of art did they do, if at all. other students fostered a bit and gave out some interesting information about themselves. but, no one said what i said. i went on to speak about my living experiences in different continents growing up, my recent japan life time, my architecture background, a little bit about my japan book, a little bit about a documentary film i might be working on, some acting work i've done, and interests i have in various fields in life. after my spiel it was this girls turn and she said with laugher and somewhat concern, "i don't think i want to go after that." she had some doubts about her being interesting enough for the class after i said my stuff. and that's ridiculous. everyone has their interesting stories and things and experiences. i just happened to stumble upon doing all that i do somehow, including this book. and the difference was i said what i felt like saying and what i find myself interested in out loud. if you write poetry as a hobby only sometimes, don't be afraid to say that. that's cool! if you like jogging at 5am every morning, don't be afraid to say that. that's amazing! if you just got had the most deliciously weird cupcake yesterday, don't be afraid to say that. that's interesting! i'm just trying to say no matter who you are i want you to know you have a lot of exciting things that have happened in your life!

   after introductions, aestan told us, "there are no exams, but there will be a lot of writing in this class. and don't expect to get a's like candy. i don't give a's out easily. so, if you don't get one, please don't be disappointed. i believe to get an a you have to be exceptional."

   aestan's little speech raised some concerns for me. i had some worries. but, since this was still just the very beginning of the class, i didn't know the work load or how i'd do or anything like that. at this point i just knew that i left a certain impression on the class, there was going to be a whole lot of writing, and that getting a's wasn't easy. then we went over the syllabus and had our first writing assignment assigned. "just respond" was written in capitals letters on the "how to go about your writing assignments" section from the syllabus. and note, this page was full of more stuff on ideas on how to respond in writing on a reading or text or film or video or so, but the main emphasis was to just respond. after class i went up to aestan and said, "what do you mean just respond?" she said, "just that, respond. just respond." i was puzzled for a moment, then went on to say, "so just respond however i want?" she said, "yes, and then we could take it from there. this is the first assignment and i just want to get a feel for your writing. respond however you see fit." i curiously said, "okay." then as i left the room i said to myself in my brain, "okay, i'll just respond i guess."

    and guess what i did for my first writing assignment? yes, just responded. i went to town with this response! wrote anything i wanted! my writing was fearless! no worries. no problems. i was me and i was going to write like me. no one writes like me. no one is me. and as i was responding and not following any writing "rules" i was taught to follow in high school and early college, i found that i was having a blast. probably the most fun you could have with writing. and another reason i was worry free when it came to the first assignment was because it was just that, the first assignment. if i did bad it wouldn't matter too much because we had something like 40 writings to do for the class. if i did bad i'd have plenty of time to adjust. but, why adjust when you are fully you and creative? i don't know. well, i wrote and wrote anything i wanted and turned in my work the next day we had class. then the anticipation started, "i wonder how i did?"

now understand, aestan has written books herself and was currently working on a book at this point in time. she's been writing for a while. and she has read so much. who knew if my writing was going to be any different from other stuff she's read. i didn't know. but, for some reason i had a feeling it would be different. why? because i cared about putting creativity in my writing. and since i was allowed to interpret "just respond" in any way i saw fit, well i did just that. i went all out with putting myself on the pages before me. kind of like i'm doing right now in this book.

it was a wednesday in february. and it was time to get our papers back. read, commented on, and graded by miss aestan herself. paper goes there, paper almost comes here, paper goes over there, papers going everywhere, and then i catch one and get my paper back. i thought, "the moment of truth is here. has my creative individual writing been appreciated or disregarded? did i make my reader thirsty for water or did i give her a clean wine glass of filtered water? let's see." i opened my eyes and saw comments here and there. there were maybe two or three grammatical corrections. my eyes wondered intensely down the page. and there it is. my grade. i got a 10. i wasn't sure what that meant. then after handing the last few papers back aestan tells us that a 10 is an a. okay. yes! success! i got a 10! she liked what i had to say! she appreciated my writing and unique way of putting a response together! i was a happy guy. i felt good. thank you aestan. but, now it was time to see if i could put together another amazing response.

our next writing assignment was to do two responses by next class. one was on a text about damien and the other was the "introduction" and "smell" chapter from diane's *a natural history of the senses* book. okay, i realized that all this was a good chunk of reading. and i'm not good at reading. and then there was a little concern in me on whether i could get a 10 for each response. but hey, i just had to keep telling myself to just write anything that came to my mind in any way i wanted to after i read what i should read.

after reading the text on damien i started typing my responsive thoughts. and since i did that there was no pressure. i was just being me and not trying to write like someone i'm not. and that was so much fun and a blast to do. so, with this damien text i was just fascinated by his titles. such long amazing titles he had for his works. and he had a great woman by his side who didn't want him to quit art. i just wrote stuff that i thought was interesting. and i wrote any way i wanted. after all, that's what i should do, right?

for the reading from diane i found smell to be extraordinary. this concept that our smell sense is the only sense we can't lose because we'll die hit me hard and came out of nowhere. i don't think i ever knew the extreme importance of smell and what different scents can do to you. and this idea that you can't really describe a smell was crazy. i wrote about my fascination with this smell sense and whatever else came to my free flowing mind as i wrote. writing was so fun. probably because i was able to write without any worries.

well, class day came. and i was turning in my papers. and i noticed something interesting, my papers were getting longer and longer. we had a guideline that told us to write a paragraph or up to a page as a minimum. there was no maximum. and these two writings i just did were about two pages each. i think i was just having too much fun writing and letting ideas out. i was like a machine when it came to writing. just producing words in sentences on pages. and well, i turned in my two newest responses and then the wait to receive feedback began again.

next class period it was time to get papers back. i had this anticipation and slight worry. was i going to pull off two back-to-back a's for these two past papers i turned in last class? and especially from a professor that doesn't give a's like candy? and super especially from my writing, which is almost like calculated reckless writing? hmm, calculated reckless writing, that's interesting. is that how i should start describing my writing? i don't know, but i kind of think there is a fit. well, okay, once again papers are flying to students here, there, over there, almost here, right next to me, and then finally me! lets see, lets see. how did myself do? i looked and saw comments and minor corrections and then turned the page from my damien response and i saw a 10. then i looked and saw comments and minor corrections and turned the page from my diane response and i saw a 10. what!? i did it again!? no, my creativity and fun and enjoyment of writing shown on the pages did it! this felt great! i really did appreciate aestan liking what i had to say. i was a happy camper who felt encouraged to keep being himself in his writing.

okay, so i was writing these responses and i kept getting 10's. over and over and over again. i was surprised, happy, and writing more and more. and it was almost like i had this pressure to not break my streak. then one day, i received a graded response paper on my hands. i immediately look at the grade and i saw an 8. no! well, okay, whatever. it's fine. no big deal. i've been doing so good for so long. i guess it makes sense i miss a 10 at least one time. right? right? or wrong? well, then i noticed the paper only being something like half a page and i thought back and didn't recall writing half a page. then i looked at the name on the paper and it wasn't mine. it wasn't mine! i didn't get an 8! right underneath this 8 paper i saw my paper. perhaps the two pages were a bit stuck together or something. i began to regroup and get a bit more calm. then this jolt of confidence came up. i turned the page on my paper and at the end of the second page of writing i saw my 10. success, success, and my winning streak continued. phew, that was a close one.

now, here's the thing. on my papers i'd get comments like: "a beautiful, exciting piece of writing. bravo!" or "another terrific piece! keep up the good work!" or "akuna, you've really dug into the heart of things here. running with ideas, questioning them, making them your own. bravo!" and more. all that sounds exciting, right? like, i'm doing something right. well, i went to aestan and had a little conversation with her. and she was more than happy to exchange some words with me. i told her, "you know, i don't know how to write." then she told me, "you're a great writer." i went on to say, "i'm just writing however i want to and it's funny because i don't really know how to write." and she continued with encouragement, "you're doing great, don't worry."

then i start turning my writing up a notch. taking it to higher levels. putting more of me on the page. turning up the level of high creativity that already exists. some of my responses were almost only questions. some of them were very personal. and in one of them i even created this sense of uncomfort when it came to the english language and proper grammar. and all i was getting were 10's on ever paper. and yes, i was doing all the assignments, which were the readings and film watchings and stuff like that. but of course, sometimes i wouldn't fully finish a reading, but i would still respond if i felt like i had enough information. i was writing and writing pages and pages. i felt like it. it was fine with me. i was comfortable. i was having a blast. the sentences were just appearing on the page. from my brain to the page. from my brain to the page. from my brain to the page. and all i'd see later on were 10's and 10's and 10's with plus' and positivity.

    then one day towards the end of the semester we had this reading to do. it was a book titled, *book of tea*. and i don't know. i was extra busy around this time of the semester or something. well, i've always been busy, but now i guess i had extra things to do and catch up on. and note, for this aesthetics class i was in, aestan allowed us to not do a response or two without any penalty. or if we did all of the responses she said she would take out the lowest grades from one or two of them when it came to determine our final grades. she wanted us to succeed and she knew she was giving us a lot to read, watch, and write about. you know what i'm saying? she basically gave us a "freebie" or two. and she knew that things come up sometimes and that there can be some turbulence in a class with an assignment or two. well, okay, so, as you know, right now i had no turbulence in this class. i was smooth sailing. and really, i almost technically didn't have to do another paper and i would probably pass the class. so, okay. i didn't read *book of tea*, hence i didn't have a response for it. i was planning on taking a freebie for this assignment. no worries for me, right? but, i felt uncomfortable not doing the work. i'm sometimes not very happy when i don't complete something that i should. yeah, probably my "structure" and "follow the rules" genes talking. but, my "spontaneous" and "what rules?" genes sometimes start yelling and begin to kick in at a higher gear. so listen, i got to class without a *book of tea* response. and note, this is what happens during our 1hr or so class - we talk about what we read. i usually had plenty to say, but this class i planned to be more on the quite side. and i shouldn't be picked on, right? i've said so much during other class discussions. well, wrong! during the beginning of our class-wide conversation in regards to *book of* tea aestan looked at me and happily said, "akuna, you've been to japan. so, how do you think the *book of tea* relates to your experiences in there?" what!? is this really happening!? for some reason i didn't want to bluntly say that i didn't do the reading. i was a bit shy to put myself in that light right then. or maybe i had fear. or maybe i was just really caught off guard. i don't know. i was on the spot. that moment felt long. what do i do? what do i say? well, i smiled and said, "yeah." then the room felt a slight pause. and that allowed aestan to give me a more specific question. so, she went on to ask me something about the relationship of time spent drinking tea and culture and something along those lines. some words connected in my head and i said, "yeah, culture there is definitely different. in japan tea is more popular than here in america. and tea is healthy. and from my experience, in japan the food portions are much smaller than in the u.s. and i think that allows for a healthier lifestyle. and just how natural and nourishing tea is for the body is something that should be more considered everywhere. japanese have a certain affinity with tea and appreciate it. and that might be a thing in asian culture - consuming tea often." then aestan agreed with things i said and since what we do in class is converse with each other, well, students intervened and spoke their opinions and i then thought in my head, "wow, maybe i got away with it, but i don't know." and note, i didn't at any time say i read the book or didn't read the book. so, it wasn't like i was lying. and what i said was what i thought. but, really i just improvised and spoke true knowledge i knew. seriously, no lies here. well, okay. so more and more discussion went around the room and i started learning what this book was maybe about. and then i thought of the most amazing creative thing that i maybe should do at that point in time. yes, i thought of actually writing a response for this reading during class. but, the reading had to be typed out and double spaced. that was the basic format of turning in papers. well, at this point there was 17mins of class left. i thought and thought and contemplated and analyzed. i found a piece of paper. i wrote on it. i figured things out. i thought, "okay this book has something to do with simplicity from my understanding via the current discussion in class. okay. simplicity. and something about technology doing whatever it's doing. and something along those lines with drinking tea. i guess." then i began my rough draft on this piece of paper i had before me. i have no idea how big my balls were at that time. but, let me tell you, something was about to go down and you have to have balls to do what's next. i somehow had the audacity to get up and excuse myself out of class with this piece of paper in hand and an empty water bottle. i'm guessing the assumption from the class was that i'll go to the bathroom or refill my water bottle or something. i wanted that assumption, hence the water bottle. well, i squirmed up the stairs of the art building where the public computers resided. i started typing my response out! and it was during class! am i serious!? yes! and then i tryed to print it out. printer didn't work. blup! time was running out. there were 7mins left before class ends. i saw my sound and vision professor and since i had a cool relationship with him i asked him if i could print something out real quick from his office. i even told him that it was a paper for a class i had right now. he laughed and said, "okay." okay, so i was in a rush, i went in his office and found a computer from the dinosaur age, like something that creative people handicap crazy difficult to use. i just wanted to type something out! whatever, i found this program to type stuff. i don't even know what it's called to this day. so, i typed my response. if i remember correctly, this is basically literally what i wrote: "response to the *book of tea*. (loading) (loading) (loading) (loading) (technology, eh? why can't we just enjoy the simple things in life?)" and that was it. and note, this was spread over two pages. two "loadings" per page. and these "loadings" implied that my actual response to the *book of tea* was loading. why was it loading? because technology is too busy loading sometimes. or because my amazing superstar piece of writing is so great that it's still loading on the page because of how big a deal it is. i wrote that last sentence with a whimsical smile on my face and a bit of sarcasm. "but, really, sometimes just enjoy simple things" i thought. and if aestan had to read all these papers from her students, why don't i give her something simple this time, right? something fun. and the most creative amazing paper i've done in her class. so, after typing my response i printed it out and i made my way back to class, but i stoped to fill my water bottle on the way before i arrived inside the room. and now note, i walked in the room almost shy and embarrassed because i was bringing in these two brilliant pieces of white paper shinning and everyone knew i didn't leave with *those* two stars. after i sat down on my seat i took a sip of water in attempt to bring back the idea that i left to fill my water bottle. then i realized class was to end in 4mins. then last pieces of conversation were spoken.

then class was over. students turned in their papers.
and then i walked up to aestan and semi-fearfully, but
semi-confidently at the same time, turn in these two
pages that appear to have nothing on them. and now
note, what i've written in this paragraph you are
currently reading i probably shouldn't be writing at all.
i'm sure aestan is going read this book and she'll learn
about what i did. i'm putting myself out there right
now. but listen, i didn't mean any disrespect at all to
aestan by not doing the reading. my creativity took over
with that assignment and i did what i felt like doing. i
had fun doing it. it was an experience for me to do that
response. and i really like telling the story. i find it
fascinating. and that response is one of my most
memorable ones, if not the most memorable one. and
what i understood before doing it was that i was
"allowed" to do such a thing. because of my success in
previous responses i was looked at as someone who
knows what he's doing. i felt like aestan saw me a
certain way and after she learned that i was doing the
readings and watching the videos and bringing fresh
writing afterwards then i was allowed to push my
responses even further. it's like once you're in, you're in
and you can do anything from that point on. maybe,
right? well, okay, so, days passed by and aesthetics class
came again. no papers were returned. next class, same.
at this point i was coming to each class with a high level
of curiosity of what i got on my *book of tea* response. next
class, nothing. and aestan apologized for the extra time
that it was taking for her to return our papers. she was
just a bit overloaded with responses from our class and
her other aesthetics class. she said she was getting
through them though, and next class we should receive
them back. i waited with anticipation. next class
seemed so far away. but, it was coming. the clock ticked

hours away. finally, class time. and papers start flying all over the room. one to her. one to him. another to him. one to the human on my left. one to the woman in front of me. then finally i catch my blank looking papers. and aestan smiled at me as i received my work and said, "i enjoyed this."

    something else, since i knew aestan was currently working on a book, i wanted to have a meeting with her. i was working on a book also, right? i just wanted to know more about publishing and releasing writing and stuff. well, her and i met one day and discussed a few things. we talked about books and writing and creativity. some nice information was exchanged. and then as we were wrapping up our meeting i asked, "how are the other students doing in class?" i was curious because i almost felt like i was getting 10's too easily. and i didn't know if i was actually a good writer or if aestan was just lenient on me and maybe everyone else or something. she went on to say that there were two or three standouts. and that she was trying to eliminate this uncomfortable structure that some students felt the had to follow. like the "5 paragraph rule" that you learn in high school and robotic writing like that. she wanted her students to be free with writing. and not feel forced to follow everything they have learned about writing. i fully knew what she was saying because when i was in high school i followed the rules so heavily and i felt like writing was so hard and uncomfortable and artificial. and super not individual. so, i really appreciated aestan giving me the opportunity to be whoever i wanted to be on the page. honestly, thank you aestan. you've really helped and inspired me. and then, before i left our conversation, i asked aestan, "if i turned in a paper with no name on it, would you recognize that it's mine?" her response was, "instantly!"

    and here's a typical tangent by me that aestan, i think, appreciates: i'm sitting in a coffee shop in shirlington writing this book right now. the sun is coming up from behind me on this crisp november morning in 2013. i have coffee to my left and there's a girl on her laptop in front of me. to my right there's a small line of people getting coffee or maybe a sweet or something. i'm sitting inside, but recently a lady opened up the "window wall" and now even though i'm inside, i'm outside. another woman is about to sit down in front of me and in front of the other woman in front of me. that would mean this new girl is in the middle of both of us. this new one is, well, i don't know what race she is. she has black headphones on and is sipping coffee. there's a book in front of her. it looks big. out of this brown bag she took out food. looks like a sweet. her purse is like burgundy red. she has a clear plastic case for her phone. she has a ring on her left hand ring finger and one on her right index finger. and wait, i was wrong, i just saw her pull out her actual phone and it doesn't have a clear case. i think the clear case thing was on her music box. like a small apple product probably. she now reads the beginning of this book as she sips coffee. to my left there is a woman and a man. they are getting up right now and are about to leave. the woman wears a black outfit with a black hat and purple pants. they are gone. i don't remember what the man was wearing. to my left diagonally behind me are two more sets of people. each have a dog. one set is a man with two kids. or maybe one kid. yes, one child. who i thought to be the other child ended up being a woman sitting around 12feet away on a bench. the other set of two people are two women. behind me are people. the sun is nice. it really is. earlier i slowly took off one jacket and then another. wow! i almost spilled coffee on my laptop! this was crazy! good thing i had only 9% of my coffee left. no damage and no spill! phew! that was an extremely close one! i was going to type something, but that near spill made me type about it. that's like a tangent in a tangent. wow! so, now i should remember what i was going to type. i'm thinking. wait one moment as i think (author thinks and tries to remember). oh yeah, okay, yes. i was going to say that i've been here for hours working on this book. and i'm still working.

arthur lugauskas

chapter 10 : drawing two professor

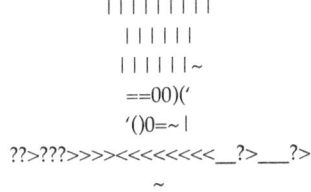

okay, picture time! i mean drawing time! let me draw you a picture of how my drawing two class was. but first, i want you to know that i don't think i'm good at drawing. i struggle with it. or at least i struggle with the traditional aspect of it. drawing the human figure hyperrealistic is hyperhard for me. i don't know.

so, well, first day in class we all introduced ourselves. and that day i learned that my professor was named drawia years and years ago in europe. i thought, "nice, we have being european in common." she was pretty blunt with a dry sense of humor. she seemed like a tough grader and not super into joking around. and that was okay. i didn't mind who she was and i liked that she wanted high quality work.

      during class we would draw and practice. and for homework assignments drawia wanted us to do them outside of class and spend a minimum of 6hours a week working on them. it made sense, right? plus, doing amazing drawings can take a really long time. when work is rushed, it sometimes tends to look rushed. i've done rushed work before. i've had my all-nighters when i did architecture models and stuff like that in the past. doing work last minute wasn't new to me. and it still isn't. but, these days i did tend to care about what i did and because of that i cared to bring high quality. but, you know, sometimes how long something takes is irrelevant. if what is made is amazing, then it's amazing, period. and then there are things that can take days, weeks, or months and look horrible. just be honest with yourself. if something doesn't work, no problem. just realize it and move on. if something is quick and spontaneous and works, cool. okay, where am i going with this? drawing. yes. so, i wasn't the best drawer, but i did want to produce great drawings in this class. and of course, not so much drawings only for the class, but really for me as "portfolio worthy pieces of art" or just for me to be amazed at or whatever the case. but, hey, how would i do that if i didn't draw well? well, maybe rely what i'm best at? and what would that be? probably being creative. because i had access to my creativity and it was on my side. but, since i want to be creative with anything, aren't i always relying on my creativeness? i guess. so, listen, my plan was to put time into drawing, but put more creativity than time in each work. i cared more about the idea and uniqueness of a drawing than skill or craft. but note, i wasn't planning on neglecting skill or craft. i just was aware i wasn't that good at it. and don't get me wrong, i did want to get better. i think.

as the class went on i cared about what i did, i was creative, i was having fun, being whimsical, and enjoying lines and images formed. i turned my stuff in on time. i did sketches in my sketchbook last minute, but tended to do a large number of them. and actually on a sketchbook review day drawia mentioned that i had more sketches than most of the class. but, she still said i had a b for the time being around the middle of the semester, despite my hard work. but, i wasn't worried. i had been working hard on my drawing projects, but i guess i should be work harder to get an a, right? and note, my sketches weren't great at all. but, i met the minimum or so required amount to turn in and that should count for something, right? maybe. i kept going with class and did work with intense care to originality in mind. i knew i was unique and i had to put myself in my work, hence i had to put uniqueness in what i did.

then we had a perspectives drawing assignment to do. and i knew a thing or two from a perspectives class i had during my architecture studies and also from drawing one at nova. so, when drawia had us do a practice perspective drawing in class, well, i was one of the shining stars that time. and for the perspective oriented drawing project drawia assigned us she allowed us to do anything that had to do with perspectives. we had free range to do whatever with perspectives! i thought, "great!" then, i wanted to turn it up a notch and do my project on a bigger piece of paper. we've been doing finished drawings on 18"x24" sheets of white paper. since i had a certain confidence, passion, and skill in perspective drawings i wanted to showcase that. this was probably going to be my time to shine in this class. and the class was told that we were going to do drawings on bigger pieces of paper, but we hadn't got to it at this point. i had to be different with my paper this time. i wanted to. i was. so, i purchased a 22"x30" white sheet of paper with deckled edges. and then i got home and began my drawing. wait, no, i didn't begin right away. i thought about what i should do. and i thought some more. and then i thought, "what would happen if i draw one perspective, then another one sideways, then another one flipped upside down, and then another right side up again all on this one piece of paper? or, something like that!" at that point i didn't fully know where i was going, but i had an idea. and i went with what i thought.

    i started on the white surface before me with a graphite dot. then i got a ruler and drew a straight line. and then a rectangle surrounded that dot. and then my first perspective was surfacing with respect to the horizon line and one vanishing point. i enjoyed putting my thoughts on paper. and once i felt like my first layer of perspective was ready to stay i went over the graphite lines with a felt tip pen. then i looked at what i just did and began thinking. i thought and thought. what next? where to next? after some contemplation i was ready for my second dot, then horizon line, and then another one-point perspective, but this time the new invented space was inside one section of the initial perspective layer and slanted sideways in relationship to that same first layer. i looked at what i had just done and liked it. then i decided to attack another open section on the page and do a two-point perspective. and then in that two-point perspective i found a space for me to do another one-point perspective. and i kept creating these imaginary spaces and places. each space would be different and have its own horizon line and vanishing point or points and angle on the paper and this and that. i was doing these spontaneous perspectives, creating unique worlds, but also having this broad structure underneath it all. and the structure i'm talking about was doing what i thought - perspectives inside of perspectives. do you know what i'm saying? if you don't, then what i'm saying is that after my thought and initial idea, the rest of the work was me fiddling around, playing, having fun, creating, putting ideas on top of ideas, etc. this was beginning to look unlike anything i've ever seen. i was fascinated! this was new! this was its own thing! there was no category of art that i felt this fit in! then i thought, "why don't i make up my own category!? right!?" plus, the drawing before me was asking for it. i thought and thought. and then it clicked. what i just did should be called "perspectives inside of perspectives art." but, that was so long to say over and over again. okay, well, why not take the first letter of each word and see what gets spelled out? so, maybe something like p.i.o.p. art. yes! yes! piop art! boom, i coined the term! and i didn't even really know what "coined" meant, but i felt like that was what went down. and i didn't plan on any of that. it all just happened. i didn't plan on inventing a form of art or whatever that may be called. it just happened because of creativity and many other reasons. and then i thought, "maybe one day i'll google 'piop art' and what won't happen is a question like 'did you mean pop art?' yes, one day."

    finally the day came when we have a critique in class for our perspective drawings. i've worked hard on mine and got to class that day full of confidence. i felt like i did something amazing. no, i knew i did something amazing! but, something so simple at the same time. or better yet, my concept had a simplicity in it and my idea had purity, but what the end product generated was intrigue, questioning, and complexity. so, we started having the critique. two students went at a time. one group, then another, then another. and for your information, i didn't have many comments on the perspective drawings that were presented. then, it was my turn to go up alongside with a classmate. i had the biggest drawing because i chose to up the notch when it came to paper size. the was the first everyone noticed. then the astonishment in the viewers' eyes began. as students gazed at what i presented before them, they seemed puzzled, curious, interested, and uncertain as to what they were witnessing. even drawia herself was shocked. what had i just done? and ever since that day people saw me differently. people knew that i knew a thing or two. people liked what i was doing. and drawia was impressed with what i had done. then anticipation started in everyones mind, "what will he do next?"

    what did i do next? well, next it was time to do drawings on huge paper. way bigger than what my first ever piop art drawing was on. actually, when i first saw the paper size for my next project i got a bit scared. but, i was excited too! because i didn't recall ever attacking such a scale. but, i was ready! or, no. i don't know if i was ready. i just went in! and i got comfortable. well, kind of. the scale was crazy for me at that time. i was drawing standing up and kneeling down and i felt like i was dancing with activity and drawing materials and paper. crazy time in my life! and i put time and effort into my large scale drawings. i had fun with them.

    and now it's time for a very important story. brace yourself. it's about to get real! what am i talking about? let me tell you. but first, wait. i have to give you prepare you. so, overall drawing two was going well for me. i had been working hard, being creative, having fun, learning, etc. and as the semester progressed i had learned more about drawia. i mentioned a few first impressions earlier, but now i have second, third, fourth, fifth, etc. impressions. first, i thought she really didn't like to smile that much. i'm not joking when i say this. and i felt displeased by that because smiling is like one of my favorite things to do. some people actually saw me as a smiling machine. now, i'm not saying drawia never smiled, but i am saying she didn't do it that much on her own terms. she preferred to be serious and often times had this annoyed look on her face when it came to her relationship with her students. don't get me wrong now, she was helpful and she had knowledge, but she wasn't playful and fun. and playful and fun were two more strong attributes to my personality. so, as you may have noticed, her and i had differences. and these differences showed in class. i tried to bring smiles out of her. i succeeded at times, but other times she felt what i had to say was wrong or whatever the case. let me tell you something drawia taught her class. she said that we shouldn't ever mix certain mediums. like graphite and felt tip pens and ink. she said those things don't marry well together and if a student would combine them she would automatically hate. now, okay, i understand they may not work well together, but why not allow students to try to make them work? why not go away from traditional thinking about what mediums should and shouldn't be mixed? why not experiment and explore? when will mixing them be allowed? when the most famous artists begin to combine mediums that don't marry, then sell their work for hundreds of thousands of dollars, then have others artists do the same thing, then wait five to seven years, and then finally mixing mediums that don't marry is the new traditional form of drawing? i don't know. and drawia seemed to be a person who didn't want her students to have that much fun. in one way you could say that she was basically promoting unhappiness. and trust me, it was uncomfortable and uninspiring to be around a person like that. and drawia didn't really like to say "hi" outside of class either. or maybe she just didn't like to say "hi" to me. and i thought we had a european connection. nevermind i guess. and here's another instance. so, in the beginning of the semester drawia wanted to see work from her new drawing two class, or i.e. us. she wanted us to bring some of our work so she and the rest of the class had an idea of what level of art making each person looked to be at based on previous work. and i thought that to be completely acceptable and fun. and the day she mentioned that i asked her if she was going to bring some of her work to show the class too. and i said that in a smiling manner. and her response was, "no." just a straight up, "no." it's like she thought i was attacking her or challenging her or something. which was not the case at all. she was a drawing professor, right? she was also an artist, right? she drew, right? okay, so, was i not allowed to be interested in seeing her work? i didn't know what the big deal was. and why was her response to harsh. i was just a curious individual who wanted to see art that he may have not seen before. well, whatever, i didn't question further or ask anymore after her "no" response. okay, so, now that i've prepared you a bit, time for the very important story i mentioned in the beginning of this paragraph. so, there was this project drawia gave the class. it was around mid-to-late semester. we had to do it on a sheet of the large-sized paper we had been working with. and there was this theme for us to go off of. everything sounded good and i brought my individuality, originality, and creativity to this project - as i normally tried to do with everything i did. i was excited with my idea, went through with what i thought of, and did my drawing. then the day it was due came. i was ready to present. critiques began. and this time it was one student at a time. student after student went. then it was my turn. i was feeling good and excited to present! i was proud of what i did! i went up in front of the class and explained what they were seeing before them, "so, lately i've been feeling like i'm about to go crazy because i've been working on all these projects. and i have all these ideas. and time is flying and disappearing before my eyes. i'm trying to catch time, but it's not easy. i have ideas on top of ideas. my thoughts keep me awake at night. inside my head is craziness right now. and as i'm trying to finish up projects, new ones are starting on a consistent basis. so, the drawing in front of you has to do with everything i just said. the person in it is me - the artist. and the concept is me building me. with one hand i'm drawing my lower body, feet, and overall foundation with charcoal. and at the same time, with my other hand i'm painting my story, adding color to my life, and becoming more vibrant and exciting. and where it's interesting is, i don't even have a foundation to stand on, but i'm already adding more elements on my structure. and there's this idea that everything starts from my brain, my thoughts, my thinking, and for some reason i don't worry so much about the foundation because i believe it will appear. so, i'm loading on top of loads without fully knowing what's in each load or what the initial load is or where it is or if it's ready for unload yet or not, but at the same time i'm believing that i shouldn't worry." drawia had this concerned and perplexed look on her face and then commented, "akuna, you should go to some museums. go see what artists are doing." and i thought, "what the blup did she just say!? is she seriously telling me this!? really!? are you kidding me!? so, you're basically telling me, 'go be a follower, go see what other artists are doing, don't be original, don't bring new thought or ideas to the table, you're not a real artist until you start doing what you see in museums, you don't know anything about art, i'm a professor and i've never seen such a drawing, nor have i heard such an explanation, so, you have got to be out of your mind, i'm here to teach you what you should do, and what you should do is not be creative, not be unique, not do things i've never seen before, and not be you.'" so, listen everyone, i took drawia's comment as a huge compliment. i understood she's never experienced a mind like mine. and i understood that what i've done she's never seen before. and that made me feel unique, individual, and amazing. thank you for that comment drawia. you boosted my "ego" that day because i knew that comment was a positive comment in disguise. i'm sure no one saw the comment like i did and that's okay. i deconstructed that comment in my head and learned what it actually meant. and i'm happy to be sharing this very important moment in my education life in art school - where creativity, originality, and differentness *should* be promoted. does this all make sense? or am i the one who's crazy here?

    okay, lets end with this chapter. a couple more things. for our final project drawia allowed us to draw anything we wanted. i was like, "yes! what a fantastic assignment from drawia!" but, most others were puzzled and confused and wanted guidance. i heard some students say things like, "what do you mean by 'do whatever'? what do you mean we can do anything?

what are the guidelines? what do you want me to do?" and i was disappointed to hear all those questions. i was just thinking, "listen people, she said that we can draw whatever! end of story! draw anything you want!" but note, i understood. and this stuff isn't uncommon. most people want guidance because school teaches you to be guided your whole life. traditional thinking is taught after your 5th birthday. or maybe sooner these days. school, for the most part, doesn't teach you how to be yourself. individuality isn't wanted *that* much. but, robots are! and that's a problem! and when you have someone who is a complete individual, he or she is hated on! blup! oh, and "blup" is a word i invented. i don't like to say certain words, so i choose to replace certain words with other words via word invention. i have a few words i've made up and use on an almost regular basis. friends of mine know the words i'm talking about. some of the words are a bit contagious and i've had plenty of friends use my words around me. it's kind of funny and interesting. and, well, they aren't necessarily my words, but instead words i prefer to use overtop certain words i don't care to use. you know what i mean? but, okay, individuality and doing whatever you want. so, yeah, it was no surprise that most of my drawing two class asked for guidance. i was one of the few that was fully comfortable with drawing anything i wanted and super excited about it. and now listen everyone, it's sad that too many people don't do what they want. you have the opportunity to do whatever you want everyday! don't let anyone live *your* life! think about what *you* want to do and then figure out how you are going to do it! it's all possible! anything is possible! but, it starts with you not being afraid to be yourself! and simply believing in yourself! i'm going off on another tangent, right? okay, back to this "do whatever" assignment. i was happy about it. and i decided to do a small scale drawing of every practice drawing and "homework" drawing i did throughout the whole semester on a single 18"x24" sheet of white paper. that size was the size we used most often, so i thought it was the right size to do this project on. and i wanted to do my final in pen and ink. that medium was fun, looked nice, and i liked it. and note, it happened to be drawias favorite medium to draw in. and understand, it's just a coincidence that i'm doing my final drawing two drawing in drawias favorite drawing medium. so, i found all my practice drawings and "homework" ones, organized them, and then i did a certain "picture-frame-type" composition on a newsprint sheet of paper. i liked what i saw. and of course, i added this newsprint practice drawing of my final that i just did in the composition because it was part of my initial idea. i then did the final and had fun with doing these "loose-hand" small drawings that i soon became fond of. final critique day came and a student found what i did playful and said, "i like it. it's interesting because you're almost mocking the class. it almost feels like you're saying, 'this is all i learned in drawing two.' it's cool and fun." and i found this classmates comment fun in itself. it's interesting what people get out of what you do. it wasn't in my intention to "mock" the class or what we have learned or make these smaller versions of bigger drawings make the bigger drawings less significant towards the end or stuff like that. i just wanted to have fun and be creative and do a project that no one else would do. of course, i didn't know if anyone else was thinking about the same thing as me, but i felt confident that my idea was going to stand on its own.

okay, *now* it's time for the last paragraph of this chapter. big problem after the last day of my drawing two class. after all my work, sketchbook sketches, practice drawings, "homework" drawings, originality, pushing creativity and projects to places where they may not be understood upon first inspection, and etc. etc. etc. guess what grade i got? did you guess a? or b? or c? well, i got a b. a b!? yes, a b! okay, now, listen, if i deserved that b i would take it. but, honestly in my heart i didn't feel like i deserved that grade. on sketchbook day i had more sketches than most of the class, i turned in all my final drawings on time, i missed maybe only one class (if that), and when i was in class i was working! and i even invented piop art! and after all that a b!? and note, i'm not trying to be a diva or drama queen or act like i care all that much about school or grades or whatever. i'm just hurt because i was wronged. i honestly, truly believe i didn't deserve the b. if i deserved it i would take it. so, this isn't about grades. please understand that. this is about what's right. i think the factor that it came down to on whether i was going to get an a or b was how much drawia liked me. and since we had some clashes during the semester i think she took that into consideration when she was thinking of what my final grade was going to be. you know, i guess she didn't like my smile or positivity or originality or care for doing unique creative art or my confidence in *my* drawings or me doing drawings *my* way or whatever the case when it came to my personality *that* much. tisk tisk.

arthur lugauskas

chapter 11 : sculpture one professor

time to get into a class that has to do with my bfa concentration - sculpture. i actually didn't know who the professor was going to be for this class because when i signed up for it the "professor box" showed "tbd." so, i didn't know what to expect. and let me take this time to tell you that i've never been interested in going to those online websites about who's the "best" or "worst" professor to have class with. when i would sign up for classes all i cared about was what classes i had to take and how i could piece together my schedule the best way. so, it was about how my schedule looked as opposed to who the professor was. and plus, everyone has their own opinions and many people are sometimes biased. like with drawia, i think she just didn't like me, but that doesn't mean she's not going to like you. and i had my experience with her, i was honest with what i wrote, but understand that my experience with a person will be different than your experience. and note, if i learn that a certain professor is good or great from a fellow student i might take that into consideration. but, i'm not interested in writing on those online professor rating sites or reading them. little tangent i took there, but now back to sculpture one class. so, i didn't know who was going to teach the class. then first day of class came around and i meet a man named ten. he said, "sellbee isn't here today because she's out of town. but, she'll be present next class." i was confused. who was sellbee? or what was sellbee? and who is this guy named ten? but, then pieces started to come together. i learned that ten basically ran the sculpture studio in a way and his office was in sort of the middle of it and he's the main man to go to if anyone wants help with tools and stuff like that. he watched over the studio and made sure people were safe and all that. he seemed cool. and during his introduction of who he was i learned that he skateboarded. i was very happy to hear that because i've been skateboarding for years and years now. i thought him and i would get along. and i learned that sellbee was a person and that she was an african woman and that she was going to be my sculpture one professor for the semester. and ten was going to be around when class was in session for help or questions or etc.

    then i was curious as to who sellbee was and what face she had. i didn't know what to expect. i didn't know if she was going to be nice or mean. and i didn't know anything about what was going to happen in this class. but, i was excited!

second day of class we meet sellbee. and i quickly learned that she was a nice woman and full of smiles. i was happy about that.

class went quite smoothly overall. my first sculpture project was me remaking my car in an abstract way from parts that came off my actual car. sidebar, i used to play around with my car a lot and take it apart like legos and do all this stuff to my daily driver. hence i had parts that no longer needed to be on the car. why? because less weight, more speed, right? so, yeah, my first sculpture in this class had a personal thing from me in it. the process of making was fun and sellbee enjoyed what i was doing and my work ethic.

the next sculpture i did was another project that had to do with something personal. basically i did a globe out of plaster and i had all these countries made out of different materials and i welded some people out of nails and put those people on the globe and each of them had "strings of life" and most peoples string was short, indicating that they haven't experienced the world or traveled that much, and then there was a nail with a longer string that has touched down in a variety of places of the globe, indicating experience, and i was trying to say that not enough people travel and experience. and the "nail person" that had been everywhere was a little bigger than the rest and that implied more knowledge simply because of travel and living in a variety of cultures. and to this day i think it's really healthy to travel. i've grown up traveling and experiencing so much. and all my travels have helped me become who i am today and i tell people who haven't lived in another continent to leave the country immediately. but, these people think i'm joking and they tell me reasons why they can't leave. but, i'm not joking and i'm trying to help when i say, "leave the country tomorrow." and blah, blah, blah.

then we had a group sculpture project to do and i had a big voice during discussions in my group. i wasn't scared to state what i thought. and in the end the piece we did was successful and interactive.

then came another project. and i had this small scale idea, but sellbee suggested, "why don't you go big? like why not do that somewhere on the stairwell?" and i responded, "hmm. yes. why not?" then i did my first large scale string installation on the main stairwell in the art building. it was with gray string primarily, but there was a bit of blue string to imply windows. i felt good after i did that piece and it opened doors for my future work and ideas. i appreciated sellbees suggestion and i'm thankful for the opportunity she presented to me. she was encouraging and let me be me. and i was working hard in her class. she appreciated that and later on in the future mentioned that i made her teaching of the class worth it. and the reason she said that was because a lot of students slacked and she had to push them to do work and some of them weren't taking things that seriously at all and stuff like that. well, the class was fun for me and helped me grow as an artist and individual. thanks for how you conducted class sellbee.

don't say anything, ever

arthur lugauskas

::: : : : : : :: :: : : : : : : : :: :::
chapter 12 : sound and vision professor
:::::::::::::::::::::::::::::::::::   ::: : : : ::: : : ::: : :: ::: ::::::::::::::::::::::

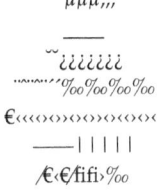

sound and vision time! actually, when i signed up for this class i thought i signed up for a different class, but didn't realize it and blah blah blah. i don't really want to get into that story. just know, this was one of the classes that counted towards my degree.

okay, so, first day of class i met the professor. his name was sunvy. i think he was african american. he had glasses that he put on sometimes and he spoke very well. i felt like he was a smart man with a lot of knowledge. but, at the same time he had comedy elements to him and was hip. i don't know if he considers himself "hip", but i feel like that word fits his personality.

this class was supposed to be about sound and vision. and that sounded good to me! but, sunvy was a bit unhappy the first day because the classroom he was given didn't have all the equipment that he wanted it to have in order to teach the class. so, he told us that he was going to improvise. and note, sunvy made music and knew about sound and had cool vibes around him.

well, in class we had listening sessions to ambient noise, we had recording sessions of music making or singing or whatever, and we even tried to fix a piano for some reason.

one time sunvy had us listen to a song. then he played another song. then he asked us to write what we thought of each song and the differences and similarities of the two. and after we turned in our papers he said that one of the songs was his own. then i thought, "hmm, i wrote what i thought. i'm not sure how he will take my comments." well, i never got my paper back. i don't know why.

so, throughout the class we did stuff here and there and learned about this and that, but there were two things the class was primarily about. and these two things would affect our grade the most and they were just really important overall. the first thing was for us to develop a sonic portfolio by the end of the semester. the second thing was for the class to be involved in some way with something called "noise awareness day."

i'll start with giving you some sonic portfolio business. so, at first i thought about actually doing a full album. like, yes, a music album. with me singing or putting words together in a creative way or something like that. i mentioned that to sunvy and he immediately got this idea that i'm going to be a hip hop star or something like that. i'm not sure why, but i guess he saw something in me. or maybe he was joking around. he did say that with a smile, but i don't know. sidebar, around early into the semester time when we had a studio session in the music studio sunvy had in the art building i decided to sing. other students brought instruments and stuff like that. i used my voice. and what did i sing? well, i was going through a broken heart, i wrote a song, and then sang it and actually almost cried while singing. sunvy was in the studio that day and also a few other classmates. what i sang was real and honest. i got emotional while singing. i'm actually not sure how i just sang so fearlessly in the soundproof room while classmates and sunvy were outside of that room listening to everything i was singing via loud clear speakers. i just let my heart out when i was in there. and after i was done i got out of the room a bit emotional. but, i didn't let my sensitivity show too much. i regrouped relatively quick, i think. and the first words out of sunvy's mouth were, "wow, that's cold man!" and what he was referring to was how the song went and what i said at the end of the song especially. and then sunvy actually showed interest in using what i sang in one of his songs. he said he'd edit my voice and no one would know it was me. i said, "okay." and he ended up doing what he said he'd do and he had a performance and used the song with my voice edited a certain way and then he told me that people responded well to the voice they heard and people felt that there was pain in that voice and sunvy himself said i had a good voice and stuff like that. and after i heard that i thought, "what!? i don't know how to sing. is he joking?" so, after sunvys positive comment i laughed a bit because i thought it was funny and said, "i don't really know how to sing." well, whatever the case, sunvy basically gave me encouragement and liked what i was doing. but, i still didn't understand what he heard in my voice. then i learned that sunvy was willing to give me the code to enter the music studio whenever i wanted to work on music if i wanted it. i felt humbled. and making music was in my bag of interests. so, i got the code and sometimes i would go to the studio and work late nights on music. i had no idea what i was doing because i didn't know how to make music. but, i was experimenting and trying to learn. sometimes i'd be in the studio all night. and yes, i would literally sleep there sometimes and have class in the morning when i woke up. yeah. and on one instance i let go and sang my heart out and i came to tears and broke down. i had a lot of pain inside me. sidebar to the current sidebar, i had a girlfriend named azza, we were together for around a year, stuff happened, tables turned, i ended up getting really hurt somehow, and i guess i was looking for an outlet for my pain and music was an option i thought of. end sidebar inside sidebar. and now, back to original sidebar, so yeah, i had emotional times in the studio. and now end original sidebar. and quick new sidebar, this sidebar business in writing is kind of fun. i just learned it as i was typing earlier in this book. i'm not sure how or why or where it came from. i just typed it on the page and liked it. okay, now end the second sidebar and back to the paragraph that was happening before any sidebar came into it. wait, you're not lost, are you? i'm not lost. this is where we left off: me wanting to make a music album for sonic portfolio and proposing that so sunvy and him thinking that i was going to be a hip hop star. back on track? cool. so, yeah, i was thinking about doing an album, but i ended up losing grip of time and no album of me singing and stuff happened. or well, how do i put this? umm, i'll tell you what i did for my sonic portfolio. okay, so, basically i went to the nga museum in dc and recorded five van gogh paintings as if i was reading them left to right and top to bottom and then i went in the studio and tried reading each of the five van gogh paintings through sound. did that make sense? maybe i'm just confusing you. i'm not trying to confuse you. well, after composing what i thought van goghs paintings would sound like i put the finished songs and footage together and made short films of my reading van gogh's through sound. that was my sonic portfolio with the integration of film and creativity.

    and now, time for "noise awareness day" business. sunvy was in charge of putting together this thing called "noise awareness day" and it was something important to him. he told us about what it was. and i learned that it was a day full of sound waves and performances and noise in any and every way. and that this day happens in the art building and often goes all day and into the night and even next morning usually. he said that last year they finished around 6am. it sounded amazing! so, first things to figure out were giving people "noise awareness day" jobs. sunvy wanted help and he had a sound and vision class to help him. the duties ranged from being a performer to doing two hours shifts of helping make sure everything is running well to security and etc. my classmates were picking different things they wanted to do or just felt comfortable with. and as for me, well, i'm a performer, right? i think so. so, yeah, i decided to do a performance during the day we will be reminded to be aware of noise. and what did i care to bring in my performance? creativity, of course! you know this by now, right? so, let me break it down for you. after much thinking and putting puzzle pieces together i came up with this idea and i did this performance: don't lose me now, okay, so i performed all five reading van gogh songs live while the footage was playing and then i told the audience that i had a performance earlier and if they missed it they should ask themselves where they were at, and then i said that my earlier performance was so good that an encore was going to be shown right now, and note, this was a pre-recorded performance of me singing on a table in the exact room "noise awareness day" was taking place, and finlay was the one who filmed it and i edited it and now i was playing it as if i performed earlier that day and i wanted for the audience to question if what i was saying was real or performance and then as the footage played of me singing on that table i actually brought an easel, some paint, and paint brushes out and started to paint myself performing and then during the footage, digital me said he was nervous and that people are watching and then alive me said to not worry and to keep going and then digital me kept singing and alive me keeps painting digital me and that's basically what i did for my "noise awareness day" performance. fun, right? i mean, super amazing and extraordinary, right!?

don't say anything, ever

arthur lugauskas

don't say anything, ever

::::: : : : ::::: :: : ::::: : : ::::::: ::::: : : :::: ::::: :: :: ::::: ::::: :: :: :: : ::
chapter 13 : visual voices professor
: : : : : :: : : :: : : : : : : : : : : : : : : ::::::: :::::::::::::::::::::::::::::::::::

.°..°°.°.°.°..°°.
°..°.°.°°
»'»'»'»'»'»"""""
¿¿˜¿ ¿ ¿ ¿ ˘˘˘˘˘˘˘˘
`»`»`»₁˜₁₁◊¥¥¥¥
¥^¥^--«æ`÷≥≥≥÷≤≤
"««"««"««æ'ææ…'ææ…'ææ…"

what is visual voices? it's a class that you have to take three times in order to get an art degree at gmu. and the way this class works is, well, it's not really a class. it's a lecture series. basically gmu invites guest speakers that are in the art world in some way and they do a 1hr or so lecture in an auditorium and there are normally 4 or 5 lectures to attend in a semester and each semester the group of speakers are different, hence the reason why it makes sense to take the class more than once. and after listening to the speakers the students are to write a 5 page paper or 1500 word paper or something like that on a speaker of choice and students are required to attend all the lectures because attendance is half the grade and, well, that's the basic structure of visual voices.

okay, now that we have that covered, time to get into a battle scene. so, the professor or the one who was involved with this visual voices lecture series or the one who was inviting the speakers or whatever the case was vivtol. and vivtol also happened to be the head of the school of art at gmu. big deal person, right? and another cool thing was that he had published books about portfolio design. wow, cool, great! so, as you know i've already had a meeting with aestan about how to go about publishing books, right? and she gave me good info, but thought she didn't help much because of her lack of knowledge on how books are published in the technology age because of self-publishing online and all that stuff. she knew more about the traditional route of publishing and shared what she knew with me in that regard and how authors went about publishing books in the past. okay, so that happened, but i wanted to know more. so, i connected some dots and used my resources. basically i emailed vivtol in regards to having a meeting with him about book publishing. i guessed he was probably a busy man, but i thought he could spare 18mins or so to give me some advice. well, i got a nice response from him via email and we set up a meeting. so, i was excited for this meeting, i wanted to learn, and i was ready for it. the day came and we meet at his office inside the art building. he was prepared for me. upon entering his office he gave me a sheet of paper with important information in regards to book publishing. and he wanted me to look over it instantly. i did. then we got to talking. and as we discussed book publishing related things we steered off into things about me somehow. he was curious what i was about and work i've done artistically - like in an object or drawing making scenario. i showed him some images of my architecture models and drawings and stuff. and then we got to talking more about my interests and what i was doing with my life. and i mentioned dreams i had and a variety of things. and i related some of my thoughts to people i was fascinated with and inspired by. one of those people being frank gehry. and i at that point i had recently saw the film *sketches of frank gehry* and was amazed by it. it almost brought me to tears. actually i think one time it did. so, i mentioned to vivtol things i learned about frank. and i said things like, "for architecture i'm not interested in doing autocad drawings for other architects for 7 years and then finally maybe at some point doing my own architecture designs. i want to be the architect of a place or space. i believe in my design. i know i could make amazing happen. all i'm missing is the opportunity right now. and my biggest steer away from architecture at the moment is just that - not currently having a given opportunity by someone to design something as an architect. and partly it's because i haven't looked for that commission and such. but, with architecture i'm not worried because i plan to design my own house someday and maybe that will be my entrance into the world of being great architect. well, if i achieve the level of creativity and amazing i'm looking for that is. but, one thing i do know is that one thing i learned and really didn't like about studying architecture is that what is expected for architecture students after graduation is to do autocad for 7 years before they just get the opportunity to be involved with a design in some way. i don't want to do that and that's not going to be me. and i've been thinking like this before i saw the film on frank. and after i saw that film i was so happy that i wasn't the only one who thought in this way in a way. like, frank 'doesn't know' how to really use a computer. frank was told that he should just quite architecture and do something else when he first was studying it. but, he didn't give up, he went his way in his life, and somehow ended up being one of the greatest living architects today! and i find his sketches to be so amazing!" and then guess what vivtol said to me. well, his response was, "how many frank gehrys are there?" then in my head i just exploded with anger and annoyance and frustration. i was thinking, "what the blup did you just say to me!? are you serious! so, you're basically telling me that there is no possible way i'll be as great as frank or even get close to his level of amazingness and that i shouldn't try to go my own path and that i should follow the 'common path' laid out for architecture graduates and that i'm crazy to think i could just burst into the architecture scene and make amazing because i believe in my capabilities as a creative and designing with experience and individuality in mind and that i should stop dreaming." and note, i know vivtol didn't say all that, but that was my interpretation based on the tone in his voice and the look he had on his face and other nonverbal details after my spiel of words. so, right then and there i learned that vivtol was a dreamkiller and that i really shouldn't be letting my dreams out to him because i felt that he felt superior than me and i also felt that he felt that i should be a robot mind instead of an individual mind. well, i answered vivtol, "one, but.." and before i could say another word he said, "exactly. only one." and as he said that he lifted his left hand and showed me one finger. i felt so disrespected for some reason. and it was like my dreams were in jeopardy and that i had to be strong in keeping them safe and protecting them. because this talk was coming from the head of the school of art at gmu! like, the person who runs a school where creativity, individuality, and dreams should be fostered and encouraged instead of bashed on, discounted, and neglected! i was just really shocked and had this crazy bad of emotions. and the main one being just hurt.

      overall, after that meeting i saw vivtol as a nice person. i wasn't interested in talking about my dreams, goals, and desires with him anymore, but i didn't mind saying "hi" with a smile to him when i saw him. i didn't have any hard feelings against him. i was just at a different level of thought and i understood that. or actually, seriously, who knows, maybe i'm the one who's crazy.

arthur lugauskas

don't say anything, ever

::: : : : : ::::: : :::: : : :: :::: :: ::: ::: :::: :: : :::: : : :: :::: ::::: :::::::::::::::::::::
chapter 14 : honors seminar professor
:::::::::: : : ::: :: ::: : : ::::: :::: : :::: :: ::::::: ::::::::::::: :::::::::::::::: :::::

$####%#%#%#%#&#&#&#&%%&#%%#%&%&#"$"$$%"$
%"$"%&#$"%$$%"$%$%#$%%"%& | | | | | | # | | # | # | | | # | # | # | # |
| # | ## | # | # | # | # | | | # | ~ | ~# | ~ | #~ | ~ | ~ | ~ | ~ | #~ | #~ | #~ | # | ~# |
~~=#=~~=#=~=~=~=~=~=#=~#~==~#~=##=#=~=~#=~=~'''=~~"=
~='''| ~# | # | ~~ | "~ | " | | " | "| = | = | = | #=#=$=$=$=%=~%~=%=~~=
%~=~==~~=&~=~=~=~=&~~=&~==~%=~%=~=~%$~$~~~$~ | # ~ | ~ |
~ | $ | ~

and now, to talk about one more class i had this semester. this class was the last one added to my schedule. it was a class that you had to be invited to in order to be part of, hence the name honors. do you want to guess who recommended me for the class? certainly one of my professors early on in the semester. who do you think? newsy? aestan? maybe drawia? or could it of been sellbee? or sunvy? or do you think vivtol? do you have your guesses? i'm guessing you had your eliminations if you were having a hard time. well, if you guessed newsy, you're wrong. ouch. it almost hurts me to write "you're wrong." but, it's funny because i don't mean that in any negative or hurtful way. i think that statement might just appear to be negative. i don't know. but, what i do know is that the statement is true if the situation i laid out was correct. and maybe you didn't guess newsy and if that's the case then you weren't even in the running of being wrong when i stated, "well, if you guessed newsy, you're wrong". but, i still feel like you may have gotten that hit of me saying you're wrong in whatever the case. do i make any sense right now? good. and i mean "good" to whatever answer you gave me or didn't give me. so, we're finding out who recommended me to be part of the honors seminar class and honors program in general. well, if you guessed aestan, you are right! wow, doesn't me saying "you are right" feel good in any case? i think it does. so, yes, aestan recommended me to join honors because of the thoughts i expressed in my written responses. i really was happy she saw something in me and encouraged me to go further and brought opportunities to me. thanks again aestan!

    so, i missed only one or two or three honors seminar classes by the time i became part of it. and the first class i attended i learned that i actually didn't miss much due to how the honors class was laid out in the curriculum. because honors was at the same time as visual voices and when visual voices met then there was no honors and when visual voices didn't meet honors was in session and honors was held only once a week and blah blah blah.

    i guess there was supposed to be this sense of prestige being with other honors students, like these are the people doing the most or whatever the case, but i don't know. i'm not sure how i felt. maybe i didn't really fit in the class because i joined it a bit late. or the students in that class were already friends from previous semesters and they had their little sort of clique. i don't know. i felt a bit off for some reason.

soon enough i met the professor of the class and his name was hon. he ran an artful library at the school of art and was involved with various projects. he was a nice person, but interesting too. he had this sense of realness to him. i never really knew what he did, especially when he spoke about his library. maybe because he was just bringing terms i wasn't familiar with or couldn't quite grasp. i mean, he'd explain things, but sometimes i just didn't get it. call it a flaw in my personality, call it something weird about me, or whatever.

well, hon was cool with me and vice versa. we didn't have conflicts. and one of the things we did in his honors class was really get involved with artists doing work outside of "school world". and we spoke and worked with them first hand.

one project we were involved with was this huge citywide exhibition in dc. i met with an artist who was putting sets of rocks all around the city and if a person collected all the rocks then they could go online and type in a code that was formed with a combination of the 7 or so rocks and then they could win something. fun, right? it was like a scavenger hunt.

another project we were involved with had to do with ten. and ten is an artist if you didn't know. and he was actually making this do-it-yourself skatepark at this bridge spot in dc. it was all about flow and pathway of a person moving around a space. one day i visited the site with actually my sculpture one class. i feel like i'm at a semi-tangent right now. well, that day ten was at this bridge spot working and skateboarding. and when he saw me gaze at his skateboard he noticed and let me borrow it and then i was cruising around the space. it was fun. very fun. i was skateboarding during class. cool or cool? okay, so i'm moving and grooving on wheels and then i noticed that there was this other man there. his name was bom. and i kept hearing about him in school, but had no idea who he was. even a fellow student questioned and said, "you haven't had a class with bom!? you should try to take your next sculpture class with him! he will blow your mind!" that was one of the first roll of comments that introduced me to this man named bom. the interesting part was that he had been like a myth or a legend to me because i heard talk of him, but never seen him or knew who he actually was. but, then again, it was my 1st semester at gmu, so what did i know? okay, so, let me give you some structure to what i wrote earlier. well, one day when sellbee told her sculpture one class, "we are going to this bridge spot to visit ten and bom might be there too." i didn't know what to think because i didn't know bom or who he was, but i was interested in seeing this man i've heard so much about. then the day came and i saw bom himself. he had a cane, i think. and as i looked at him i didn't know what the big deal about him was. i noticed that he was an older man with a beard. but, not *that* old. and the beard wasn't *that* long. i didn't talk to him much after sellbee introduced us to him. i don't know why. then later on when we made it back to gmu i asked sellbee about bom and who he was. she said that he ran the sculpture department at the school of art at gmu and that he was currently on sabbatical. i thought, "okay. and what is a sabbatical? sounds bad or something." and then i asked sellbee, "what's a sabbatical?" and she said it was some sort of leave for the semester. and i still didn't get it nor understand. sellbee mentioned that

bom should be back next semester. i thought, "okay." and that was that.
    and another big part of the honors class was a trip to a living museum in nc. that was a crazy experience that involved a lot of stuff. and i mean literally stuff on stuff on stuff.

arthur lugauskas

don't say anything, ever

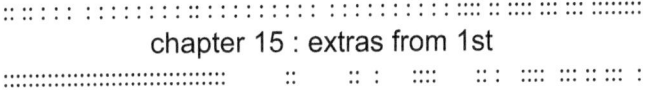

chapter 15 : extras from 1st

while a lot of things had happened with my classes, projects, and professors in my 1st gmu semester, understand that there was plenty more going on.

well, for one i decided to work on a couple of paintings. of what, though? let me tell you. so, since i really liked my first ever piop art drawing i thought, "why don't i make a painting with this same piop art idea?" after that thought i went to the art store and bought a 36"x48" canvas. i don't know why i thought i was ready to attack such a size when i didn't even know how to paint and the biggest canvas prior that size that i painted on was something like 20"x20". but, well, i guess i had confidence inside me somewhere. so, next thing i knew i was in my room and starting to make piop art on a huge canvas. when i was working on it for the first hours i thought what i had in front of me was gigantic. at this point i was pretty oblivious to a lot of the "art world" and as to what sized paintings existed and all that. so, i was working on this canvas and learning about how my process for this would be because another layer other than drawing with graphite and pen was going to be added. and that layer was, yes, paint. acrylic paint to be exact. i didn't really know the difference between oil and acrylic paint at this point. and i didn't really know what oil paint was because the few painting projects i did at nova were with acrylic paints. so, there i was, drawing my second ever piop artwork without even really knowing what i was doing other than the basic idea i had in my head. it was an intense and scary moment. painting on a canvas was like going into a battlefield for me. or a war! and even though i didn't really know what i was doing, nor did i know how to paint, nor did i have full blown confidence entering this canvas physically, i think for some reason i had confidence in my ideas and what i thought would and should work and i was just having fun making something of value in my world.

    one day at school i had a little incident. remember fundofdne? narcissist thing? right? okay, so remember he taught at gmu as well as at nova? yeah, so i saw him at school plenty and we had our conversations here and there. and it was funny because when we interacted with each other we both had this blunt, fun, and dry sense of humor. fun moments those were. well, one day there was a moment that was a little bit different from the others. what happened was one day i mentioned to him that i was doing an amazing painting, even though i didn't know how to pain. and yes, i'm talking about the first ever piop art painting i was working on that i stated in the paragraph prior to this one. and then i said, "yeah, i want to have paintings in new york that are worth so much and have such high value and not necessarily for the money, but for fun because i don't know how to paint. you know, i'm not interested in being an artist who's painted for 20plus years and then just starts to get recognized. i want my paintings to be worth thousands or millions and i don't know how to paint." and he said, "you don't want to be that guy." and i kind of laughingly said, "yeah, i kind of do. maybe." and that was the incident, moment, memory.

      then i got to a point when i realized that i've been working on a lot of new things, but didn't have them documented just yet. i thought and thought and then called finlay and said, "hey, lets have another filming session. i'm thinking another interview, but this time in this music studio i have access to. and i have a string installation, new drawings, and me making music that i'd like you to film. could we make it happen?" and he said, "sure." so, that's what we did. the interview was long and actually not really like an interview. finlay just threw out questions to me in order for me to start flowing. but, then it got to me telling stories and talking about how i was at a "make it" or "break" point in my life due to all the projects i was working on. i was at a crazy time period and literally felt like i was possibly close to going crazy. we were filming until 2 or 3am for hours and hours. and note, the first interview finlay recorded of me i actually put together in an edit. it was something like around 5mins. i showed finlay and he liked it. and i actually showed the edit to a couple of professors at school and maybe one or two other friends. i still saw it as too exclusive and not ready to go out into the world. and the edit was a rough draft. not a super rough draft, but a rough draft that was close to what i thought would be the final look of that segment of the possibly larger film that i might be working on. and note, for that first edit i put in a lot of time, but some fine tuning was missing. well, the response for this edit was good from just about everyone. or i should say that the response was good from the less than 10 people who saw it.

i also was so excited about my first piop art painting that i was working on that i asked finlay for another filming session of me working on this painting. he agreed and we did just that. the documentation was great and i soon started hinting to finlay that we actually had a lot of footage and that what he was filming may not quite be an interview anymore. he thought similarly, but wasn't quite sure what i was exactly saying.

okay, i still have a few more things i want to cover in regards to what happened around the time i was attending my spring 2012 gmu semester. hang on.

for one, earlier in the 2012 year i started having meetings here and there with finlay and another friend of ours named ki oni. these meetings were intended for us to showcase things we've been working on and then use each others honest thoughts to critique what we see and suggest ideas for improvement or encouragement to keep going or stuff like that. we three were basically hard working people who had creativity, ideas, and work to make and give the world. you already know about finlay, but you don't know ki oni. well, ki oni makes music that is juxtaposing with his personality. and well, ki oni also made short films at one point and i've actually been involved as an actor in a couple of them. but, now his focus was music and creating in that sonic medium.

    for two, i spent some time with another close friend named mattata. him and i normally had "out-of-this-world" conversations. and in those our brains would often literally leave earth and create these imaginarily amazing mind blowing thoughts and ideas on things and life and all sorts of stuff. yeah, those were healthy dreamkillingless moments in my life. those conversations enforced my layers of believing anything is possible. mattata also battled traditional thinking and had a heavy interest in choosing the life he wanted to live, as opposed to what he thinks society may suggest him to become. and mattata is a friend who i worked on cars with. we used to go to junkyards and find parts for our small compact cars that we drove. and these cars we'd take apart and do all sorts of things to without knowing if we were going to break them or not. we were just having fun. and we've been working on a collaborative book that has to do with cars, or more specifically *our* cars. and we've also had a few meetings here and there in order to work on characters for us to have in our arsenal when it came to acting. sidebar, mattata and myself were in a play together in high school years and years ago. so, for a while we have been into entertaining people and performing for an audience.

    for three, i started loosing touch with a close friend named vier. he happened to also be in the same play as mattata and myself in high school. and all three of us were like a crazy trio of friends when we got together. and note, with vier, we actually never completely lost contact or whatever the case with one another, but we had times where we didn't speak for months sometimes. but, when it came back to us getting in contact with one another it wasn't ever awkward or anything like that. and just so you know a bit about vier, well, he's probably one of the best martial artists in america and very well respected and cares about bringing creativity in that medium of expression. and note, him and i never really quite went to intergalactic conversations like mattata and myself, but we did have good talks. i'd say vier is a bit more on the safe side maybe. i don't know. don't get me wrong now, vier takes chances and is very successful in his field, but i don't know if he believes in himself as much as i or others believe in him. i think he's one of the best actors i know. and yeah, it's funny, he does act and i've done paid acting work with him. but, i don't really know how to act and he does know very well. but, i don't think he knows that. and i know he has so much skills and has the ability to be amazing and great at a global scale, but something had happened to him around around early 2012. it was like he was distracted or something. i don't know. like he slowed down and cared more about school than his dreams. it was like someone killed some of his dreams. and note, i've tried to revive them with my talks to him. and when i would say what i said he'd get inspired, but then something would happen and he wouldn't keep going with everything he wants to. or maybe i'm just wrong about what i'm saying. what do i know? well, what i do know is that around the first few months of 2012 i didn't see him much, nor did i speak to him much. i want to say that our lack of contact had to do with him having a girlfriend around that time. and i don't know if i even want to get into this. maybe a little bit. okay, so vier and i have definitely had our conflicts. or maybe i should say "bumps on the road". one day years ago vier got into a relationship with anita, a girl he met in high school. sounds good and that's cool and all, right? congratulations! well, after a year or whatever they breakup. ouch! sad time! vier calls me. i meet up with him and tell him not to worry and talk about hard times i've been through after my breakups and all this. i knew vier was in a delicate place after his breakup. and i knew it was going to take time for him to recover because he loved her. i was there for my friend. and vier knew i was there for him. i tried to encourage him and give him good thoughts and positivity and different possibilities to think of after he vented and let me know what happen. okay, a little bit of time passed and then vier and anita were back together. okay, umm, if both of them are happy, congratulations again! i want people to be in happy relationships. but, them getting back together was not part of the plan. they broke up, right? okay, they were done! but, they are back! okay, cinderella story. good for them. as much as i want my cinderella story, i'm not here to bash on theirs regardless of the advice and conversations i had with vier on how he should go about the situation. fine. cool. no worries. well, then vier and myself don't talk much. i guess he was busy with his girl. or this is a coincidence or whatever. no problem. i was busy. it was cool. well, then next thing i knew after however much time passed by vier and anita breakup again! and who's the first person he calls? me! yes, me! and what do i do? i do what i did last time! i was there for the man and gave him a shoulder to cry on and tried to help him and let him vent his heart out! this time they shouldn't get back together again, right? or why breakup twice in the first place!? and understand, i understand fighting, i understand problems in a relationship, but, i also understand talking and fixing things without getting to a breakup point. so, after vier and i were meeting up here and there and being interested in doing big things in the world together, umm, next thing i knew was, well, do you want to guess!? yes, they are back together again! blup! i almost felt like my words went in one ear and out the other! i'm giving him honest advice and trying to help him as a human and individual and friend and then he basically neglects all the time i gave him and encouraging words on how to be strong and he basically disrespects me and spits in my face and does the complete opposite! whatever, no problem! he has the right to do whatever he wants and it was *his* relationship! but, the problem was that after he got back with her again i basically loose contact with vier again! coincidence!? i don't think so! and then we get to where we are now in the first few months of 2012. and actually something funny happened. so, one of the few times i met with vier in early 2012 was at this restaurant. but, i didn't just meet him. his girlfriend was there, so was mattata, and vier's brother ne. and well, we all got to talking and having conversation. and i call out vier on our lack of friendship. like i told him, "yeah, we're like hardly friends." and mattata was surprised of the lack of interaction that existed between vier and myself. and i knew i had a lot to do with our lack of interaction because i had this weird thing where i liked it when friends contacted me. yeah, call it diva or whatever. call it a flaw. call it arrogance. but, no it's not really any of that and it's not like i wouldn't call a friend or whatever the case, but just when it gets to being weeks of no interaction i get busy and to not get distracted i choose to not call people sometimes and i think that if they were interested in having a conversation or talking that they could call me. whatever, maybe that's just an excuse. but, back to this restaurant. so, anita tells all of us that she asks vier about how i'm doing and how his friends are doing. then that got me all confused, like i thought she was breaking friendships apart, but now it was vier who wasn't keeping friendships together? i didn't know. probably it was ultimately my fault, right? if that was the case, then okay, that was the case. but, i think vier had a certain level of weakness when it came to being with a girlfriend. and i think i did too when i had a girlfriend. and i think that's the case with a lot of men. why? i don't know! girls are amazing or something. but, okay, then in this restaurant we all got to talking about school. and i express my views on life and anita thinks i'm attacking her or something. she says, "you don't know me! you don't know about what i've been through!" and stuff like that. and i respond, "yeah, i don't know you, but you're assuming things about me right now as if you know me and you have this idea that my life has been easy, but you don't know that my whole family at one point in time shared a room in my uncles home and we slept like tacos on the floor and at that point in my life i didn't cry because all i wanted to do was play outside and listen, i'm not trying to act like i know you, but something about me is that once i know someone a little bit i tend to befriend them quite easily and i become really honest and be myself without hiding anything and i'm open and speak truth." and yeah, i guess i just jump leaps and bounds in friendships sometimes or something. warm up and then full blast i guess. i don't know. well, anita and i were having this heated discussion about how she's working so hard to get through school and i'm saying how i'm working so hard and trying to do amazing things in this world and all this heavy loud talking kept going back and forth and then mattata intervened with a, "stop you two. quite. wait. wait. just let me explain. okay, first of all (looking at anita) akuna isn't attacking you. please understand that. and second of all (looking at me) akuna i know you and i know what you're saying and i know you have good intentions, but sometimes the way you say what you say is with such passion and almost intimidating that some people may feel like you're attacking them even thought you're not. so lets all just stop arguing and talk about something else because this arguments isn't going anywhere." and then i thought, "wow, thank you mattata for understanding." and i think from that day anita hated me. and maybe it had to do with what i said or maybe because she is super structured with life and in her mind and doesn't believe in dreamers like me or whatever the case. wow, i didn't plan nor expect to get into all that. but, okay, you kind of know vier now and the tension him and i may have sometimes. but, it probably had to do with me being jealous of him being with the woman he loves and for me *not* being with the woman i love, nor knowing who she necessarily is, nor knowing if i'll ever love again if i loved, nor knowing if i'll ever have a cinderella story like him, etc. or maybe not. it was really probably more like a situation where i've been there for a friend and tried to genuinely help him out over and over again and him just neglecting everything i said and doing the complete opposite basically. or, maybe it was just a combination of things, or really i probably don't fully know.

    for four, i decided to write some short stories. then i thought they may fit into a book a certain way. and these stories were entertaining, funny, and exciting, but real and intense at the same time. i still have more of them to write and if my balls are big enough i'll release them at some point. and you could note this, they have to do with creating artistic masterpieces. whatever that means.

and for five, one day aestan told me about this japanese artist that was doing a live painting performance on stage at this theatre that existed on the gmu campus. she thought i'd be interested since i had been to japan and all that. and i thought, "sure, why not check it out?" so, i ended up going to the thing and it was cool and interesting. after the artist performed i spoke the little japanese i knew to her. she didn't know much english, but we shared a few laughs. then a person from a japanese newspaper or something photographed the japanese artist and me. i then tried saying a few things to him in japanese. then, next thing i knew this guy asked me where i learned to speak japanese. i said, "i don't know japanese. i just know a few words." and then he wondered what i did. and then i was really real with him, "i do a lot of things. i studied architecture and have a strong interest in designing houses and buildings. i'm just missing the opportunity right now. i've done acting work and still have heavy interest in being in films and movies. and i've worked on films and might have a big project in the works right now. i also write and am working on books. and i have this painting i'm working on and et cetera." he was a bit puzzled, but interested in knowing more. i then asked what he did and he said that he painted, was working on making a lot of money so he could move to nyc with around $15,000, and that he was graduating next semester from gmu and stuff like that. and then i think he was trying to see what i was going to do for money in the future and i kept saying that i wasn't too worried about that and that what i cared about was living my life doing what i want and bringing amazing creativity into what i do and that i thought things should work out if i was just me and followed my heart and what i believed. and i tried to tell this guy that anything was possible and stuff like that. and then he asked what my name was and i said, "akuna." and his response was, "i'm walter." then i learned that he was interested in working with me. i let him get my contact information after he asked, but i didn't have collaborative work with him in my plans because i didn't know how serious he was.

don't say anything, ever

arthur lugauskas

chapter 16 : summertime practice

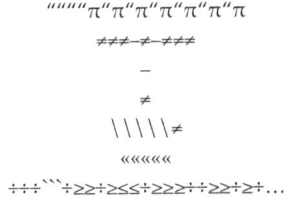

well, turned out walter was a bit more serious than i thought. one day he invited me to stop by his house for a cookout that he was having with his roommates. i decided to go. when i got there he showed me some of his art. and i learned that he actually did a lot of art. and he was good at drawing. then i saw that he had these huge wooden panel paintings and incorporated money in his art and the colors gold and black a lot and etc. and then i learned that he even had this persona that he created and all this stuff. "maybe he has huge dreams like me," i thought. and when walter and i would discuss some certain things i discovered that some thoughts connected quite well. of course, there were differences here and there, but overall at this point we had somewhat similar views on things.

      one big thing that happened in the summertime of 2012 was walter and myself going to a variety of places to practice conversation with strangers. we basically wanted to get better at talking and communicating certain ideas and stuff. and well, this is going to be tough to say here, but, umm, i actually started another book. another book!? yes! i have problems with starting projects on top of unfinished projects! i was just inspired and had to write! i want to release this book i talk about at some point. but, for now, it's still unfinished. just please patiently wait. thank you.

      and well, i also did some traveling around this time. and to a variety of places. from local trips to nyc to a trip to jamaica to etc. but, i also worked a lot to have some financial stability for a little while. what did i do? i taught kids how to skateboard. i was a director at these camps and basically had staff and all this stuff. the kids were fun. they ranged from 6-13 years old. i enjoyed making them laugh, teaching them, helping them, keeping their dreams alive, etc. and i worked all over the place. different locations for different weeks. different sets of kids each week. different staff. and that was good because it kept things exciting and new. and i made some survival and lunch money while i was at it. but, the best part was that i was surrounded by dreamers and visionaries. and yes, i'm talking about the kids i was working with. and i encouraged them to further believe that they can do what they want.

especially on the skateboard. i was there to help, give positive support, and watch them succeed and complete challenges with a smile on their faces. sure, many of them fell a whole lot of times, but most of them were warriors and got back up like nothing happened. and sure, there were crybabies and wimps and kids with killed dreams that only cared about money. but note, not that many of them were like that, but the few that were hurt me. so young, so contaminated. not cool!

arthur lugauskas

don't say anything, ever

: ::::: :::::: :::: :: : :::::::: :: :: :: ::: ::: :: ::: ::: :: ::: ::: :::   ::   :   : :: :   : ::
chapter 17 : fall 2012 semester
:::::: ::::::::::: :::::::::::: :::::::::::::::::::::   :   ::   : ::   : : :::::::

#########
%$%$%$%$%$
&'&&'&'&'&&&&&&
§§∞§∞∞∞∞∞∞¢'¢∞¢∞∞∞¢∞$%$%
&%%&%&%&$%$%$%$%
))()()()((''('(&'&&&%&%%$%$%$%$%$%$#$#$#$
|¥¥¥|¥|¥|¥| | |¥|¥|~^^¥^¥^¥¥^¥^^¥|~||~^¥¥¥^¥^|~~|~||~

second semester time! so, first day of classes i entered the soa building like a boss! wait, you do know what "soa" means, right? yes, "school of art." okay, so i was ready! i felt great! and now lets just get straight to business, shall we!? or i mean, straight to realness with new professors!

arthur lugauskas

don't say anything, ever

chapter 18 : art now professor

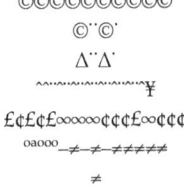

and it's "art now" time! i'm not sure why i'm so excited writing all this right now. but, okay, "art now" time. this class was an art history course. and you know i wasn't good at history. i just didn't grasp it. so, i had concerns going into this class. well, maybe not concerns, but i just really didn't want to go over art history. or, no, not necessarily that, i thinks it was more like i didn't want to read a lot and do exams and have a lecture course. and sad enough, first day of class i learned that the course was going to consist of lectures, a lot of reading, three exams, and one huge paper. great. blup! didn't want all that! but, the class was required for the degree and blah blah blah. i just had to go through it.

well, since i was dealing with lecture after lecture after lecture on a consistent basis, there was not much room for my talking.

wait, let me tell you a good thing about this class that i didn't really want to be in. the professor was nice. she was a young lady named arni. and she was super smart and knowledgeable when it came to art history. her brains had so much information in it! and she did promote talking and asking questions during lecture to an extent. but, i think i just wasn't the biggest fan of the lecture atmosphere. i don't know. and note, "art now" had a primary focus on art post-1940s, i think.

well, overall the class went well for me. i didn't read much. i studied for the exams last minute and did all-nighters if i had to. i learned during lectures, but didn't remember most of the information for some reason. i was just weak when it came to learning about certain things or something. but, some information of heavy personal interest from my part stayed with me.

i remember learning about the avant-garde and being really interested. i kept asking questions about it. and i wondered if there can be an avant-garde today and all this stuff. i remember one thing in particular arni said. and that sentence was this, "i don't think it's possible to have an avant-garde today." then, soon after my line of questions were done a classmate/friend who sat diagonally behind me semi-jokingly asked, "akuna, are you going to be the one man avant-garde?" i laughed and said, "maybe."

and when it came to this huge paper that was due at the end of the semester with a presentation involved the guidelines were: choose any living artist who's done work post-1970, do research on him or her, write a 10-15page paper, and prepare a 10minute presentation to present to the class. first artist i thought of was akuna lunersks. this was an artist of all mediums. a complete persona! an avant-garde in todays art world! but, no one knew. so, how did that work? i don't know. so i proposed that artist to arni and she laughed a bit and said, "no." i guess this kind of proposal worked half way with newsy and no way with arni. and there was a reason arni said "no", but i don't really remember it. i was probably too crushed by the "no." actually i'm joking. i really wasn't too sad about her "no" for some reason. i let it be and did my paper on an architect. but, didn't she say to do the paper on an artist? yes, and this architect was an artist! you know who i'm talking about, right? just think of an architect who does amazing sketches, hangs out with artists more than architects, designed buildings that are basically sculptures, and who designed a museum that some people complained about and hated because they thought more visitors were going to the museum to see the architecture instead of the art. yeah, crazy right? all this controversy in regards to the architecture of this particular museum outshining all the millions of dollars of artworks from past and present and this idea that architecture "wasn't allowed" to do that and this and that and blah blah blah.

arthur lugauskas

don't say anything, ever

chapter 19 : advanced composition english professor

    and now, time for another class i was dreading to take. i really, really, really, really, really, didn't want to take this class! not english! no! didn't want to deal with english classes anymore! blup!

    i don't know how do describe how much i really didn't want to take this english class. but, this was the last english class i had to take if i wanted a bfa from gmu. this class was beyond required. the curriculum i was following in order to achieve the degree basically said, "there is no escaping this advanced english class." ugh!

"fine! whatever! i'll take the class! but, i'm going to write my way!" i thought. apparently i'm a good writer, right? yeah, maybe for people outside of english class. i don't know. blup! blup! blup me!

so, there i was, my first day in the class that i wanted to take the least. and the location i was at was definitely not in the art building. there were students from all sorts of majors anticipating the pain of english with me. and in the front of the room stood a man with tattoos and muscles. he was a short guy, with a beard, and a nice haircut. 10:30am he introduced himself and the class as follows, "hi everyone, my name is englue. welcome to my class. we will have an overarching theme for the semester which has to do with monsters. and we'll be watching and analyzing films a lot. from old ones to new ones. and short ones to long ones. and one very important thing, we will be in groups a lot. so, if you can't handle being in a group, this class is not for you. during class we will primarily talk via discussions. if you don't like talking, this class isn't for you. so, if anyone wants to leave right now, please do so. other than that, i think this class will be fun. so, lets get started with the syllabus." then i was like, "what!? if i'm taking any english class at this point in my life, this is the class! how did i end up with probably the best english class a student could end up in? i don't know. but, i'm liking what i'm hearing."

i quickly learned that englue just had a book published with a co-author and that he had a heavy interest in the film world. i found him to be for creativity instead of against it. and note, there was plenty of writing that went on inside and outside of class. i was writing how i wanted to write and noticed appreciation from englue. he was a cool professor. and he let me be me.

don't say anything, ever

arthur lugauskas

don't say anything, ever

chapter 20 : fundamentals studio lighting professor

°ΔΔ°Δ°ΔΔ°Δ°ßΔ°ßßßß˜ˆßˆßˆßˆ∑∑ˆ˜˜∑¨ˆ
∑π∑ππ∑π∑π∑π∑πøøπ∑πø∑πø∑øøπ∑
∑πøœπøøπœπøøπø∑øππøœøπ
∑ππ∑π∑π¬¬ßππ¬ßπ¬∑¬π¬ß¬ππ∑πß
≠–≠–≠—≠–≠–≠–≠∑–≠≠–≠∑–≠–∑–≠∑–≠–≠—≠≠–
\≠∑≠\\≠≠\≠\∑≠\∑≠\∑≠\∑≠\∑≠\
iiiiiiiiiii

sidebar, i'm at a cafe in annandale right now. i've been here for hours and hours writing. and writing isn't that easy sometimes. or maybe i'm just nervous thinking if i'll complete this book and other things in the time frame i want to. i have my concerns sometimes. i should worry more probably. if you saw me right now i'd look normal. but, in my head the craziest activity is going on. it actually gets hard to sleep when my brain keeps thinking all the time and all the little-brain-people continuously keep working. do you know what i'm saying? well, okay, so i'm at this cafe with some coffee on my left. when i arrived here hours ago at one point i was the only one upstairs. literally emptiness and me. then people started coming. that made a little noise. then more people. and more. and more! and more! and now the place is jam packed! crazy packed! so loud! a group of humans were just singing "happy birthday" to someone. two people to my left are just talking and talking and stuff. earlier one of the guys was saying to the other guy that you had to have money to have good education. and i thought, "no." but, wow, there is so much noise here. so many groups of people. some with girlfriends, some with boyfriends, some just girls, some just guys. it's kind of funny because i'm the only one here alone on my laptop writing. and what's crazy is that i'm working so hard right now that when i don't pay attention to my surroundings i don't hear the noise. when i'm so focused i'm just in my own world creating a world that you are in right now as the reader. interesting, eh? end sidebar.

    wait, not end sidebar. originally i wanted this book to be done by around now, but it's not! and it's november 15th right now! and apparently i want to have this book ready and released by december 15th! but, i still have 4 piop art walls to do, a sculpture or two or three to finish, photo shoots and video shoots pending, fine-tuning to get done for this and that, and blah blah blah! blup me! now, end sidebar. reopen sidebar, seriously blup me! end sidebar.

    so, times are crazy right now, but now lets go back to the past. this fundamentals studio lighting class was basically a photography lighting class. or a class that had to do with beginner studio lighting. the professor i had was a woman named lily. and joining my class was her studio lighting two class. so, yes, studio lighting one and studio lighting two were combined into one class and met at the same times but did different projects and worked on learning or improving how to manipulate light in photography in different ways. get it? if you do, good!

lily was a nice person and did do photography herself. and she was actually working on a photo series that had to do with the last thing she saw at random times of the day three times a day for a year. was that too confusing? i had a confusing time writing it, sort of. but, yeah, lily was active, fun, and ready to teach about lighting and photography and all that.

i was just excited to do photography that *i* wanted in the lighting studio. and now note, lily gave assignments out, but left a lot of room for students to be creative and put their own ideas into the images they wanted to create. usually there would be a basic structure of what she wanted and then it was up to the students to do what they wanted.

one thing i want to tell you is that i learned about light! i was fascinated when lily one day showed us how to paint with light. that was an amazing moment just seeing light paint an object via getting a certain something in the way of light a certain way. eye opening experience!

well, when it came to the assignments i did them my way. and i remember talking to some students and telling them to not worry so much about the technique and to instead just do whatever they wanted. but, what i was saying didn't resonate. they cared more about grades. and then it came to our first class critique. and i was surprised! i saw so much garbage! like horrible photography! careless creativeless last minute "i'm just trying to get a grade" or "i was to busy partying last weekend, so i'm just going to put something dumb together" photography! blup! the photography was worse than my first paintings i did last year! or, maybe not, my paintings were probably worse! or not? i don't know. but listen, seeing what i saw in this first critique was hard for me. and what confused me more was how lily treated each presentation. she never said anything bad. she just suggested improvements. i wanted to speak up, but i bit my tongue for some reason. after the critiques and after most people left i couldn't hold it any longer. i went up to lily and said, "most of the stuff we saw was horrible! like do these kids not try or something!? i don't get it." and her response was, "yeah, i agree. a lot of the work is really undeveloped and lacks care. but, the reason i don't tell the students what they are doing is bad or yell at them and stuff is because i had a professor when i was in school and that's all he would do and that wasn't productive for the students because a lot of them took it personally and felt attacked. so, what i do here in my classes is try telling students their work sucks the nice way. and that was is suggesting ways they could improve and get better. and i do get personal with them, but not in front of the class. because if i were to call them out in front of everybody that would be bad and embarrassing and really hurtful." i saw justice in her explanation, but still i didn't know what to really think. i was probably just mean and picky. or maybe i was just a jerk sometimes, right?

     okay, as the semester went on more assignments were given and more images were taken. but, the mentality i had going into all these assignments was, "i'm not here to do assignments. i'm not competing with students in class. i'm here to do straight-up projects for the world. and if i'm competing then i'm competing with the leaders in the photography world right now. i'm here to do work beyond school. i'm not playing around with my photography. why? because *i'm* doing it!" and note, by me saying "not playing around" i mean "i'm not interested in producing ugly garbage that's whack." and understand this, i actually stated my intentions and mentality in regards to going about assignments to lily early on in the semester and she agreed with my way of thinking and thought that more students should think like that.

     so, just so everyone knew how much i wasn't playing around, when it came to a certain assignment i went all out. here's the framework: lily wanted her lighting one class to produce 2-4 well composed technically apt images that involved glass, metal, white, and black. those were the only guidelines. the final images and how we put the materials together in one image frame was up to us. great! wait, think real quick what you would do. and for fun, why not go and do this project yourself in the most creative manner you could think of. or not. whatever you want. but, now, let me tell you how i took this assignment. so, i went through experimentation of white and black acrylic paint in a bottle with water froze up and this and that and ideas here and there on how i could go about this project. then this is what i ended up doing: i wrote a poem, rolled it up, had metal wire wrapped around it with the incorporation of broken pieces of glass, then i got a water bottle and slit a cut into it the long way and then put my poem, wire, and glass in the water bottle and then poured water inside and then froze up the whole thing and then took it out the freezer and then had around a 4hour photo shoot session in the lighting studio with around 12 carefully placed lights all around the object and after over 808 images the poem finally melted out of the ice and revealed itself. then i spent hours picking and choosing the best images for this series that came out of this project because there wasn't just one amazing image. eventually finally i had got down to the final 43 images and then 23 images and then after a couple of meetings with certain people and one final meeting with finlay the image count made it down to a total of 10. then i did some minor basic edits to each image, but nothing crazy because i was horrible and lacked so much knowledge when it came to photo editing programs. but note, most of my editing occurred before i even pushed any button on my camera. then i thought to do two different versions of this series and what happened was one set of 10 images was primarily black and the other version of 10 images was primarily white. so, yeah, two sets of 10 images in a sequential series. then i went to class the day we had our critiques for this assignment with my finished images and revealed the title of my series saying, "this is *pome in ice*." and i asked the students to tell me the bad they saw in my work. i asked for criticism! if someone thought i had garbage, i wanted that person to tell me. i wanted to know how i could improve! after all, i didn't really know how to do photography, i wasn't a photo major, but for some reason i thought i had produced some of the best photography work in class. but, maybe i was crazy for thinking that was, hence i wanted to know what was wrong with my images! nobody said anything! or, wait, i think someone said something, but they were quite about it! i wanted truth! i wanted people to be loud and tell me they hated what they saw if they hated what they saw! but, no! nothing, except for a comment that had something to do with something i forgot. other than that i got compliments. and i really do appreciate those, don't get me wrong now. i did work very hard on this series and spent a lot of time on it. a lot of thinking was involved and process and learning. i did want a good response from people and that's why i asked for how the series could be improved. there were something like 13 brains in the room and all of those brains had knowledge and ideas and individual thoughts and certain opinions in regards to what i was doing and what they didn't like and what they thought could be done for improvement. and i wanted that feedback. and now listen to what the problem was, if i didn't get that feedback i was left to assume that my series was on point, good, great, amazing, and fantastic and mind blowing, right? well, okay, then it was time for other students to show what they produced and, well, the images i saw i thought ranged from great to good to nice to okay to horrible to tasteless. and i encouraged and complimented what i liked. but, when it came to the works that really annoyed me i got called out by lily to state what i thought. she wanted me to take the hit and tell the student that had bad work what i thought. and i said what i thought. but, i wan't that mean. i thought about what lily said and putting people on the spot. so, i really didn't come off hateful. but, i definitely didn't say the work was amazing either. i went lilys route and mentioned how the image could be improved and spoke about what i thought wasn't working and stuff like that. looking back now, i was a hypocrite in a way and i didn't say the harsh feelings i truly felt towards some images. but, then again i think about it and realize that no one asked for harsh criticism like me. i think i was one of the few who cared about doing amazing photography. i was one of the only few, if not the only one, who wasn't looking at getting some desk job in the art world in the future. because instead i had my ideas that my art would take care of me. and i think the reason students were lacking in making quality work was because they thought they couldn't "make it" in the art world or whatever. i felt like someone killed their dreams somewhere along the road of life and they believed those dreamkillers. but, then again maybe some of them were studying photography for a reason other that actually really liking photography. i don't know ultimately. but, what i do know is that i was really disappointed that the studio lighting two students and photography majors were generating worse photographs than studio lighting one students who were primarily biology majors and majors outside of photo. and that was what frustrated me! i was just thinking, "why are you studying photography in the first place!? you don't even actually like to do it! and you have no confidence in your work! and you're apparently about to graduate!? what the blup!"

after that uninspiring critique lily had to review all the images and grade them. but, it was crazy because it was like the work produced was a reflection of what the professor taught. and i saw lily as a professor who wanted better images than what the class was giving her. okay, now i'm about to give you another one of my proudest moments. so, the day lily was giving us our grades each student received a piece of paper. except me. and i was stumped. i spoke to a few classmates and they got either an a or a b or whatever the case, but i had nothing, yet. i went up to lily and asked if she had a grade slip thing for me. and she told me, "i don't have one for you. i'll tell you why after class." i confusedly said, "okay." and then i was concerned and worried a bit and not sure what to think. but wait, there was also a sense of no worries too for some reason. yes, mixed emotions you could say. well, finally class ended and i approached lily. then she went on to explain, "the reason i didn't give you a slip of paper is because on these slips that i've made i have different things i use to grade the images. as you could see (she shows me a slip) there's technique, composition, iso, contrast, depth, etc. and i put numbers beside each category so students could see where they did well and where they could improve. and the reason i don't have a slip for you is because if i did i'd be just making up numbers. because it's not like you really followed all this stuff, nor were you concerned with it. so, that's the reason i don't have a slip for you. and plus, i'd rather have a conversation with you and tell you what i think in regards to what you're doing. so, don't worry, you have an a. and we know it's not grades you're worried about. so, lets look a few of your images and talk a bit." i was stunned, humbled, and appreciative of everything lily just stated to me. and i had a certain confidence boost and felt like my individuality was respected. then lily and i spoke about some of my work and she gave me good information and advice. thank you lily!

    then it was time to see who will be part of the the wall of best works. lily had her section and it was small. so, she told the class that everyone wasn't going to fit on this hallway wall section of hers and that those who aren't chosen shouldn't take it personally. then she had all the images she wanted on the wall on her computer screen. everyone went to see if their image made it. and then people were excited to of had two or even three images chosen. and then i look at the screen and see my images. how many? i count, one, two, three. wait, another one. that made four. four!? wow! but, it was funny because i think the students thought that only two people or so had three images and that three images was the most a student was asked for. i don't think anyone knew lily wanted four from me. and i didn't bother stating it out loud. i was honored. and i felt like i was doing something right. and note really quick, these images were expected to be displayed on the wall until students did new work that could be chosen for the next new wall-time session.

     and well, after a few weeks passed by, it was time to change the images on the wall. and of course, everyone produced more and new work. this time lily personally told students the images she wanted from them; if she wanted anything at all that was. and listen to this, i remember hearing this photography major who was in studio lighting two ask lily if her images were ones that were wanted. and lily kindly responded, "sorry, no, not this time." the student was a bit sad because she had spent money and printed something like four images or so. then lily said with a laugh, "yeah, sorry, only the best." and note, there was no animosity in her voice. but, then this is where things got interesting. after that incident a few minutes passed by and i wondered if lily wanted any of my images. i didn't mind if she said "no" because that would mean i didn't have to print any. and the reason i say that is because printing was a bit expensive and the more images you printed the more it costed and i was borderline broke. or maybe i should say that i was not fully broke due to my summer money, but my funds were scarce. but listen, i didn't really expect a "no" from lily. and, well, i didn't get a "no." instead lily said, "yeah, print three of your images out." and i said, "which three? any three?" and she said, "yeah. choose three."

     and i do want to mention really quick that there was this one girl who i thought had phenomenal images. each time she would produce greatness. i really liked her work. her aesthetic, ideas, color, etc. she really had very well done photographs! and she was a photography major and in studio lighting two. but, i didn't really care about those logistics. i just really liked her work.

arthur lugauskas

don't say anything, ever

chapter 21 : sculpture three professor

⁀⁀⁀⁀⁀⁀⊘⁀⊘⊘⁀⊘⁀⊘⁀⊘⁀⊘
......

'‰'‰'‰',,,,¢¢¢∞∞∞∞∞∞∞∞∞∞∞∞∞
oo

o

aa

≠≠≠≠≠

      was that a typo or mistake? sculpture three? not a typo nor mistake. and yes, i skipped sculpture two for the time being and was in sculpture three in my second semester at gmu. why? well, don't get me wrong, i still had to take sculpture two at some point, but, with sculpture i guess there was a certain allowance to jump to different "levels" after sculpture one was taken. probably one of the only concentrations, if not the only, where students were allowed to do that.

sidebar, i'm now in a new location writing and it's november 16th, 5:24pm. where? soho. where in soho? at a cafe. and i have some hot cinnamon apple spice tea with five spoons of sugar in it to my left. music is paying, but i find the overall atmosphere inside here okay. or well, i actually don't like it that much. and as for outside, well, people are everywhere. a lot of motion and activity in the city right now. and the weather is fantastic for november. not cold, just chilly. and i actually feel like going somewhere else to write. so, time to leave even though i just got here. sidebar close.

okay, another sidebar, so i went a couple of blocks down the street and then around the corner and now i'm at my new destination. and where i am now is a place i had amazing raw vegan sushi earlier. this place is great with a healthy scent of fruits and vegetables roaming in the atmosphere. i feel good, but exhausted at the same time due to my heavy lack of sleep last night. but, whatever, back to writing. end another sidebar.

so, yeah, it was time for sculpture three for me because it worked better with my schedule. because remember that i planned my classes according to my schedule and not according to which specific professor teaches the class. so, now you know why i was in sculpture three. and now, do you want to guess who my professor was? well, who else other than bom. i now had class with the man who i thought was a myth. crazy, eh? i guess he returned from his sabbatical. and well, the first day of class we all introduced ourselves. and by "we all" i mean me, fellow classmates, and bom. i don't really know how some sentence structures exactly should be or if there is implied understanding in some circumstances or whatever. okay, whatever, so after introductions bom started talking a bit. and he spoke about this thing called "thingness." he was telling all of us to find our "thingness" and he was super cool in his approach with how he spoke. i don't know, but bom had these good vibrations around him. and he had plenty to say. and plenty thoughtfully interesting things. i felt good to be in that atmosphere.

    then bom went on to tell us what our first project should be like. and all he said about it was, "i want you all to make 20 things, but have each one be different in material and scale from one another." and that was all. some students wanted more, but bom had already given all the information he knew and wanted to give. and he let us do whatever we wanted with those super broad guidelines. or are they super broad? i don't know. well, i'm guessing you could guess what i wanted to bring in this project. right? yes, full blown creativity. i wanted to manipulate and twist and tangle this project in the most amazing way in where no one else had ever thought of before. i wanted to bring mind blowing business to the table. or something too hard to grasp, but if observed closely you'd see the essence and honesty to what was asked for. but, to do all that i had to think and think and use my brain and connect dots in new ways. and i did all that.

    so, to break down the project, let me tell you what i did with the assignment sentences framework i was given. i started collecting one piece of hair from different girls in my classes. and i happened to have one last skate camp going on, so i managed to get a strand of hair from a few of the tiny skateboard girls. i ended up getting a total of 20 pieces of hair from females of different age, race, size, etc. then i got these small planks of wood and picture frames from an art store. and i started cutting box and/or rectangle openings on one piece of wood and then i took the glass out of a 4"x6" picture frame and put that on top of the wood that had the opening or openings and then i put one piece of hair on the glass and then i flipped all that over onto another piece of wood that was the same size as the initial wood piece i started with. then after some glue action i made my first piece. then i kept going like that with 9 more hair strands. and as for the remaining 10, i did something else with them that also had to do with glass and wood. but, then when it came to present i told bom and my class, "so, i approached this project a certain way. and the way it works and makes sense is that each strand of hair is from a different person. and well, the people who allowed me to have their piece of hair for art ranged from 6-67 years old. and note, each hair is different in length, but also by age alone each person is a different size. and actually in any case every person is a different size in scale, right i don't think there are people of the exact scale anywhere. and the way each hair piece is different from one another in the material aspect, well, each person has different dna, right? so, dna is the material that i'm using and each hair is different because there is different dna in or on each one. does everyone get it?" and i think some people may have thought i was a bit crazy, maybe some thought what i did was stupid, and maybe a few kind of got it. bom went on to say with a slightly perplexed face, "okay. yeah, i didn't quite expect that. i was interested in you kind of experimenting with materials and scale and stuff, but okay, good." and that was when i realized that i maybe had taken the project too far. well, i was happy i did. but, then again, maybe i missed some lessons when it came to understanding about materials more and how various ones handle manipulation differently and stuff. either case, i ultimately don't regret what i did.

    well, after my hair pieces it was time for another project. i thought and i thought. i didn't want to make a huge "thing" because if i did i questioned where i would store it. because note, i wasn't that interested in making something and then getting rid of it at the end of the semester. or at least getting rid of it on my own terms that is. i tend to get attached to many of my works. i'm not sure why. and don't get me wrong now, i certainly would like to make huge things for the world and places on earth. but, that opportunity had yet to appear. or maybe i just had to catch it. but, plus, anyway, i didn't have that much money to spend on a lot of materials to make something huge. and not that i had to have a lot of materials to make somethings huge. blah blah blah. okay listen, i did want to make an impact still! so, what did i do? well, i wasn't at school to make assignments, right? if i had work to do in a class i wanted to take whatever project i had to do beyond the classroom and in line with the best living artists today. i was ready to make pieces that were part of my build. my build? yes, my ultimate artist build. or something like that. i feel hesitant to say that i wanted to make "portfolio pieces" for some reason. lets just say i was interested in making amazing work in order to prove to people that i can do greatness and in return the idea was that these works should help me get opportunities to do more and greater work for the world on a larger scale. does that sound better that "i was interested in making 'portfolio pieces'"? yeah, well, that was how i looked at a lot of early projects i was doing in my "early art career".

    well, what did i do next in sculpture three that fit in a "sculpture" project category, but was beyond "just an assignment"? before i get into it let me tell you something. after the first broadly worded curious and intriguing assignment bom gave us, the next project or work for us to produce he left open to our imagination and ideas. and since this was sculpture three he thought of us being advanced enough to be able to generate projects from our own thoughts. and i thought, "great!" but note, bom did provide some guidance to those who weren't yet sure what they exactly wanted. but, the amazing thing about bom was that when someone would ask "what should i do?" bom would respond "well, what do you want to do?" and when i heard those things i thought, "wow! what a great way to teach!" you know, bom would really get into searching for what your ideas were and what you wanted to bring to the table. he wasn't interested in telling you exactly everything you should do. he was interested in people thinking for themselves and doing their thing. i respected that and soon learned why bom was so known and so liked by my peers and his peers alike. after some conversations with bom and hearing what he had to say and listening how he said what he thought i realized that he was the man!

    okay, okay akuna, what was the next project you did!? okay audience reading this book, i'll tell you. i decided to do another string installation. but, this time it was going to be more amazing, more string, more genius, more more. and i thought installation was like a subset of sculpture or sort of fit in with sculpture in some way or whatever. it was like installation and sculpture had similar dna or something. yeah. so, i was going to do the biggest piece of work that costed the least amount of money, but also has the biggest impact in the art building. i decided to use the main stairwell again because that space was available. and since there was nothing on it or around it, well, i decided to take over. and note, i was just using my surroundings and using existing space and then generating projects as if i was doing a commission or museum exhibit or just something creative in a mall or literally anywhere. and in this case i was going to be able to have a piece done that could potentially help me revolutionize stairwell experiences in the future. and i was ready to show how i could evolve a stairwell with no damage to surrounding territory or walls or whatever and no obstruction to human traffic flow. and i wanted a straight-up experience oriented installation. and i did just that to the main stairwell in the soa building at gmu in 2012.

      okay, so, first i bought a few rolls of gray sting. and note, at this point in time i was wearing only gray tones. but, i had a small heart on the lower left of my gray button-down shirt. sometimes the heart was red and other times it was gray. i wore a different heart everyday to school and just anywhere i went really. people asked what the heart meant and why i wore it and stuff like that. and i had different answers that ranged from "no girl has my heart right now" to "it's my signature". so, you could say that my outfit was all gray tones and a touch of color. i saw myself as a walking piece of art. and much of my art in general was gray tone oriented with a touch of color around this time too. and think about it, since i didn't know much about art and stuff, but believed i was one of the greatest artists or something like that, well, i was doing major amazing work but starting with what you might learn first, which is how to use gray tones. does that make sense? i maybe wasn't ready for much color because i wasn't sure how to incorporate color into ideas that were still being built and fine-tuned. do you know what i'm saying? so, with all the gray string i bought i looked at getting a color to touch the gray installation i was going to do. and i decided on that color being red this time. remember the last string installation i did had the color blue to imply windows inside? yeah, so for my second string installation ever i decided to incorporate the color red. why red? well, i thought i might want to incorporate a red heart in my installation and do something with perspective. and that's what i did. the whole installation was very much thought out and it was basically an abstract reflection of myself. there goes one possible artist statement, right? but, let me tell you more. so, the red heart was elongated when you stepped into the third floor or halfway between the second and third floor on the stairwell of the three-story art building. but, when you were at the very bottom of the stairs and looking up to the heart it shrunk and felt more tender and soft and complete. i also played with the concept of seeing a heart that felt so out-of-reach sometimes. something else, the stairwell was primarily gray. and my string installation blended in so much. it was like it wasn't even there. and i think some people completely didn't even know of its existence. why? because a lot of people didn't pay attention to details. and a lot of people were too focused on their phones and didn't even know what existed in their surroundings. especially a three-story string installation wrapping up a stairwell sometimes! it was crazy! but so fun for me. another thing with the installation was this idea that when straight lines readjusted according to a certain calculated patter, well, what began to happen was a beautiful curve. and that certainly was another thing that was visible to those paying close attention and taking the time to experience the piece in full. and i played with this idea of timelessness because since the installation felt "invisible" to many people, well, when those people did discover its existence via friends or just "happening to notice one day" then i had this feeling where i thought they questioned how long it had been up and if it had always existed or not because they never noticed before. and when the installation would be taken down (because it had to even though i didn't think it should have been) then the question for some would be, "did it ever exist?" and to those who knew of its existence, they could have the memory of something that came as a myth to others. and one more thing about this installation was that it really looked like it was elevating the stairwell if you saw the activity and interaction of the string planes from the top floor. and that caused this juxtaposing thought of something so delicate and soft elevating something so concrete and heavy. and really, just the points of view and thought generation this piece generated for my mind and to those who gave it time fascinated me. and one particular reaction i received from many was that it looked like a musical instrument. and that caused another juxtaposition of something looking so musical, but when touched being so soundless. overall the installation was one of my greatest works at that time and was, in my opinion, one of the best installations that ever existed in the soa building.

    and when it came to critiques in boms class and everyone gathered to look at what i had created, well, it was interesting. but, the most interesting part was what bom found interesting. and what i'm talking about is what i'm about to type next. i said, "yeah, the elongated heart shrinking thing based on point of view came from my experience of seeing words shrink in the back of a cereal box game. because sometimes when i would eat cereal i'd look at the back of the box. and some boxes had these little games or whatever. and one time the game was to read something. and that something was really literally long words that were super hard to read if you looked straight at them. and from that game i learned that if altered my point of view a certain way then the words would be easy to read." and then bom took that as a key element in the whole installation i did. he said, "you know, i like this installation and i think it's a great piece. but, what really fascinates me is that you got this idea from a cereal box."

don't say anything, ever

arthur lugauskas

::::: :: :::: ::: ::::: ::::: :::: :: ::::: :: :::::::::: :::: ::::: ::::: ::::: :::::::
chapter 22 : visual voices professor again
::::: ::: :::: ::::: :::::: ::: :: :::::::: :::::: : ::::::::::: ::::: ::: ::::::::::::::

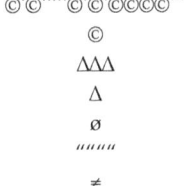

i'll provide a little story in this chapter that doesn't have that much to do with visual voices, but in a way does. or no, yeah, it kind of does, in a way. so, i somehow stumbled into a certain conversation one day. and the peoples involved were san (he was one of the visual voices guest speakers for the semester), vivtol, hon, and a couple of undergrad sculpture students. and note, these students were among some of the harder working crowd of students at the school. well, i didn't completely stumble into this conversation. i guess i got an invite from hon via email or something. well, i'm not really sure right now as i write this story. but, okay, lets say hon invited a few "high end" students or whatever to have a special conversation with san. i was one of the few who took part in that. and after that conversation of specialties and getting to know how amazing san was everyone got up and it was time for dinner. and note, san was going to give his lecture in a couple of hours at that time. so, the location to eat was going to be near by and after everything was figured out, well, somehow myself and a couple other undergrad students got invited. and next thing i knew i was eating dinner with the top dogs of the school of art at gmu. i'm talking about dinner with the guest artist san who was expected to give a lecture to something like 300 students later on that evening, the director of the school of art vivtol, the person of high prestige hon, the man running the sculpture department bom, a lady heavy into photography and respected as a photography professor at school named web, and a couple of other big names. and then you had me and a couple of hard working high achieving undergrad students. wait, there was one more person who i should mention. i'll mention her in the next paragraph.

okay, so, to dinner we went to a nearby restaurant, right? though it was walking distance, some people wanted to drive. and among the drivers was a woman named fume. now, let me tell you who fume was. to my knowledge at that time, fume was a sculpture one and sculpture two professor at gmu. maybe she taught other classes, but if she did i didn't know. she was an active woman with high energy. a lot of students knew here and had a good relationship with her. fume wasn't afraid to speak her mind. and i learned that if i wasn't in sculpture three with bom, i probably would have been in sculpture two with fume. and at this point her and i didn't really know each other. we may have seen one another walking around the sculpture studio or the art building, but we never really had a conversation. well, since she was driving to this dinner and a couple of undergrad students were going to hop in the car with her i thought, "maybe i should do the same?" and the reason was because i knew these students. because they were my classmates actually. and there was space in the car and i thought i would have an opportunity to actually meet fume. and something like that happened. well, she was welcoming when it came to me riding along with her and the other students in her car. i appreciated that. now learn, when i got in the car fume immediately put some music on and put the volume up. this was an upbeat girl. she was excited about life. then in the car ride we all got to talking. and fume knew about the other students, but she didn't know me. well, first topic of conversation was about one of fumes sculpture one students who was this girl who was doing this massive volcano-like sculpture and who was writing and doing all this stuff. fume was saying how impressed by this student of hers she was and how she thought she would go on to do big things in life. or i.e., fume was talking highly of a student because of what the student produced and because of the potential she saw in the student based on all the work and excitement and ambition the student portrayed. after her description i thought, "interesting. i'm doing similar things." then i jokingly, but maybe not super jokingly, thought, "fume doesn't know that the next big thing is in the car right now." well, it got to the point where fume wondered who i was and what i did. because i was after all in her car with her and she was a stranger to me and vice versa. i thought i'd go almost all out with my description of myself. well, since there was greatness of students being talked about, i thought i was in that category and should state why i was a big deal. right? for first impression? good idea? bad idea? i don't know. whatever, i spoke my mind. fume first asked, "what are you studying?" i replied with, "sculpture, but i'm not so interested in describing myself in a single category like that." the she went on, "okay. that's interesting. i didn't know you were studying sculpture. because i normally know all the sculpture students. but, okay, what else do you do?" then i went on to say, "yeah, i probably would've been in your sculpture two class because i understand that you're the professor for that class. but, due to my schedule i had to skip sculpture two for now. but, i'll probably be there at one point. and yeah, i'm working on books and on a variety of projects that have to do with art. from paintings, to drawings, to sculpture, to installation, to film. and i studied architecture before and i still have high interest in designing buildings and houses. i've also done acting work and still care to further pursue that. and recently i've worked on photography and have some series' in the works. i'm just juggling a bunch of things." then she went on to say, "okay. what are the books about?" but, when she asked that she showed lack of interest. and i felt like she felt i was saying that i was great. and i don't think she liked that. i answered, "the books vary in subject matter and they are still in progress. i know the basic ideas for them, but i'll see what happens." then the conversation shifted to other things for some reason and next thing i knew we arrived to the restaurant.

  well, that was my first actual conversation with fume. then at the restaurant i sat with my fellow undergrads and the bigger dogs of the school of art sat around san. i was just excited and humbled to be in the presence of all these people. i felt special. i was around people who were a big deal and that made me a big deal. or something like that. then after dinner vivtol payed for all of us. that caught me by surprise and i was very appreciative. i thanked vivtol with a smile. i really did appreciate dinner and being in conversation with of all these individuals. good experience.

      then we got back to school and all of us went to sans lecture. and i thought jokingly, "yeah, i just had dinner with the man on stage and the people who put that man on stage. i feel cool."

arthur lugauskas

don't say anything, ever

chapter 23 : honors seminar professor again

why honors seminar again? well, after speaking with my counselor i learned about how this honors program worked. basically, i was supposed to take the honors seminar class each semester i was at gmu (or a total of four times) in order for me to graduate with honors. if i didn't do that then taking the class one time wouldn't of really meant anything. i thought, "ugh." but, then i thought, "whatever. it's a 1credit course and hons cool and it's not like there will be an overload of work or anything like that. actually, i don't mind. it's cool." so, that's why i'm in honors seminar again. and i planned to be in it again and again.

plus, each semester honors class was different. because the students would change and hon would think of different things to do. hon was open to ideas and i don't think he had a definite structure to follow. there were main points for him to touch on, like research, doing a trip, having us meet artists, etc. but, overall it looked like hon was going to adjust when the time came and then what got done would be depending on how the class was and how things were and that was why the class was expected to be different each time. and plus, honors was a class for students who were working hard and were good and were given the honor to be in that class, right? so, just conversations in class with great minds would be acceptable and helpful. or just bouncing ideas around would be healthy, i thought.

so, this semester hon started off with having everyone present what they've worked on in the past months and what they were working on currently. this was good because it allowed us all to learn about one another more and more. then hon wanted us to research and learn about artists similar to us. he gave out names he thought fit with each students interests. and i learned that hon started to see me as being the art. like my life was the art. like i was in performance at all times. i was a bit stunned and curious as to how he got to that point. but, i went with it and said, "yeah. i see myself as a walking piece of art. and everything i do i feel is art." then he told me to check out marina abramovic. i didn't know this artist at the time, but hon said that there may be similarities with her and me and that i may find what she did interesting. could hon really have possibly seen me as someone who was in performance at all times of the day? and could i of possibly been i in performance at all times? or was i in performance at all times since a certain time in my life when i decided to make my life a performance for a certain time?

arthur lugauskas

chapter 24 : extras from 2nd

ææ«æææææææææ«′′′′′′′′
′′′′ ′′

≥÷≥≥÷÷≥≥≥≥≥≤≤≤≤≥≥≤≥≤≥≤≥≤≥
≤≥≤≥≤≥≤≥≤≥≤≥≤≥≤≥≥≥≤≤≤≥≤≥≤≥≥
\≠\≠\-°å\å\\å\å\å\œ\\œ\œ\œ∑\\∑
%"%'&(%))$(%)$(&)'$('(%)&)('&()%$)(
``¿˜¿˜↙↙↙⁄⁄⁄⁄⁄↙↙↙↙⁄↙¿¿€¿€¿€¿↙¿↙´€↙´€↙´¿˜€⁄↙⁄

well, of course there was so much more going on other than the projects i did as a part of "school" or a "class" in my second semester at gmu. i mean researching and learning more about frank, watching films and writing about them, doing multiple photography series', generating a three story string installation, having important dinners, and being looked at as a living piece of art was cool and all, but i wanted to do more. i had more ideas. i had more to do. i wasn't satisfied with all that. i had more to give. i had more to grow. i had more to practice. i had greater greatness to achieve.

and note, i've just mentioned highlights of my classes in the previous chapters. i found what i've written to be some of the more important stuff, but understand that more projects and conversations and interactions and blah blah blah happened in school. but, also much blah blah blah and stuff happened outside of school. and i'll write about a few.

for one, i started to get aggravated and annoyed at how opportunityless school could be sometimes. i started really realizing that what i was making with finlay was a full-blown documentary. i knew it was more than an interview. and i started wanting to bring the film to fruition. but a few more filming sessions were missing. and i planned to do those during my semester inside and outside of school. and around this time i was discovering that the content and imagery and footage was more powerful that i had originally thought and as i edited more and more of everything together i started seeing the bigger picture that it could possibly turn out to be. i mean finlay and i filmed in the photo studio, more of me painting my first ever piop art painting, me working on sculpture in the sculpture studio and then skateboarding over the piece i had just created, and etc. so, i was excited and was feeling ready to edit and complete this now prototype called "documentary film of my art" that was coming together slowly. i wanted to speed up the process and work more. so, i decided to begin trying to find somewhere i could premiere the film at school. i knew gmu had a movie theatre on campus and i thought my film should get an opportunity to be played there. this theatre normally showed movies from movie theaters that were no longer in the movie theaters. i felt that at the completion of my documentary everything should be of high quality and if i presented my idea and what i wanted to do i'd be appreciated for generating a full-length film. and i was legally a full-time student of the university. how could they say "no", right? so, i started with the film lab. they gave me information on who i should contact. i called the person who i should call and spoke of my idea. and then she asked, "are you a film student?" i said, "no." and then i started getting the cold shoulder. and she wasn't trying to help me out at all! she acted like she didn't know anything anymore and that i should try out this other contact person and see what they say. i felt so degraded. but, i kept going. next location i went i proposed my general idea of having a documentary film premiere at on campus and i was sent to go somewhere else. "really!?" i thought. so, i went to this somewhere else and that somewhere else took me full circle back to the place prior to it that told me to go to the somewhere else. so, okay, i was frustrated and annoyed. but, i went back and asked. then the lady at the desk went on about how i have to be involved in a group of some sort to use the movie theatre at all and that it had to be an event and that it could only be on a weekday because the weekends are only for big films and blah blah blah. i thought, "are you blupping serious!?" and then i learned that if i wasn't involved in any group apparently i could make up a group, but if i did it would have to meet a certain minimum number of people and have to get approved and all this stuff. basically i understood this, "i.e. don't try to have your film premiered at school. who are you anyway? i don't know you. you're not a film student. what makes you feel so special? and you probably aren't doing anything good with quality. you still have to learn how to make films. like really, who do you think you

are? you're just some kid. no one cares about what
you're doing, including us. we don't have help for you.
even though you're a full time student and giving the
school all this money. yes, we don't take that into
consideration. we just see you as a little worthless
person who probably doesn't even have a documentary
in the works. after you leave we'll laugh at you and your
request. but, for now we'll just have this look on our face
that shows how confused we are with your request and
say, 'yeah, sorry'." and thought to myself, "wow, is this
really happening!? they had me running around in
circles and at the end they just don't want to help. i'm
here delivering high end product. i have a segment i'm
ready to show anyone right now just for them to see i'm
not playing around. everything in this film is original. no
songs or music or this or that is stolen. everything is
done from scratch! i'm just looking for an opportunity to
showcase something i've been working on! i'm just
trying to bring amazing visuals connected with words to
an audience! is that too much to ask for!? you can't just
give me an opportunity!? really!? i'm not just a kid doing
stupid things! i don't do assignments for class anymore!
i don't need to be a film major to make amazing movies!
i have creativity and amazingness on my side! i have
something amazing for the student body to see and i'm
just asking for a chance to show it. i'm putting myself
out there. i'm not waiting on someone else to tell me i'm
ready to make films. i'm making films because i feel like
it and because i can! what the blup!?"

    so, yeah, we covered a bit of things in the
paragraph previous this one. you now know i had been
filming with finlay and that i was working on my first
ever piop art painting. and what else? well, i had been
writing of course. working on different books and
stories and stuff along those lines. i had been organizing

and taking part in a couple of photo shoots. and for those who don't know, i do prefer being in front of the camera more than behind it.

and walter and i had continued practicing the art of conversation with different people. we started to get really good at it. we also learned a lot about lies and deception and how fake some people could be. and we also started developing new ways to get into conversations with strangers. we really were becoming great at talking and improvising, but with all the good also came bad. walter and i had a couple of huge fights. not physical, just verbal and experiential. well, this was his last semester at gmu as you may know, right? yeah, so, he had been working hard on his senior project which consisted of three big paintings all about perseverance, never giving up, being strong, and fighting for what you believe. and one day i walked in a painting studio room and found him working on his second painting. then i was honest with him because i didn't care to give him lies. but note, i also didn't have any bad intentions in what i said. what did i say? i'm about to tell you. so, i saw what he did to the background of the second painting and said, "that looks amateur." and i didn't say that in any mean voice or anything like that. and after i said what i said walter completely flipped out and said, "you don't know anything about painting! i'm a great artist! you're just a kid! i've been painting for years and years and practice every day!" and of course i got super mad and annoyed at the immaturity and stupidity that he showed me and went on to say, "listen! i'm just trying to help you! i see the first painting you did and i find that background to be amazing! but, this one, in my honest opinion, looks amateur! and yes, i know i don't know how to paint! i've openly admitted that and still do to this day!" then he went off more and said, "yeah, that other paintings background took way longer than expected and i'm at a major time constraint! and you don't know how fast acrylic paints dry and i even mixed something to make the paint dry-time longer, but it didn't work that well so i had to work fast! and all this paint costed a lot of money!" and blah blah blah he went on screaming at me. and i didn't feel like dealing with his childish dumb behavior after i thought he was a friend and that i could give him an honest comment. i was really annoyed because i had no intentions of disrespect or anything like that. if anything, i was just trying to save him the embarrassment of horrible work. or i was just trying to tell him something *i* didn't like. and note, if he would have understood that and decided that he liked what i didn't like then great. no worries. and if others liked it what i didn't like, cool. was i "not allowed" to say what i didn't like? and he said things about how the piece wasn't done and blah blah blah. but, in any case, his response to a simple comment that i blatantly have used to describe other friends' works' when i thought that way was what appalled me. like, for instance, with finlay, one day when he showed me a short film he had just made and i didn't like it. so, i told him that i thought it wasn't that good and blah blah blah. and what did finlay do? he took what i said, but counteracted my opinion with his continuos liking of that short film. so, to this day i don't really like that finlay film, but he does. it's all cordial and good. no problems. just opinion differences. and that's good because people should have different points of view. and plus, it's not like i was trying to hate what finlay did or anything like that. he was interested in what i thought and i told him just that. but, yeah, i didn't want to deal with walters behavior and raised voice anymore, so i was done with him after that moment. then a few days passed by and walter found me working on some images at school and he came over and apologized for what he said and for his reaction. this time he was calm and polite and was just explaining how he was nervous and concerned if he would finish his paintings on time and that he ran into a lot of problems with trying different painting techniques and that he knew the other background was better, but that first background took way longer than expected and this and that. i decided to accept his apology, but i went back into our friendship with caution.

   and actually since i was very close to wrapping up my first piop art painting, i decided to start my second one. oh, and something else that was incorporated with these piop art paintings were separate excess paint paintings on a separate canvas. what am i talking about? well, since acrylic paints dry relatively quick and sometimes i overcompensate on how much paint i expect to use for a section of canvas i didn't want to just throw the paint out or put it to waste, so i decided to do these excess paint paintings. so, yes, i used the paint that was about to dry or the extra paint after i was done painting a certain section of a piop art painting on a separate canvas. and the way i did that was just taking a paper towel, pushing through the paint of the "palette" with that paper towel, and then just scrubbing paint on the canvas. so, the idea was to have one excess painting for every piop art painting of a series of possibly 7. and for starters, all these first piop art paintings i thought would be painted in various gray tones, but each would have a touch of color. and each color would be different. and the color was to serve as the instructions for how one would go about replicating the finished images.

when it came to my second piop art painting, i ended up getting to a point where i was in the painting studio working with walter. we had music playing and we would be just jamming out. he was working on his senior show work and i was working on my career work.

and i did a bit of traveling around this time. mostly local. and one trip in particular was a trip i went on with walter to audrey's show in new york. and note, she showed her beautiful paintings in a gallery in chelsea. and the place was packed when we arrived. audrey was kind of like a superstar in the painting world. but, it was strange because i don't think that many people knew her. because when i would ask students and especially painting majors at gmu if they knew who audrey was i would get the response, "no, i don't know who she is." but, then when i would see her in new york and open the book that had basic information about her paintings and, well, all i remembered seeing were red dots. listen, on audrey's opening show day all of her paintings were sold. that was something crazy for me to see. and she had something like 22-38 paintings that were either around $8,000, $15,000, or $23,000. audrey was really making an impact in the fine art world, but people at school weren't in tune with that. or maybe i was just seeing an illusion.

don't say anything, ever

arthur lugauskas

don't say anything, ever

chapter 25 : wintertime warm

in this chapter we'll touch on a few things that happened in late november, most of december, and early january.

to start things off, it was walters birthday in november. and he wanted to go out and celebrate on a weekend. though i was busy, i found time. and plus, walters best friend of the last couple years was in town. his name was slan. i quickly became friends with him soon after we met. he was a funny guy. always smiling and joking around. the vibes were good. all three of us went to dc for the evening. and when we got there we started talking to strangers, primarily beautiful women. well, slan wasn't at the level walter and i were, so we took him under our wing. and note, slam had it all, but all he was missing was the confidence to go up to a girl and introduce himself, sometimes. you know, sometimes shyness takes over. and that's okay. walter was actually originally a shy guy. but, he overcame his shyness by dancing in front of people in public transportation locations, going up to people and asking if he could draw them, and just saying "hi" to random strangers for starters. walter and i knew slam had it in him, but all he was missing was a little push. and that was what we did on that november evening. we tried to improve slams "conversation with strangers" skills. and little by little it was working, but slam didn't become a monster overnight. well, we all kept bouncing around dc and going from place to place. we met some people, but focused on meeting girls, getting rejected by girls, rejecting girls, and more girl interactions stuff. why? because the idea was to get walter a possible girlfriend. it was all about walter on this evening and even though slam and i would talk to girls here and there, we wanted walter to pick who he wanted to not get rejected by and it was our job to just help out the cause. then we got to a situation. there were three girls walking down the street. it was approach time. walter chose who he was interested in. cool. it was then up to slam and myself to distract the other girls via conversation while walter worked on getting a connection with his girl of interest. well, no connection was made, but i ended up connecting with the girl i was talking to, so i got her number. and slam sort of connected to the girl he was talking to, but didn't ask for her number. then as slam and i were walking up the street we noticed that walter was a bit ahead of us for some reason. then we saw two ladies walking to the left. i wanted to help slam with trying to raise his confidence real quick and said, "let's talk to them real quick." he said, "okay, let's do it." and we drifted into the direction the girls were going. and then we all got to talking very comfortably. slam was killing it! and i was happy to be learning more about the girl i was talking to. well, this ended up not being a quick thing. we ended up walking the girls home somehow. yes, conversations was that good. and note, towards the end of my conversation with this girl walter was calling. and i think he was calling slam too. but, neither slam nor i picked up the phone. i didn't want to be disrespectful in picking up a phone call mid-conversation, you know? and plus, i was going to call walter right back. there should be no worries, right? well, wrong. after slam and i finished sharing words with the pretty ladies we got their numbers and then left and called walter back. we soon discovered that walter actually was really annoyed at us and then said, "lets just leave." i was puzzled. walter didn't need anyone i thought. he was fully capable of meeting people, girls, or whoever alone for a few minutes, right? yeah, i thought so. so, what was all the fuss about? well, as slam and i walked back, we ended up finding where we parked. so, we got in the car and decided to drive and pick up walter. then as we were driving we joked with picking up these three girls we saw on the street. you know, like "happy birthday walter, we maybe found you a girlfriend" or whatever. and when we were on the phone and told that to walter, he just got more mad. i really had no idea what got into him. well, we found walter, he got in the car, and then was completely furious! slam and i were shocked! i was thinking, "what is this guy so mad about?" and then long story short, basically walter didn't want to be my nor slams friend anymore. yeah, it was ugly. maybe i'll have more of the story in another book or something.

so, then december was walters senior show. and we had still sort of been in conflict and had issues with one another despite his apologies to me and stuff. but, i knew this show was important for him and that he worked really hard on it. i didn't want to bring any negativity or any thing like that. so, i kept my cool and went about the showcase evening party cordially. and i thought walter had one of the better works in the group show. him and a couple of others stood out to me. and that was coming from a neutral stand point. and a cool thing was that my abstract reflection string installation was up during the show. stuff like that doesn't normally happen. what i mean is that this was the senior show and works by only the ones who were graduating should be up, hence no other work by students who weren't in the show or graduating or whatever. i wasn't graduating, i wasn't in the show, and it was only my 2nd semester at gmu. but, in a funny way, i technically sort of kind of was in the show. and yes, i thought my strings were one of the best pieces being shown, despite them being overlooked. well, after the show finished and all that walter and i still didn't talk much.

to celebrate the new year i went to new york with finlay and we stayed at my friends place. do you think we had a flashy time? do you think we saw the ball drop? no and no. somehow finlay and i entered into the new year in a train inside an underground subway station. yeah, crazy. but, the funniest and saddest part was when a friend we were with said, "i can't believe it. i spent my first ever new years in america in the stupid subway."

then in january 2013 i got an email from walter about this art contest thing. he thought i should do a piece for it because it was free to submit. i left off the thing until last minute. i was busy with other stuff. then on the submission day i decided to do something. and note, the premise was to do any kind of artwork about gun control laws. not really my forte, but i decided to just take a shot at it. so, i really didn't know what this contest or submission or whatever thing was actually about. since i didn't watch the news or know about gun control laws or anything in that world that was really going on, i was lost. but, the contest was open to anything. so, i thought and thought. and then came up with something. i just did a painting where i literally wrote "gun control laws seem to be invisible" with clear acrylic paint on white bristol board paper. then i did some gray tones of paint on the boarders to make boarders sort of. all that probably took me around 10-17mins. and i took a snapshot of my piece and submitted it worry-free. then next thing i knew i got an email stating that i was one of the 32 chosen artists out of the 148 that submitted. i thought, "huh!? wow!" then i got back to working on art that was taking me longer to finish.

    well, after all that i ended up getting the exclusive invite to the "artists only" party before this group show i was now involved with opened to the public. and i decided to go, meet some people, make some contacts, and eat some food. when i arrived, the owner of the space had a concern with my piece. reason being because i just dropped off the piece of paper with dried paint on it. no frame or anything. apparently i was supposed to have it framed, or no, the owner of the space thought it was going to be framed. in my head i thought, "i don't know this stuff. i thought maybe you had a crew that framed works or something. or i don't know what i exactly thought." so, what happened was, i ended up taking the artwork back home later that evening and i was going to figure out a frame and bring back the framed version before the show opened. but, while i was at this party event thing i didn't see walter. i thought he was going to submit. but, interestingly enough i ended up getting a text from him. at this point i didn't really have anything against him nor was i interested in doing much with him. i basically saw him as an acquaintance. and i didn't mind talking a bit. so, we had a phone conversation after the his text and he said that he didn't submit to this show and that he was surprised that i was at this event because it wasn't advertised online and that he was happy for me and this and that. then he wanted to go to dc and practice conversation with people again. well, i was already at this show in dc, so i thought, "why not for a bit?" and plus, walter has been my best wingman yet. and a reason he was so good was because of all the practice we've had in the past. we basically both had lots of experiences with interactions with strangers and we've learned goods and bads and we maybe knew what it meant to "take one for the team" and stuff like that. and yes note, walter and i have had our horrible arguments, but we've also had some great achievements working together. so, after the art party event thing i met up with him. and we got to business. talking to people, giving off positive vibes, high-fiveing strangers, smiling and giving sunshine to beautiful women we saw, etc. and then i met ae min.

    well, some time passed by and walter and i became friends again slowly. and we decided to start a headshot business. like, i'd be the photographer taking headshots and he would edit them slightly. we worked on all that for a little while and were building our headshots portfolio. but, then arguments came again. basically i wasn't that interested in doing these headshots and i just saw them as a quick way to make lunch money, but walter was trying to take this business more seriously than what i thought we had initially discussed. and then he didn't want to do all the editing because it took too long he said, despite me telling him to just edit a little bit. he wanted to do some of the photography too and wanted me to learn all this photo editing software. i wasn't interested in that field because i don't like computers that much. i'd rather interact and talk with the model while i did the photography. i guess he preferred that to, despite his years and years of skills and experience editing images. and complications and disagreements like that came about. eventually we stopped doing this headshots business thing. but, this time we didn't have and explosion of an argument. we noted our differences and let it be after some relatively minor arguments.

     and on another occasion in early 2013 walter and i went to new york for this huge art fair. there were galleries from all around the world there. and i ended up getting quite disappointed after seeing many of the works in the show. and that wasn't coming from a hateful place at all. i just was genuinely appalled at how the art world was looking when it came to the artworks being produced. it was like everything has been dumbified. and not in a tasteful and thoughtful way. doors stacked up on top of doors in the ugliest manner wasn't cool. putting an onion on a table in a particular location wasn't that great. more mirrors and lights wasn't new. wait, wait, i'm sorry, i'm wrong, all that stuff was amazing if you had a certain name behind it, right? despite the many things i really didn't like, i did end up seeing some stuff that ticked my fancy. anish had a fantastic piece. and um, yeah, i remember a lot of disappointment. and not that many standouts. maybe it's because i'm a picky jerk or maybe i just lack art world knowledge or maybe the art world was hypnotized or something.

don't say anything, ever

arthur lugauskas

chapter 26 : spring 2013 gmu semester

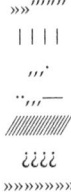

well, it was time for another semester full of classes, stories, and adventures. i felt good coming in. i was ready to take over in 2013. and after this semester, the next one was going to be my last one. well, if i didn't dropout for some reason. why do i say that? well, because those thoughts were coming into my head. i was just feeling like i shouldn't be in school. i mean, in one way that didn't make sense because all i received were a's in all my classes, except drawing two. but, then again, maybe that was exactly why it made sense for me to dropout. was school too easy for me? i don't know. i was lost and found around the beginning of my 3rd semester. well, time to get into what went down.

don't say anything, ever

arthur lugauskas

don't say anything, ever

::: ::: ::: : :: : :: :::::: :: :: : : ::
:::::: :: : :: : : : : : :   :   : :   ::::::::
chapter 27 : critical theory in the visual arts professor
:::::::::::::::::::::::::: :: : : : : : : : : ::
::::::::::::   ::   :   :   :   : : ::::::::::

....
.........πøππ......
""π"π"π"øøπ"
—≠—≠≠——≠
≠—≠—≠—≠—≠—≠⁰—ᵃᵒ
—

«‹«‹«‹›»›»»«‹«‹«›»›»»‹«›»

    so, critical theory in the visual arts was a class i had my concerns with. it had writing involved and papers. but, i should be comfortable with writing, right? yeah, but i didn't know. maybe i worried if my writing would be accepted and if i would be allowed to write however i wanted. but, i did hear good things about the professor of the class. her name was citi and she was an upbeat lady with fun nerdy qualities. i think she even admitted how much of a nerd she was. there were plenty of laughs and smiles and jokes that surfaced in the classroom. and i liked citi because she was just "hip" in the funniest way. and note, she also had lots of knowledge and knew what she was talking about.

    in class, we broke into small groups many times. and what do you think i desired when it came to a group project where we were allowed to do basically anything we wanted? what do you think i wanted when citi told us, "hypothetically speaking, lets say i have billions of dollars or unlimited money and resources and i'm looking for a project proposal that can have anything to do with nature or creating a utopia in any way and this can be anywhere in the world and lets say the four groups in this room are the only ones who i care to provide me with the best idea for me to bring into fruition. it can literally be anything your imagination can think of. there are no limits."? of course i wanted to bring the most creative "out-of-reach" genius idea possible. i wanted to have fun because we were allowed to. i was excited! so, i started talking to my group and proposing some of the craziest ideas. i thought the conversation i was having might go to places where mattata and i often went. i thought everyone would build on great ideas and take them further. i thought people in my group would propose their own craziest imaginatively creative ideas. but, no! none of that happened! they looked at me like i was crazy! they just wanted to "keep it real." and they kept saying how it wasn't possible. and i said, "why not? we are given permission to do literally anything in this project! we can take our thoughts anywhere we want to! this concept of something being 'realistic' wasn't in the description of what we should or shouldn't do! why would we limit ourselves when we are given no limits!?" and sure i was proposing stuff like rollercoasters across continents and tubes that wrapped around the world and different things at that caliber. but, all i kept hearing was, "that's not possible. we can't do that. we don't have the resources. etc." oh, and more excuses. but listen, of course i understood this as a brainstorm session that was going on and i knew it was a group project and i was fully aware that i was not the leader of this group. so, after i spoke with all my excitement and energy it was time for others to say what they wanted to do. and well, they weren't sure where to take it. it was like everyone was waiting for everyone else to say something. and this idea of "thinking what to do" was going in circles. but, don't get me wrong now, my group did show me my respect and i think was appreciative a little bit after they heard what i was saying, but they just wanted to be more grounded. or something. but, i was ready to fly sky high. if i had the opportunity to go global or universal or beyond, why wouldn't i? my group was trying to keep things local and what they believed was possible, which was a limited number of things. so, then finally we would get to an idea we all kind of agreed on. then, even with that idea i would get excited to take it to new levels. but, ultimately i realized that i had a different mentality than everyone else. and my thoughts were at least right next to the stars or beyond. so now, two possible things. one, maybe i was just crazy and not a real person. or two, maybe most people were boxed in to thoughts that didn't go beyond what was known and didn't want to be open minded to possibilities. wait, person who is reading this, who are you? if you have a hard copy of this book please write your name under this sentence so you and i know this book is yours. and if you're a reader who doesn't own this book, it's okay, i give you permission to write your name under this sentence. and if you're a reader who is reading this book digitally or electronically or whatever, well, please write your name on a sticky note. why do i ask this? well, it's just me and you here right now. and i want you to remember who you are if you forgot somewhere along the line of living life. and i want you to have the experience of writing and seeing *your* hand written name on a surface. and i just want you to know that no one else is going to write your name exactly like you. and yes, i really am asking you to write your name if you haven't already. and of course, if you don't want to, no problem. if you did write your name though, well, thank you and you're welcome.

don't say anything, ever

arthur lugauskas

don't say anything, ever

::::::::::::::::::::: : ::: :::: ::::: :::: ::::: : ::: : ::: ::: :::::::::::::::::::::
chapter 28 : writing for artists professor
:::::::::::::: :::: ::: : :: ::: ::: : :: ::: :: ::: : : : : : :::::::::::::::::::

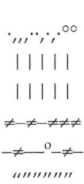

     guess which professor was signed up to teach me and my class about writing for artists? the man who likes sounds, the man who makes music, yes, sunvy the man himself. i was in his class again, but this time it has to do with writing.

     okay, so, in our first class of the semester i learned that sunvy was a big deal when it came to writing. like, he knew how to write and he knew how to do it well. and i'm talking about really well. sunvy was almost a full blown big time author, but he messed up this one time on a pretty huge piece of writing and that damaged his career as a writer pretty bad. or so he said. but, i believed him. and sunvy also said that many students have bad writing and that he was interested in all of us getting better. he didn't plan for us to be the best writers once we finished with this class, but he did expect to correct certain mistakes that most students make when it came to writing. and i was just blown away for a bit. i really had no idea the level of writer sunvy was. and he really knew how to write. so, i was honored to have this class with him. and me and sunvy were really cool with one another. how great!

now, i want to tell you something sunvy told me after our first class. so, i was having a small conversation with him about how he looks at writing and what he kind of expects from students and well, he said, "akuna, i like you, but i'm concerned with how your writing is." i guess he didn't see me as a writer. so, i responded, "well, i don't know how to write, but aestan said that i was a great writer. so, i don't know. but, she gave me confidence in my writing despite me telling her what i just told you about me not knowing how to write." then sunvy responded with a puzzled look on his face, "aestan!? she's like the best writer in this school! i look up to her when it comes to writing!" then i got really puzzled and thought, "what!? so, the best writer in school thinks i know how to write and could recognize my writing from a pile of pieces of writing with no names on them!? is my writing that special!? i don't know what to think. maybe everything i do is just an illusion?" then i told sunvy, "wow, um, yeah, i don't know. maybe she said what she said about me and my writing mistakingly? i don't know." then i went on to question sunvy if i could just write all my pieces of writing for class in lowercase letters. and he said, "no. i don't want you to do that." then i said, "i like lowercase and is it not cool if i just be an individual?" and he went on to explain, "yeah, i just really don't want you to do that because when it comes to grading i want to grade without knowing who wrote the piece. i'm interested in grading and analyzing the writing itself and not knowing who's it is. and that's why i'm very stubborn about the basic format i want written work to be turned in to me from everyone. that's one of the few things i really care to get from students. having the work double space, full punctuation, in arial font all the time, and name and date and class on the upper right side of the page." i took that explanation sunvy gave me as a valid one and didn't bother fighting with him. and plus, sunvy was the man. we didn't have beef with one another and had respect for each other.

and what made me really enjoy and appreciate sunvy's class was that he honestly wanted us to produce good writing. he didn't care how long or short each piece was. it was all about quality. one day sunvy said, "i want all of you to see each project assigned as something that you plan to publish. take your work that seriously. get it ready to the point where it would be ready to be published in a newspaper or journal. i want you guys to have pieces of writing and not just class assignments." and that moment i thought, "yes! yes! you're talking my language when it comes to how kids and people and students should view this class, their other classes, school in general, and life as a whole!" and yeah, around this time, as you may already know, i had already stopped doing assignments. i didn't believe in assignments anymore. when i had an "assignment" for a class or whatever, i turned it into a project. or i did whatever i wanted and was able to throw words together to make it fit the "proposed assignment" if i wanted to.

    then there would be times i would stay after class to simply converse with sunvy for a bit. sometimes another classmate would do the same. on one of those instances sunvy, myself, and the other student were catching up a bit. and sunvy would continually ask me, "are you getting enough sleep?" he would say that jokingly, but seriously kind of. he knew i worked all the time all day all night if i had to and if i wanted to. and of course, plenty of times he'd see my eyes red from lack of sleep. but, he appreciated my work ethic. so, on this day that i'm writing about, sunvy told the other student in the classroom, "you know, akuna doesn't sleep. watch out for this guy. i'm telling you he's going to make it. and i'm not joking, akuna is going to be rich and famous." then i intervened with smiling and laughing, "yeah, then i could give back to people like you and give you some money for your bills." and with good vibes sunvy went on to say, "yes, please just pay my bills. i'm getting nothing here." but then i had to change the subject and ask sunvy what that something was that he was up to secretly that he didn't want to tell the class. what am i talking about? well, sunvy said in class that he was working on something big, like really big that might allow him to be done with teaching. but, he still had much to do and go through and all this stuff. so, i was curious and thoughtful and i connected some dots and then i felt like i may have possibly figured out what sunvy was up to. so, then i asked him after i changed the subject from me to his big project. but, he still didn't fully tell me, but he gave me hints of the project being a book. and to this day i think i know what the book might be about and what sunvy wants to say in it and i do think it could be very successful. and note, i didn't want to tell him exactly what i thought he might be doing because i wanted him to tell me first so i could see if i made the connection correctly or not. and if i did or didn't i wasn't that interested in writing what i thought he might be writing. i had a lot of other unfinished projects that wanted my attention. i was just curious and wanted to know and i think that was it. but, he didn't tell me. and it was okay. there were no hard feelings.

arthur lugauskas

chapter 29 : sculpture four professor

```
           ¬¬…¬…¬¬
     …¬¬…¬¬…¬…¬…¬…¬…¬…¬…¬…¬…¬…
øπøπøππøπøøππøøπøπøπøπøπøπøπøπøπøπøππøøπøππø¬……
…¬¬…øπ¬…πø¬…πø¬…øπ¬…πø≠≠≠≠≠≠≠≠≠≠≠≠≠≠≠≠
  ≠≠≠≠≠≠≠≠≠≠≠≠≠——≠≠¬¬π≠≠≠¬≠¬≠¬≠¬≠¬≠¬≠¬≠¬≠¬≠¬
 ≠¬≠¬≠¬≠¬≠¬≠¬¬¬¬≠≠¬¬¬≠¬¬¬¬¬≠¬≠¬≠≠¬≠¬≠¬
              ≠¬¬¬¬¬¬¬————¬¬¬¬≠≠¬
```

     we're still postponing sculpture two because it didn't work well with my schedule again. so, definitely next semester (if i don't dropout this semester) i better be in that class. and note, sculpture four worked great with our schedule. yes, our. if you're this deep in this book it's now about us. we are looking at my journey and experiences and stories together. cool?

     guess who i was also back with, professor wise. yes, the man who wants students to just do their thing. the legend, the myth, the artist, bom!

i'm just going to get straight into my not giving a blupness. i wanted to make a moving painting. or a painting that could change and be re-arranged. so, i did just that. a painting in sculpture class? yes, because i wanted to and i decided to. and anything can technically be sculpture. even air itself. actually, this book is a sculpture. are looking at a sculpture right now. sculptures can be imaginary. and hey, in front of you boom i just made an invisible sculpture. do you see it? of course not, it's invisible. do you want me to describe it? well, not now. maybe ask me when you see me. even if you see me on the tv feel free to ask me that moment. it would be pretty cool if i was doing a live interview on tv and you actually asked me and somehow harmoniously i just stopped mid interview and said that i had to answer this question that you asked me about describing this invisible sculpture. then the interviewer would probably think i was crazy maybe. but what if that really happened in order and in harmony with me and you. wow, the experience that could be! that would really be truly amazing! and what if you recorded it!? that would be some next level stuff! maybe one day. but, okay, back to what i was saying or writing or whatever. so, yeah, moving painting would be a sculpture because it would be interactive and it would be something that was on something or on a wall or so and blah blah blah. must i explain and put words together to justify that a painting or a moving painting is a sculpture? all these boxes and categories. and this and that. okay, well, bom let me do whatever i wanted in sculpture four and i did just that. so, this painting was going to be my third piop art painting. remember i basically finished my first one and started my second one? yeah, so i hadn't finished my second one, but i was already going for a third one. stupid? maybe. why do i

don't say anything, ever

chapter 29 : sculpture four professor

¬¬...¬...¬¬
...¬¬...¬¬...¬...¬...¬...¬...¬...¬...¬...¬...
ØπØπØππØπØØπππØØπØπØπØπØπØπØπØπØπØπØπππØØπØππØ¬......
...¬¬...Øπ¬...πØ¬...πØ¬...Øπ¬...πØ≠≠≠≠≠≠≠≠≠≠≠≠≠≠≠≠
≠≠≠≠≠≠≠≠≠≠≠≠≠≠≠¬¬π≠≠¬≠¬≠¬≠¬≠¬≠¬≠¬≠¬≠¬≠¬≠¬
≠¬≠¬≠¬≠¬≠¬≠¬¬¬≠¬≠¬¬¬≠¬¬¬¬¬≠¬≠¬≠¬≠¬≠¬≠¬
≠¬¬¬¬¬¬¬————¬¬¬¬≠≠¬

      we're still postponing sculpture two because it didn't work well with my schedule again. so, definitely next semester (if i don't dropout this semester) i better be in that class. and note, sculpture four worked great with our schedule. yes, our. if you're this deep in this book it's now about us. we are looking at my journey and experiences and stories together. cool?

      guess who i was also back with, professor wise. yes, the man who wants students to just do their thing. the legend, the myth, the artist, bom!

i'm just going to get straight into my not giving a blupness. i wanted to make a moving painting. or a painting that could change and be re-arranged. so, i did just that. a painting in sculpture class? yes, because i wanted to and i decided to. and anything can technically be sculpture. even air itself. actually, this book is a sculpture. are looking at a sculpture right now. sculptures can be imaginary. and hey, in front of you boom i just made an invisible sculpture. do you see it? of course not, it's invisible. do you want me to describe it? well, not now. maybe ask me when you see me. even if you see me on the tv feel free to ask me that moment. it would be pretty cool if i was doing a live interview on tv and you actually asked me and somehow harmoniously i just stopped mid interview and said that i had to answer this question that you asked me about describing this invisible sculpture. then the interviewer would probably think i was crazy maybe. but what if that really happened in order and in harmony with me and you. wow, the experience that could be! that would really be truly amazing! and what if you recorded it!? that would be some next level stuff! maybe one day. but, okay, back to what i was saying or writing or whatever. so, yeah, moving painting would be a sculpture because it would be interactive and it would be something that was on something or on a wall or so and blah blah blah. must i explain and put words together to justify that a painting or a moving painting is a sculpture? all these boxes and categories. and this and that. okay, well, bom let me do whatever i wanted in sculpture four and i did just that. so, this painting was going to be my third piop art painting. remember i basically finished my first one and started my second one? yeah, so i hadn't finished my second one, but i was already going for a third one. stupid? maybe. why do i start things without finishing other things? blup me. but, whatever. so, yeah, i had to figure out how i was going to make a moving painting. what the blup was that anyway? well, okay, after some discussion with bom, friends, and classmates i was getting closer into making something happen. then i went about experimentation and finally stuff got figured out. so, magnets in the back of twelve 12"x12" canvas'. then have all those magnetized onto a sheet of steel that would be a bit bigger than 36"x48". because i wanted this painting to be part of the series of my other two piops art paintings and one of the main cohesiveness things of these paintings was for all of them to be 36"x48". so, twelve 12"x12" canvas' arranged in a way where there are four columns of four and three rows of three would make the rectangular size of 36"x48". get it? so, i did all that and went to town painting.

    well, here's another thing. i was looking to have space to work, so i made my own space in the sculpture studio. sidebar, there was this thing called "backspace" in the sculpture studio area. and basically "backspace" was a room that held 5-7 undergrad students and gave them this sort of private studio space. and how a student got into "backspace" was by invitation only. and to get that invitation a student had to be noticed by a professor or bom or someone of high status as a dedicated person working hard and long nights. "backspace" was a special prestigious space that allowed the shinning stars of the school of art to work on shinning more. are you asking why i wasn't part of that group of people? i don't know. maybe i just wasn't doing work that was that big a deal. or maybe i wasn't a shinning star. or maybe my timing coming into the university was off. or maybe i just didn't deserve extra space because i wasn't working hard enough. or maybe i should have asked despite it being invite only. i don't know. but, whatever the case, no worries, i started a new movement. i generated my own space whether i had permission or not. i became the originator and first man to be in something i decided to call "frontspace." i felt worthy enough. i felt hard working enough. why not try, right? what's the worst that could have happened after i made my space? bom telling me to not do such a thing? in any case, "frontspace" came to existence this semester. maybe i should have called it "avant-guarde-space"? and i typed that last sentence jokingly. really, i just was appreciative with the support i had from bom and ten when it came to me creating my own space and working station. and i was just happy to have a private space to work in. and i did work there countless nights. this third piop art moving painting took a long time. but, it was well worth it. probably one of my most genius paintings ever. from the "moving" concept, to the playfulness and interactivity, to the actual "drawing" or "image" put together with all twelve canvas'. i blew my own mind for a moment during the making of this work of art and really amazed myself with my abilities in creating. and like, the image itself was mind boggling, but then when you re-arranged the pieces the image became more crazy, and then trying to put everything back together playing the game properly was just another "destroy your brain with genius" scenario and blah blah blah. yeah, i was really proud of what i did. and yeah, i still didn't know how to paint, but i think i did a much better job on this piece than my first piop art painting. and actually, since i was such a nub when it came to painting, well, it was such an intense battle scene every time i picked up a brush and was getting ready to paint another section of the canvas. and i'm talking about super intense war zone battle in my head and mind and just all around. seriously! it was crazy for me! i was nervous and had to prepare and get myself together every time i mixed some paint and was about to put some brush strokes on the canvas'. wow! i don't really know how do describe it, but yeah, painting was crazy!

    well, i actually did more work that just a "moving painting" in this class. what? well, more installation business. so, i had these boxes from things, right? i did't want to throw them away for some reason. so, i bought three different gray toned spray paint bottles, then brought the various sized boxes to school, and then spray painted them a gray tone each. sidebar, the moving painting was all gray toned and had only cyan colored dots when it was finished. end sidebar. and sidebar, i didn't end the sidebar when i went into the "backspace" sidebar. it's okay. don't worry. end sidebar. um, confused? yeah, don't be. or do be. either or. so, boxes. yes, gray boxes. well, i wanted one small box to be colored. and then i wanted another small box to be colored. and then another. so, when i installed these gray toned boxes arranged in some way i liked i did so on a three separate walls above lockers. and each composition of boxes had one colored box among the gray toned boxes. and the piece was all about experience. that's what i care about doing with almost all my works, i think, if not all. giving people experiences that can last forever. so, with the boxes as you walked down the hall from one direction and kept looking at the boxes, well, after you got to a certain nearby point then the colored box would be revealed. and that same experience went on as you went down the hall and encountered each of the three installed gray toned multiple box compositions. wow, did anything i just write make any sense? if it didn't then maybe you're reading senseless writing. hmm, that's interesting. senseless writing. is that what some of my writing is? maybe senseless to some and sensed to others? what am i saying!? what am i writing!? blup! next chapter time.

      wait, no, not next chapter time just yet. another thing. so, bom wanted the class to have discussions on tuesdays about topics of choice by different students. so, each week one student would bring something for everyone to talk about for the beginning of class. and this was just to have conversations, share ideas, and learn things. i thought it was cool. so, different students picked different things. then when it was my turn to pick the topic of conversation, well, i chose to speak about fame and superstardom. i simply questioned why people were so afraid to say that they wanted to be famous. like it was a bad thing or something. because i learned that the dictionary definition stated that fame was just being known. that was it! if five people know you then you are technically famous! but, once someone says "i want to be famous" then someone else usually rolls their eyes and laughs at your belief that you somehow think you could possibly be famous one day. and you see, those people have allowed their dreams to die and now want to kill your dreams. blup that! famous is simply being known! but, it has been made out to be bigger than the dictionary definition by society! and most people don't believe they will ever be famous even though technically they probably already are famous. and if you live in your world and your reality and you say you're famous then you are right. all this labeling and politics blurs peoples vision. most people think they'll never be famous. and most people think that wanting to be famous is a bad thing. and you know what, when bom asked each person in class if they wanted to be famous during our discussion no one said "yes", except for two people! do you think i was one of those people!? to be honest with you, no. and to be honest with you again, i am overly disappointed of my "beating around the bush" answer. i don't know what got into me. of course i didn't say "no". but, blup, i didn't just say "yes." i for some reason felt like blah blah blah. i was going saying stuff like, "yeah, i want to be known, but blah blah blah." i don't even want to go over what i said. i am really disappointed in myself for not just saying "yes." i really don't know what i was scared of or whatever. blup! blup! sorry for being so frustrated right now. but, what i really should have just said was, "yes!" and you know what i really think when it comes to fame and myself? well, i think i won't avoid fame. i think it will just happen regardless whether i want it to or not. that's my relationship with fame. it's coming for me and there's nothing stopping it. but, okay, the only two people that said "yes" to boms question was bom himself and a fellow classmate/friend. remember the guy who was in my art now class and questioned if i was going to be the "one-man-avant-guarde"? yes, he said "yes" to wanting to be famous. tisk tisk to my response though. blup me! now next chapter time.

arthur lugauskas

wanted to be famous during our discussion no one said "yes", except for two people! do you think i was one of those people!? to be honest with you, no. and to be honest with you again, i am overly disappointed of my "beating around the bush" answer. i don't know what got into me. of course i didn't say "no". but, blup, i didn't just say "yes." i for some reason felt like blah blah blah. i was going saying stuff like, "yeah, i want to be known, but blah blah blah." i don't even want to go over what i said. i am really disappointed in myself for not just saying "yes." i really don't know what i was scared of or whatever. blup! blup! sorry for being so frustrated right now. but, what i really should have just said was, "yes!" and you know what i really think when it comes to fame and myself? well, i think i won't avoid fame. i think it will just happen regardless whether i want it to or not. that's my relationship with fame. it's coming for me and there's nothing stopping it. but, okay, the only two people that said "yes" to boms question was bom himself and a fellow classmate/friend. remember the guy who was in my art now class and questioned if i was going to be the "one-man-avant-guarde"? yes, he said "yes" to wanting to be famous. tisk tisk to my response though. blup me! now next chapter time.

arthur lugauskas

don't say anything, ever

chapter 30 : sociology professor

```
         ¬
         æ
       ¬¬°Δ
  ≠—≠¬≠¬¬≠≠π≠π≠…¬…¬πø°…
 πø…¬^øΔ°ΔΔ°Δ°Δ°Δ°Δ°Δ°Δ°Δ°Δ°Δ°
$$$$$$$$$$$!$$!$!$$!$!$!$!$!##!#$$#!$"#$#!$%$#!$"#!$
~==~=~==~~=!=~=~!=~=~=~=~!==~=~=~!=~~=||||!¥¥
```

so, i was missing two general education classes that i had to take in order to complete the bfa i wanted. and they had to *not* be art classes. so, after looking through a list i found sociology to be one of the few that i thought i'd find interesting and beneficial. and so it was.

one of the biggest things i received from this lecture class was about one of my biggest interests in life - creativity. shim was my professor and he was a very knowledgable man from new york. at one point during the semester he told the class about a certain research that was conducted not to long ago. and this research had to do with what students qualities were encouraged in school environments. or something along those lines. and the number one thing that professors and instructors and teachers cared about was perseverance. like, "just make it through. persevere please!" and do you know what was the least cared about quality for a student to have? well, i say this with tears in my heart, but that quality was creativity. blup that and in a way blup school if that was really the case! creativity is one of the best qualities people have the ability to have. creativity runs the world. if it wasn't for creativity there would be more suicides. if it wasn't for creativity life would practically not exist. think of everything you own. your phone, your laptop, your clothes, your glasses, your blupping pencil, your furniture, your entertainment, your everything is thanks to creatives! everything you like is because of creativity! what do i mean by creativity? i mean innovation, design, architecture, art, image, composition, aesthetics, arrangements, nature, cars, invention, "add anything here", and "add everything else here." just think and do. don't look and follow. look and learn and then push and create further. blup that was a crazy thing to hear from shim! and it's so saddening. please, if you're reading this book right now, i want you to know that one of the biggest messages i'm trying to portray is that i think not enough people care about creativity, hence i would like more people to put creativity first before anything else when it comes to a project, an artwork, a piece of writing, acting, singing, making music, going out on dates with girls, or if you're a girl and like a guy maybe take him on a date that is the most creative date he has ever been on and give him an experience to remember forever and give him something new and whether you two work out or not or whatever happens just think that he will remember the date you took him on because you did something different for a change. did that sound like something i want from a girl? it's funny, but yes i would like a girl or my girlfriend or whoever i'm with or dating to take me on an amazing creative date. just something different. just try. don't be afraid to fail. one date i'd like to go on with a girl one day is like just really looking into fruits and vegetables and analyzing and what a i saying right now. this book isn't about me and girls. how did i get here? okay, back to where we were. sidebar, i'm at a cafe somewhere in the usa right now writing and there are two pretty ladies in front of me working on whatever they're working on and maybe i should go up to them, give them a smile, start a conversation, etc., but no, i don't plan to do such a thing at a time like now because i'm at a severe time constraint with trying to finish this book and i have project overload and etc., but they have the opportunity to say "hi" and smile at me, but i don't think they will because it's, according to society or whatever, the man who should approach the woman, and i have no problem doing that, but in a case like this i don't want to get distracted because i'm focused and am on a writing roll right now and it's interesting because me being a guy i'm like at a "safety" because i could work in cafes or places without girls trying coming up to me to start a conversation because of what society or whatever tells them about girls and guys and what am i saying again!? well, i'm just not getting approached because i'm not that famous yet and i understand that i should enjoy my not-really-famous days before it's too late because i don't know when fame plans to come after me at full speed. or, really, maybe i'm just not good looking enough. and that's why i rely on my ideas and thoughts and speaking abilities to get the girls. hey, seriously, what the blup am i saying!? okay, sidebar end. but, yeah, creativity can save the world and make it the best place to live in ever and put smiles on faces and bring the sun out and bring people together and help anyone and everyone. real talk!

so, yeah, sociology worked out. and note, i didn't do that well when it came to the multiple choice exams. but, we had the option to do a written essay instead of a multiple choice scantron sheet. and the only grades for the class were going to be four exams. and i wasn't a fan of exams. i didn't think i was good at them and stuff. so, after getting a c or a b on the first two multiple choice exams i decided to take my chance and write the essay on the third exam. and note, the essay was like "punishment" for those who wanted to make-up the exam if they missed class on exam day. and note, practically no one chose to intentionally do the essay during exam days. and i didn't go for the essay on the first two exams because i thought i'd do better with the multiple choice exam version and i had my fears on whether shim would accept my writing. because in classes other than ones that had to do with art i felt like there was this structure that professors wanted in writing and i wasn't really comfortable with that if that was the case. but, maybe i was wrong. well, i took my chance on doing the essay for the third exam. but, wait, of course i usually procrastinated until the last day or two when it came to studying all these chapters from the book and i still didn't fully grasp or get everything. so, when it came to the essay, i think i just knew how to put words together and sentences in a way where it made sense and i don't know, whatever the case i ended up getting an a for the first essay exam i did in shims class.

then for the next and final exam i realized that for me to get an a in the class i had to basically get something like 99/100 or possibly higher than that. so, i realized that if i got a b for the class i'd be satisfied. but, well, final exam day came, i wrote an essay like none other and next thing i knew when it came to me seeing my final grade it was an a. i was super surprised! i didn't know if i deserved that grade. but, if shim found what i wrote to be that good and amazing or whatever that case that gave me and a for my final grade then wow, thank you. but, i really would have understood if i received a b or even a c for that matter. i really didn't expect an a.

arthur lugauskas

don't say anything, ever

chapter 31 : african dance class professor

(()()()()(
~=~=~~=~=
$$##$#$$##$$#$%$%$%%&%&%&%&&'&'&'&''(
((('('(&%$%&'()'&%$#"$%&'()'&%$#"$%&'(&%$#
~|~|~|~|~|~|~|~|~|~|~|~|~|~|~|~|~|~||~~|
`'['['['['['['['[|>??>>?>?>?>?>?<>><<><><><><><><>
<><><><>>?<><><>><??<!!'""!!""!!"!""!!"!""!""'!"!

      am i serious when i say i was in african dance class? certainly. yeah, this was another general education course i found to be possibly interesting, active, fun, and stuff. and i thought it could bring more dynamism when it came to my thoughts on doing things. like, body motions and all that. and i also thought this class could help me make fast or moving art.
      well, african dance class was amazing! the professor was from ghana. her name was adku and she

was pretty old, but looked super young. so much energy she had! it was fascinating! we danced so much in her class. and the workout was real and intense. this class really tested my stamina. usually most people were sweating after class and super tired. oh, the african dance class days. wow! we learned about africa and african culture and eight different dances and so much more. but, the energy in class was the craziest! i was really happy i took that class. and yes, i didn't really know how to dance when i signed up for the class. but, i started to learn how to african dance once classes were in session.

overall this class was good and great. but, actually i think adku didn't really like my writing when it came to the few writing assignments she gave us. or, no, maybe it wasn't that. i think i took the assignments to more complex places than she wanted me to. i kept getting b's on the few papers i turned in. i guess i didn't really get the simple thing that was asked for me to write. and since i'm oblivious to the obvious sometimes i guess it made sense. but, adku did start noticing me more and took interest in who i was after reading what i had to say. she started calling me a philosopher. and with the few conversations her and i had after class i learned that she liked what i was about.

and during class i did well. not the best. not the worst. just well. there were others who danced much better than me and adku noticed them. she often would give the title of mr. and miss africa each class. i was never mr. africa. and it was because my dancing i guess just blended in. or it was just okay. and i had troubles doing certain moves despite my trying hard. but, i did get better and better. but, still never mr. africa. or, well, until we had our final exam. and our final exam asked each student to do two solo dances (from the eight that we learned) in front of the whole class. well, i picked my two dances and practiced. then when it came to show time i went all out. i'm talking about literally all out! i went to straight up africa! it was performance time for me and i wasn't playing! seriously, i danced so hard and fast and went so high and low and just straight up killed it! like, i'm saying that i did the best solo performance period! the cheers and claps and screams and standing ovation was like none other! and i danced so hard that i felt like my balls went up to my stomach or something! i don't really know how else to describe that moment. there is no description. you just had to be there. it was like, "what the blup just happened!?" people had no idea what i had in me. and now note, there's this quality or characteristic i have. and it happens with acting work or filming skate tricks or artwork or whatever. during practice i might just do things and do okay or good or whatever. but, when it's time for action or the cameras are on or the audience is in front of me, then is when i just evolve and come out of nowhere and just own! of course, i don't "own" all the time. but listen, something happens to me. like, i might do things that no one expects. i'm not sure why or how. but, that's something about me. i remember an acting job i had where i played young levi. there was a scene where the director wanted me to cry and scream and break down because my father was dying. and in rehearsal i would kind of do it. and i think the director had some concerns with my acting abilities, but i also think he thought my rehearsal was okay or just good. but, then when he decided to try the scene with the cameras rolling, well, wow i went all out ballistic! i was screaming, "father! father!" i was sad, angry, crying, and letting out my character like none other. once again, no one expected me to do any of that because i wasn't that loud or passionate or in character during rehearsal. so, yeah, the scene went well and i killed it! same with this final two solo dances exam in adkus african dance class. i just showed straight up domination! everyone was caught by surprise, even myself. and after class some people were speechless and others gave me props.

    and one more important thing that i got out of this class was my african name.

don't say anything, ever

arthur lugauskas

chapter 32 : visual voices professor again again

$$\Delta^{\circ\circ}\Delta^{\circ}\Delta\Delta\Delta^{\circ}\Delta^{\circ}\Delta^{\circ}$$
$$^{\circ\circ}\Delta^{\circ}$$
$$\Delta^{\circ}\Delta\Delta^{\circ}\Delta^{\cdot}$$

πøπøπ
π"π"
\≠\\≠≠\

     i really don't have much to say about visual voices or vivtol when it comes to this semester. other than this was my last visual voices and i got an a and i learned that vivtol might resign from being the chair. what chair? you know, the director of the school of art at gmu chair. yeah, he might no longer be in that position next semester.

arthur lugauskas

don't say anything, ever

chapter 33 : honors seminar professor again again

$$æ\dots$$
$$π-$$
$$\setminus \neq$$
$$^a¶$$
$$Δ©$$
$$\sqrt{\int}$$
$$\tilde{μ}$$

    i also don't have much to say about this semesters honors seminar class. other than we went on another trip to nc and did whatever else we did. nothing too crazy happened i think.

arthur lugauskas

chapter 34 : extras from 3rd

$$¨©fff©f©f©f©f$$
$$´´\Sigma´\Sigma\Sigma œ\Sigma\Sigma ¢∞∞∞∞§$$
$$^{ao}\bullet^o\bullet^o\bullet^o\bullet^{oo}\bullet^o\bullet^{ao}\bullet^{ao}\bullet$$
$$oaa$$
$$^{o\_o\_a}\bullet^{o\_oa}\bullet ¶§¶\bullet^{aoa}§$$
$$\setminus\neq\setminus\neq\neq\setminus\setminus\neq\setminus\setminus\setminus\setminus\neq$$
$$\textit{ııııııı ı ıııı}$$
$$...\ ...$$

in this chapter there is a bit to cover. one thing i think i haven't mentioned much about, if at all, was artbus. so, what was artbus? well, it was basically a bus trip to nyc that all art students at gmu had to take five times in order to graduate and get their art degree. and three artbus trips took place throughout a fall or spring semester. and the way this whole thing worked was simple. basically students went on a bus to nyc and got dropped off at chelsea and that was kind of it. if they wanted to check out the galleries they could, sometimes a faculty from the school would give a little two hour guided tour, and the only thing each person really needed to know was that the bus left at 8pm from the met. so, technically students were allowed to do anything they wanted in nyc, but just had to be on time to take the bus back to gmu. unless they planned to stay in the city, then all they had to do was tell a faculty that was on the bus they took and then the student was to be on his or her own after initial drop off. simple. or, simple for people who have things to do and live their life the way they want to. some people were just lost and had no idea what to do when they touched down in nyc. so, yeah, this artbus thing was something i've been doing during my time at gmu.

    on my first trip that i took semesters ago i spend some time going to different parts of the city with some drawing two classmates. we all brought our cameras and were doing some photography while we were there. i actually balanced videography and photography because i thought to maybe do a short film about the trip. it was a good time on a cold day.

    on my second trip that i took semesters ago i planned to skate the city. but, when the bus arrived my plans were ruined in a way because it was wet outside and was still raining a little bit. so, plans changed and i ended up spending time with walter and this artist girl from school and this other artist guy who lived in nyc. he showed us around and took us to his studio and all that. we went to a few other locations and told stories and shared experiences and memories of the past and etc.

    on my third trip i took semesters ago i was on a straight up skate mission. i went with a friend whom i've known for years. and we skated all over the city and filmed for october sequence too. the weather was beautiful and the day was jam packed. and we ended up staying in the city overnight at another friends place and then we left the next day.

      on my fourth trip i took earlier in the semester we just read about i was on a hefty mission. and it was all about art and the art world. i basically went to all these galleries in chelsea and asked them how they went about choosing their artists. and all i was getting was responses like, "just email us" or "we have a full roster" or "the gallery owner hand picks his artists" or "we have established artists in this area, but you should check the lower east side because i think they are more welcoming to emerging artists" or "our youngest artist is 36 years old" or "i've never found an artist good enough who came in cold" or "blah blah blah." i was doing art that was on another level and i knew it, but the art world didn't want to see it or accept it. it was really frustrating when i went into so many galleries and saw weak work. i had something new to bring in. but, all the galleries only looked at was how young i looked. no one gave me a shot right then and there to just look at what i had to offer. and i thought the art world was interested in new things and creativity and stuff that was pushing boundaries. and you would think that if an artist had the balls to go up to the front desk at a gallery and ask about how they selected artists then the desk people would just give two minutes of their time checking out what the artist had, right? or am i wrong about everything? why can't i be 20something years old and be an "established" artist? why is everyone going with the flow and boxing people into categories based on things that are irrelevant? like, blup, i don't plan to wait until i'm 36 years old or older to final get a show at a gallery or whatever. blup that! i have the amazing work right now! i'm already on that next level! i'm just looking for a chance! some people in the art world are so close minded! just open up your eyes and stop being a robot! why is everyone following everyone else? oh yeah, because of politics! because it's easier to follow than to lead! it's easier to not take a chance than take a chance! blup! my mission was just disappointing for the most part. but, yeah, there were maybe a couple galleries that were somewhat nice, but overall it was more like "you're too young, we don't want you, get older, you don't know what you're doing, we don't have a chance for you, who do you think you are thinking you could come up to us and think you'll get a shot when there are hundreds of thousands doing the same thing, blah blah blah."

and my fifth trip i took on the semester coming up and it was good and successful and i spend some time writing this book in soho.

so, i was really going at the art world heavily. not just ny, but chicago too. around this time i was dating a beautiful woman who i met in dc, but she lived in chicago. she soon became my girlfriend and an inspiration to me. so, i would occasionally take flights to chicago and spend time with her, but also work while i was there. one of my jobs was going full force at the art scene in that city. and as i went about business i quickly learned that chicago had the third biggest art scene in the america. it was ny, la, and then chicago. it was like a win-win situation for me when i flew there. i spend time with an amazing woman that was in my life and i went hard at the art scene over there. from galleries to art spaces to museums. i went and started conversations. and i'd say similar things i said in ny. from asking how these places went about selecting their artists to just looking for a chance to show my work to a larger audience with their backing. but, all i was getting was, "we have a full roster of artists" or "sorry, we can't accommodate you" or "yeah, we're not interested" or "just email us" or "you have to be referred to be with us" or "(add excuse here)". it was frustrating again and annoying. until in one gallery i finally got a shot to show a little bit of my work on the spot. and i had my flash drive with me in my pocket. i was ready and i showed a couple of the piop art paintings. and the response was good. but, since the series was't finished, the gallery owner told me to just email her when the series gets done so she could see how all the pieces together looked. so, it was like a tease. but, other than that i didn't get much love from the art world.

    then other business in school included me talking to another student about my moving painting. i was confident that it could be sold for over $37,000 or whatever. i believed in my work and the worth it had despite me being young or whatever. and he just laughed at me.

    and the more i learned about pricing artworks i began to understand that it was just location thing and how people saw it. like if my paintings were in a gallery in dc right now i could maybe sell them for $3,000-$5,000. if they were in a gallery in chicago then maybe $6,000-$7,000. and la would be similar to chicago i think. but, if they were in ny then probably $10,000-$18,000. but, if they were in a particular art fair then maybe $100,000-$147,000. and these prices are with me not being known in the art world. these prices are just for the worth of the art without the name behind it. but, after people would know more about me and my persona and abilities then the prices would go up easily. and i say prices like that because i'm doing quality work. i'm not playing around. i'm not joking or doing garbage art. i'm bringing newness and innovation. so much art has been untastefully dumbified in stupidity. and i'm not saying there's something wrong with stupidity, but there's a way to do high quality stupidity that's tasteful. i'm just annoyed with dumb stupidity that is dry and tasteless and annoying. now, don't get me wrong now. there are amazing mind-blowing things that exist by creative unique innovative artists. i have seen some art that was truly fascinating and astonishing and wonderful. that does exist, but i'm just concerned with how many other artists have gotten lazy or whatever the case to the point where they feel like doing low quality things. but, then again i could be the one who is overly picky and just doesn't know and is too young and blah blah blah. yeah, it's easier for the public to bash on me and say i don't know things instead of fixing the major problems. people act like everything is okay and there's no bad art and that things are going swell because that's the easier way to go about things, right? why change when you're comfortable, right?

don't say anything, ever

arthur lugauskas

don't say anything, ever

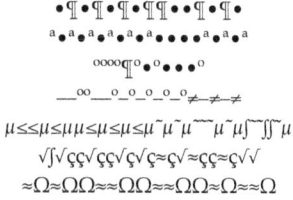

chapter 35 : coldest summer

in june things were okay, things were good, no, actually things were great and fantastic. i was writing quite a bit and working on projects. the main project of focus was my documentary. i finally went to town on it. i got heavy into editing and getting it nearer completion. but, i also had skate camps i was working at to get my money up and inspire kids in the process. and the kids really loved me. even when i wasn't their instructor they still saw me as their favorite. and the reason was because i knew how to play. i knew how to laugh. i knew how to have fun with them and get smiles out of their faces. i ended up being part of an art fair also, but it was the wrong one for me to be in i realized upon set up. walter was the one who told me about it and he was also part of it. and the reason i say it was wrong for me is because it was more about "common cute things" and not "creative innovative art pieces". note, i had the most minimalist set up and most everyone else had these "standard" tents and awnings or whatever. some people had been doing these fairs for years and knew what things sold and didn't. this was my first time being part of one of these. and though people showed up and liked what i had, i did't sell anything. and note, i didn't have my bigger paintings displayed or my "serious" art. i just had some "picture frame art" that i did relatively quickly and had fun doing. and when i did these pieces i was interested in throwing ideas on them and of course, creativity. and really note, seriously my table was the most different and diverse. most other people typically had one thing that they would replicate in different ways. and there was a lot of good stuff. and understand, i'm not bashing on the things i saw. there were good paintings, interesting clocks, fun computer chip jewelry, etc. but, then there were other "crafty" things that just blended it. i don't know. i didn't feel like i belonged there. and there were probably two or three other people who were more "fine art" than "crafty" or whatever the case. but, still, good and fun experience nonetheless. i enjoyed conversations with different people. and towards the end one guy came up to me and looked at what i had and was interested to know more about me and my art. i told him that i had my bigger stuff and works that i put more time into elsewhere. then he was extra interested in seeing what i was talking about. i had a portfolio thing with some images. he liked what he saw and said he owned eight galleries. he asked, "how much for these paintings?" i said, "depends on location, but around $6,000-$10,000 for now." and he then said, "you could sell them for a lot more." i told him, "yeah, i know, but now i technically don't have the 'name' to back the higher price because people just aren't believing in me. and maybe i don't have the right connections also." he went on to say, "i could sell them for $150,000." now note, of course i didn't know how serious this guy was. i was aware that he could have been playing around or whatever the case. plus, for some reason i myself didn't feel ready to sell my piop art paintings just yet. but, he gave me his card and number in case i was interested in talking with him further. and then i spoke to walter later on and learned that he sold one of his paintings to that guy. still though, i wasn't sure on how i was going to go about business just yet. i don't know, i was just happy. at this point i wasn't rushing being a superstar. just living life was the best. my life was the best. i was on top of the world and just had overloads of positivity and joy to give to the world. i really didn't care that much about anything other than happiness because i was just the happiest man alive! my life really was amazing! maybe too good to be true because i had it all!

      then in july i lost everything. one specific phone call basically ended my life. i began having trouble breathing. my inspiration was gone. i didn't care about eating or anything. i just started not giving a blup about anything. why? because nothing matters when you are no longer alive, right? blup art! blup writing! blup it all! nothing mattered! and i "died" at the worst time! but, then again, there is never a good time. so, after death, i don't know how i kept going. i really didn't care about anything, but somehow i just felt like i had to focus on completing certain unfinished projects despite all the pain i had. and i especially wanted to premiere my documentary film on my birthday that took place in late july. but, half the reason i wanted to premiere it was no longer an existing reason. so, i didn't know how to go about even finishing. but, for some reason i kept going and trying to complete what i set out to complete. so, weak and vulnerable i went further into editing the film. those nights were so lonely. i had no motivation often times to keep going. but, i had to. i wanted to. but, i really didn't want to. but, i did keep going. day in and day out. all night if i had to. i was on a deadline. my birthday was a little over a week away. time was ticking fast. and i still had no place for the premiere. so, i began looking for venues and sent some emails out and did some phone calls and all i got was "no." then i went into my memory bank and thought of a particular friend. his name was emdo. and i used to have acting meetings with him and vier. i hadn't seen him in a while, but i remembered that he had a martial arts school which promoted doing creative martial arts. and i remembered there being creative events held at his school at times. so, i thought to propose to him my interest in wanting to premiere my documentary at there. and note, i hadn't seen him in a year or two at this point. so, i drove to his school and found a note saying that the school had taken up a new address and name. but, it was only down the street. so, i drove down the street. and the new place was probably five times the size of the old one. i walked in, saw some friends, asked for emdo, he wasn't there, i came back later, he was there, and we got to discussion. i said what i said and he was on board. and note, during our meeting i wanted to premiere the film on my birthday which was maybe a week from that day. and emdo knew i wasn't fully done with the film because i told him. so, he asked, "how far along are you?" and i said, "well, maybe around 43% done editing wise. but, i still have to film 1/3 of the film really soon. don't worry though. i just have to not sleep." emdo laughed, showed slight concern, but took my words and planned on going through with the premiere plan. so, right after my premiere location was figured out i called finlay and urgently asked for our final filming session. i was ready to document the grand finally. from showcasing my piop art paintings, to my *pome in ice* photography series, to some *timeless clocks* that i made. finlay was on board and the next night we were about to embark on a hefty mission. and note, i didn't want to really film or do anything still. i was destroyed already. i needed nothing. no sleep, no rest, no food, no anything. so, i didn't know why i was even trying to film. but, i was. and plus, finlay knew what was going on with me. he wasn't sure how everything was going to go. neither was i. this was just something neither of us wanted to do, but knew we had to. so, the filming day came. finlay and i both packed up two cars with my artwork and drove to our filming destination. we started around 12am. we ended at around 12pm. yes, all night or all morning or whatever you want to call it. and i don't know how we did it. i don't know how i managed to say everything i said. i don't even really know what happened. but, thanks finlay for muscling through that 12hour filming session. and now, it was up to me to edit and edit and edit and figure out how to concise over 300gigs of footage into a 50minute or so documentary film. much had been edited, but much more had to be done. so, at this point i only had a lot of work to do, but my biggest job was not giving a blup about anything. but understand, i did care about delivering high quality amazing creative product. this documentary was a piece of art in itself. that was how i looked at it. and every aspect was thought through. i don't know how to emphasize enough on how much time it took me to get the film done. every night i was working four hours and hours alone. and yes, i was working during the day too! i knew i could get it done. i knew there was no such thing as impossible for me. but still, it was so hard for me to work because of my horrendous pain. i'd break down many nights. sometimes i couldn't keep going. but, i'd try to regroup and go regardless. and i kept going at all times until the premiere date came. and even then i was up all night since the day before doing touch ups and final edits on the film to get the film together on time. and just days before the premiere i started to invite friends and family. and somehow i pulled everything together. i don't know how, but i premiered the "akuna's art" documentary film on the evening of my birthday. and yes, my whole birthday prior to the premiere i spent working on the film. and myself and emdo were both surprised at the overall outcome. somehow i pulled off getting a location to premiere my documentary when it wasn't even half way done and i had only around a week until the premiere date, had to do a 12hour filming session, edit so much, fight through ridiculous pain, put everything together, invite people, and have a nice audience of friends, family, and even people i didn't really know to support and see what finlay and i put together. afterwards everyone was happy for me except me. i really appreciated everyone coming, but i still wasn't happy. and it also didn't matter that i won a skate competition the day before for the second year in a row. somehow all these victories weren't that sweet.

    and before my premiere i went to la for a bit. just to get away and whatever. i had family there to catch up with, but i also had galleries to visit and talk to. well, for one my outspokenness affected my relationship with a childhood friend because i just wanted to help her follow her dreams, but she looked at what i was saying as something other than helping her be herself i guess. on the flip side i caught up with some cousins and got to experience la as an older individual. and when i went to galleries i was interested in a one particular place that i wanted to show at. and well, i ended up speaking with a gallery owner of that gallery and then i showed him my piop art paintings and he literally had nothing bad to say about them. he said, "i don't see anything wrong with these. the only thing i have to say is that they are too smart for la. they belong more in ny." and i said, "yeah, thank you, but no one is giving me a chance in ny. do you know anyone there?" and he said he didn't, but he did give me advice and was open to possibly showing my work at his gallery. and i appreciated that. but, still, what matters when nothing matters?

    then in august i got to talking with emdo again and we brainstormed ideas of having an art show at his old school because the space was still available. and after talking to a few artists about doing a group show we learned that many were either traveling or too busy or whatever the case. so, i decided to take the opportunity and do my first solo show. and i had family from my small country of origin coming in a few weeks, so i was excited to spend time with them after not seeing them for years and years. and what better way to show them what i've been up to than inviting them to a solo art show that i put together, right?

    then a death happened. a literal death. my cousin whom i've just reconnected with in ca ended up getting hit by a car while he was at work tutoring people. and he was one who really started to take interest in my art and what i was doing. and note, i've known him since i was a small kid. and after hearing about his death i didn't know how to react and especially since i just saw him weeks ago. i didn't know how to treat death. and he was a great guy, full of life and smiles. and he helped me with advice on how to go through my pain. but, really, i just didn't know how to treat death.

then, yeah, with all that had happened i still had a show to prepare for. so, that was all i did. i had no money, no time, no life, but, i did have an opportunity to show what i was capable of in that kind of situation. so, i was ready to make the best solo art show i've ever been to. and as i was working on it all the time i realized that i was the future of art. because this show was like none other! i incorporated five mediums! five! i had installation, sculpture, painting, photography, and performance in one show! and i did all that with nothing. i was broke, busy, and dead inside. so, yes, despite all that i pulled off one of the best shows i had been to. but, to make the show the best ever i thought of an idea. and that idea was this, "what if on the opening day of the show, when everyone is there, i just stand in the middle of the room and say 'thank you all for coming' and then shoot myself." then i thought my idea was better for a movie. so, any movie directors out there reading this book who are interested in making a movie with that concept feel free to contact me and lets make the best art movie in the world. so, yeah, i didn't kill myself. i didn't think i was "allowed" to die just yet. i had too much to give to the world. too much good and amazing and creative and etc. but do note this, i did get sick during the installation of my show. i was coughing, my head hurt, and my eyes were watery. but, despite all that i still worked. and yeah, really understand this, despite me saying i didn't care about anything i want you to know that when it came to things i was doing i cared about putting out the best most creative and influential and innovative and amazing stuff. so, yes, through sickness, through pain, through all my hardships i still somehow some way worked. i think i just put off certain thoughts and feelings for later. when i was working on my show i wanted to just focus on making amazing. it wasn't time for me to cry or feel bad or whatever. but, the pain did come at times still. and i did have my breakdowns during my install process. and after everything was in place and ready, on the window of the space it said, "akuna lunersks - 'first look' - 8.30.2013 - 8:13pm". and just a week or so before the opening/ closing day of my show, school started for me.

arthur lugauskas

chapter 36 : fall 2013 gmu semester

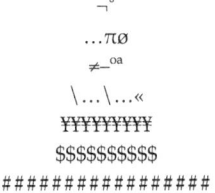

      i was in no condition to go back to school. but, this was my last semester and grand finally, right? well, because everything that had happened i think i finally had the freedom to go all out with honesty and against "common" thought. i mean, for the past semesters and months i had been doing that, sure, but, now i think i had grown to caring even less about what i "should" do and say. i had gotten to the point where i was going to really say how i felt even more, where i was going to show who i was even more, where i was going to do whatever i wanted to do, and no one was going to stop me because nothing affected me anymore. i felt like a robot or a machine of realism and truth. and now quickly understand this, there are many people who don't lie and tell truth, but only to an extent. i was ready to not hide anything. even the toughest things to say i was going to say. i had nothing to lose because i had already lost everything in july. and by me losing everything i gained everything. and what i mean is i gained a sense of fearlessness of expression. i gained this freedom. there was nothing anyone can take away from me anymore. it no longer mattered if i graduated or not. i no longer was interested in following any "art world" rules or "rules" society tell you to follow when it came to thinking. and once again, i've been thinking like that, but now i was built to a level where i had no fear in expressing exactly what i felt in a way i felt like. i was going to be that kid in tiananmen square in front of the tanks. i was going to put my career, my education, my degree, my whatever you want to call it on the line for honesty, truth, and what was actually real on a level i had never done so before. and so, my biggest semester of turmoil began.

don't say anything, ever

arthur lugauskas

don't say anything, ever

::::::::::: :::::   : : : : : :   : : : : :   : : : : : : : : : : : : : :: :   :::::::::::::::
chapter 37 : under the blade
:   : : : : :   :: : : : ::: : :   : ::::::::::::::::::::::::::::::::::   ::::   :

~='&
%$$$%&
}{}{}{}{|~|~|
|~|~|~|~|
≥÷+≥÷+≥≤≥≤≥≥÷+≥÷
`÷``«÷«÷«æ«÷«æ÷«÷«æ~
¶•¶§§¶¶•§¶¶•¶¶¶¶¶¶¶•¶¥¥¥¥¥¥¢¢¢

i'm just going to get straight to it. well, a couple of family members from my small country of origin in europe were finally here. one was my cousin and the other was my aunt. and it was their first time in america. so, first day of classes i decided to bring my cousin along so she could see how gmu was. so, first class i brought her to was my senior project class. my professor ended up being fume. remember her? so, i was excited to finally get to know her a bit and see what she was about. and remember, senior project was basically a class where all the students did high quality work that they cared about and then showcased it at the end of a semester in a group show setting. and note, the goal in senior show in a way was to know and have an idea of how to install and put together a show that would be for public viewing. and that was something the art world was about - art shows. well, as we all went around and introduced each other i was excited to tell the class about my solo show that i installed and put together literally all by myself not long ago. and right after i mentioned that i had my first ever solo show in existence, fume interrupted me and said, "we're not talking about shows right now, we're just doing quick introductions. and plus, this is about *my* solo show that's coming up." wow! that just hit me. i was confused. i thought, "really!? i can't be excited that i have something that this class is all about - an art show!?" so, yeah, apparently it was all about *her* show!? whatever, i let it be.

    then i had sculpture two later on that day. and guess who my professor was? fume again! once again i mentioned to the class that i had a solo show and i was inviting anyone who wanted to come. and i really thought fume should check out what i had done since i had two classes with her. makes sense, right? if she checked out *first look* then she could know what i was about and what i was capable of, right? and i planned to be in her classes for the next few months. why wouldn't she come? so, i invited her. then she said to give her a flyer. well, i was planning on making flyers anyway, so later on that day i made a flyer and started inviting more people from school and i even tried to give fume a personal invite. you know, her being my professor for two classes and all. we were going to have a lot of face time i thought and she was interested in helping her students with things, so i would guess she would be proud of my big achievement of having a solo show. well, despite all my wanting her to come and inviting her, she didn't come. and honestly, she never asked me how my show went or anything like that. it was like i never had a show in her eyes. well, i let it be. maybe she was busy with her show or something.

next time senior project came around fume showed the class her sculptures. she began with saying she was in love with sculpture and that she didn't like doing pretty things for rich people. and note, fume wasn't that old. but, she was active and excited and passionate for art and especially sculpture. she was hungry to do more in the art world. and she wanted her class to think that way. she wanted us to reach for the stars and unbelievable heights. she wanted us to push ourselves and do the best project possible. she wanted us to go beyond the call of duty. and as fume showed us some of her work she mentioned that her first ever solo museum show that was coming up had a lot of research that went into it. she believed that research made art amazing. i had a smirk on my face after i heard that. could someone of been researching and performing for the past two years? maybe. but, yeah, fume wanted us to go big, go crazy, get excited, and just do an amazing show. i was excited and ready. i was thinking and sketching and trying to figure out how i could make the biggest impact.

then it came to a senior project individual meeting. it was me, fume, and another lady named micky. and note, micky was helping fume with her senior project class. i wasn't sure exactly who micky was, but i knew she was involved with fume and senior project pretty heavily. so, on this individual meeting i showed some of my previous works. from architecture models, to some photography, to my piop art paintings, to even images of *first look.* then fume asked me, "what's piop art?" and i said, "it means perspectives inside of perspectives art. and it's basically this art form thing i invented because that's where i thought certain art pieces of mine fit." then fume nodded, and said almost sarcastically, "okay."

    on the next individual meeting i had to bring my idea of what i wanted to do for senior show. well, that was what i did. i said to fume and micky, "i'm thinking about doing piop art on a wall or something along those lines." then fume asked, "well, what wall are you imagining?" and i said, "i'm interested in doing my art on the first wall you see when you enter the main gallery of the soa building." then fume laughingly said, "so, you imagine having your work be the first work that everyone sees upon entering the gallery space?" i said, "yeah." then she said, "what is piop art even about and what would you write in your artist statement?" and i went the full blown honest approach and said, "honestly, i don't even really know. i have ideas on what it is, but the ultimate truth is that i don't really know. and i know i'm 'not supposed' to say that in class or art school or in the art world or whatever, but i'm choosing to give you the honest answer right now." then fume went off loudly with, "so, you invented this grand art form called piop art and you don't even know what it is!?" and i said, "yeah. you have the right to invent anything you want. i'm not here to be boxed in or put my art in a category that someone else invented if i don't feel like it. and i don't have to know exactly what piop art is. like i said, i do have my ideas and i've developed it far enough to know the basics. and understand, i could tell you all sorts of things right now that would fit and make sense and be true about piop art and my thoughts on what it might be, but i'm choosing to go with the underlying truth and tell you that i don't fully know." fume kind of rolled her eyes and just seemed like she wasn't interested in hearing more that i had to say. then micky intervened and said, "but, what would you have in your artist statement?" and i said, "i'll figure it out. i'm not that worried about it. i might just say that i don't know. and both of you, please understand that i know i'm 'not supposed' to be saying what i'm saying to you according to 'popular thinking' or whatever. but, i'm trying to give you underlying honesty. what more do you want? i'm being real with both of you for a change." then fume went on, "okay, but why walls? what if you did these perspectives that were wooden panels that were at weird angles and what if you played with light and stuff like that?" then i went on, "yeah, i think what you're saying is a good idea and that could be something for me to experiment with, but i don't know. i think i just want to do walls." then our short meeting was up and we would resume next time.

      early on in the semester in sculpture two class fume would talk and try to get students excited about making sculpture. but, she never really seemed interested in talking with me. one day i went up to her and asked for a few minutes of discussion because i wanted to show her some sketches of what i was thinking about doing. but, she was too busy for me that day.

      then on another sculpture two day fume was going around again and seeing what people were thinking about. she never came to me. i didn't know why. it was like she didn't like me. but, i didn't know. maybe she was just busy, right? and i wasn't in school to make enemies or anything like that. so, i went up to fume again with my sketchbook and checked one more time if she had time to see what i was doing and give me her input. and also just to see if she cared at all. and once again she was busy. then i said, "it's fine, don't worry about it." and right away she felt guilty or something and then felt the need to talk with me. but, i really felt like she didn't want to and i hated how fake the interaction felt when she did give me a couple minutes. and i wasn't motivated at all to speak to her at that point. but, we did have our little talk about my project ideas and her advice was, "yeah, just start. start playing around with materials and stuff."

     i was tired of people being fake or whatever the case. it was time to get real and let things out for me. so, i approached fume during a sculpture two class and just said, "could i talk to you for a bit?" and she appeared too busy for me again as usual, but said with a smile, "yeah, okay, what's up?" and i just got right to it, "i don't think you like me." that was like a whirlwind that hit her face. she was stumped for a bit and then reciprocated, "well, no, i just didn't think you needed to be babied. i thought you were doing good all on your own." and i said, "yeah, i'm not looking for help necessarily, but instead i'm just interested in conversation here and there since you're my professor. and the reason i say you don't like me is because you don't say 'hi' to me or really smile when you see me. and of course, you don't have to. i'm not asking you to. but, you are active and energetic and loving to everyone else. just not me. and i don't know what it is you have against me?" and she went on, "it's just that you say all these things, but i haven't really seen any of your work." and i said, "well, i invited you to my solo show where i had lots of my work displayed and i really wanted you to come, but you didn't seem to care about it at all." and she said, "yeah, sorry, i was busy working day in and day out on my show. i just didn't have the time." then i went on, "i'm not asking you to like me. if you do or don't it's fine. i just don't want fakeness. and i realize we have two classes together and have to get through this semester somehow. so, i'm not interested in fighting with you." she said, "yeah, it's fine. i just thought you were good on your own."

then it was time for another individualized senior project meeting with micky and fume. and my idea developed further and i was set on doing piop art on the main entrance gallery wall. and fume sill was wondering if i was sure that i didn't want to do something portable. listen, i didn't know why my request wasn't getting across, so i said, "i'm interested in doing piop art on a wall. there is something interesting about doing it on a wall. and an actual wall is different from something portable. like, i want to do it on a wall." and fume went on, "i totally get why you would want to do art on the wall, but i'm just seeing if there are other options." and then i went on to further state my idea of actually doing five piop art walls all over the art building with maybe a sculpture in front of each wall. and i wanted to do at least one wall on every floor. but, the most important wall for me was the main gallery wall people see upon entering the gallery. and you would think fume should be excited about this, right? i mean i was basically going huge and really pushing myself with trying to do the best and biggest senior project. and that was what ever student should want, right? and if everyone was aiming for the stars and beyond, then we could possibly have the best senior show in the world! then fume said, "i know what this is about. this is all about you becoming famous."

now, let me be really honest with you here. i've said this to fume and micky and even all my classmates.

it wasn't about senior project for me. i just wanted to do piop art on walls. i wanted to do that. senior project or not. it didn't matter to me once i thought of doing these walls. regardless of school or this or that or whatever, ultimately it was my desire to do these walls. grades or not! i didn't care! i just wanted to create amazing!

    okay, so, of course i didn't know exactly how i was going to go about doing any of these piop art walls. i had never done one before. i didn't know the process. i didn't know what was going to happen. but, i was ready to try and see what happens. so i went to fume with my proposal of doing some walls early on in the semester. and she said that i couldn't have walls for the whole semester because other professors or so would complain. okay, so then i just wanted one wall to make sure i could achieve what i want on a wall. and she still had her concerns. i pointed out which wall i wanted and it was a 37.9'x8.8' wall. she said that i was able to have it for the time being, but what i did might have to come down in a couple weeks. and note, she did something with one of her others classes on the stairwell where i had my string installations. and what her class did was this huge rainbow thing that took up much of the stairwell. and since fume said that you can't have things up all semester i pointed out to the rainbow installation. and she said, "yeah, that's only up until the end of september." well, umm, now as i further complete this book were are in late november and the rainbow installation is still up. and i don't have problems with the installation. i think it's pretty cool. but, it didn't go down at the end of september. i'm just saying. i felt like fume didn't want any of *my* work to be up all semester long. and for me to get that huge wall that no one was using she said that she had to send out an email and all this stuff. and i then said to her, "with all the other installations i just did them. none of my professors sent out an email or anything." she was surprised with my answer and said, "well, i don't know, but these walls get reserved." and i knew nothing about that. walls got reserved? okay, i let it be. fume sent the email out and then i guess people knew that i had the wall. and note, when i was working on that wall ten would walk by often and on one of the times he said, "yeah, i don't question what you're doing. i just let you do." i found that statement interesting.

     then another full senior project class meeting came about. at this point some people should know what they were probably doing and where they wanted to show their work. and this was helpful for everyone to see if there were any location clashes or whatever. this class was informative to know each others desires and plans. and note, this class was basically the students proposing what they proposed during their individualized meetings with fume and micky. and understand, there was nothing certain at this point. fume and micky simply wanted to know what everyone wanted. and everyone was allowed to request any location or thing they wanted to. the doors were open to anything because this was just sort of the proposal stage of what everyone wanted for their art in senior show. so, as fume went around the room hearing what the students had to say, well, things were pretty broad. no one knew exactly where they wanted to be. some people kind of knew or had an idea, while others literally didn't care where their art was displayed. then when it came to me i stated exactly what my vision was. no lies. no gimmicks. and then fume put me on blast as she reiterated what i just said by saying, "so, akuna, you want to have five walls all over the art building and one of them being on the main gallery wall, which would be the first thing people see when they enter the gallery and you also want *your* sculpture to be in front of *your* wall?" and i said, "yes." and from that point everyone hated me in the room. if you were only there. the tension was crazy! my chair was pushed back away so far from the table and i saw everyone's eyes beaming at me with disgust. no one said a word for a few long moments after my "yes" statement. i'm sure fume loved what was going on. i really don't know how to describe that moment in writing, but it was ugly. i felt like everyone ganged up on me. like, no one wanted to talk to me or say anything. it was like, "did he really just say that?" then one girl finally spoke up and said with annoyance, "what makes you think you're going to get all that space?" i responded, "i don't know if i'm going to get any of that space. i'm just proposing what i want because that is what we are here to do." it felt like lighting and thunderstorms were happening in that room. and i was getting hit hard. it was like i was a monster or someone crazy for asking what he actually wanted. you didn't want to be me that day. and now you know, that is what happens when you're real.

don't say anything, ever

arthur lugauskas

don't say anything, ever

chapter 38 : stop talking forever

so, now there was all this tension when i arrived to school. yeah, really intense. i was the most hated student in my senior project class. but note, i did have a couple of friends in that class actually. one friend was a girl named rali. and one day we discussed the day everyone tried to kill me with their laser beam eyes in senior project class. and i told her, "i'm just interested in doing a great show. everyone should aim as high as possible, right?" and she said, "yeah, but you shouldn't say it. like, when i do my projects i try doing the best stuff. i want to win. but, i never say that i want to be the best. i'm just quite." i responded with, "yeah, i used to be more quite, but i'm here to be real these days and say how i feel. so, i now understand that you think just like me, but don't say it." she went on, "yeah, you're not supposed to say the stuff you said." i went on, "i was just being honest. and why didn't you back me up? you think like me and you want to do great things, so, why didn't you speak up for me when everyone ganged up on me with throwing all this hatred at me?" and rali said, "like i said, i'm quite about it. and yeah, the room was crazy that day, but i just sat there and smiled and thought, 'wow, akuna. you're really saying this stuff?'" and i went on, "honestly, i don't think i'm going to get what i want. or especially that gallery primetime location wall space despite being literally the only one who had the balls to specifically ask for it this early in the semester with a specific plan of attack on how i plan to do my project. and what's worse is that i was put on blast about wanting it and i didn't beat around the bush. i said 'yes' and everyone heard it." then rali went on, "yeah, that's why you be quite." and i went on, "another thing, on the real i think you are fumes favorite student. if you ask for primetime gallery space i bet you'll get it." and she went on, "i want my setting to be a bit darker, so i don't really want the gallery. i'm thinking about having this critique room, but i think another girl already has it. and the problem is that i've been dreaming about doing my senior project in this critique room. so, i don't know." i said, "just ask for it. i honestly think you'll get it. and if you've been dreaming about it, then go for your dreams!"

     another friend from senior project was a guy named ant. and i thought he had one of the better senior projects. i really liked his concept and what he was doing. we spoke a bit about my situation and yeah, he knew i wasn't in a good place in the eyes of everyone in senior project class.

so, at this point i was working day in and day out on my first ever piop art wall. i've never attacked such a scale, but i was just going at it. and then a sculpture two critique day came. and well, after some students showed their projects in progress it came time for all of us to go to the wall i was working on. and, so, well, we got there and what i honestly wanted to know was what students thought without me explaining things. i just wanted people to be honest whether they knew or didn't know what was going on. because sometimes i see art and i just don't like it, but then i read or learn about it and i start to like it. and other times i see art and i just like it. so, for my time during this critique i was just genuinely curious about what others thought upon first inspection. if people didn't like it i wanted to hear that. if people liked it i wanted to hear that. i just wanted honest thoughts without words explaining what my work was about. does that sound like something okay to ask for? well, once is stated my desire to hear the classes thoughts, fume right away went off and loudly said, "i hate (she really emphasized the word hate) when students do that! i just hate that so much! every semester one student wants to not say anything and have everyone else talk! i seriously hate it when people do that!" and note, she had this disgusted look on her face when she said all that. like i did the worst thing in the world. and i was just so shocked at her reaction. she basically bulldozed my honest request to the ground and off the face of the earth and to the middle of nowhere and then spat and vomited on it. i was so much in awe and thought to myself, "what the blup just happened!? is this seriously happening to me!?

i can't just ask a question without being hated on so much!? what did i do to deserve this!? oh yeah, i was honest!" then i went on to ask fume, "why do you hate that so much?" she went on, "because that's such a wimpy move to do and disrespectful. you're work is still in progress! and of course, who doesn't want to get peoples opinions on what they are doing before the work is done!? i just really hate it when students pull that move!" and i kept thinking, "what am i pulling!? like, i don't know the experiences you've had with other students, nor do i know your perspective on how critiques should go! and yeah, maybe people want feedback, but who actually asks!? i'm asking right now and getting attacked! like, if no one wants to say anything then fine we'll move on! i honestly just want to know what people think and that's it! if they have questions or whatever they are free to ask, but i just want honest opinion without words to 'back up' or 'support' what i'm doing! blup!" and i don't know why fume was trying to put me in this box of prior students who have said that in critiques. i wasn't one of those students! and to be honest, is there a format for critiques!? i didn't think so! so i went my way! because it was my time, right!? do i have to be a follower and do what everyone expects you to do in a critique!? i myself thought of asking what others thought without saying a word about the work! i didn't know students did that! all this implied knowledge was being spat at me. like i had to know exactly what i should and shouldn't do in a critique! like there was critique etiquette! i didn't know all this "proper art school" behavior. i was in school to be me, to be real, to be honest for change! especially when it came to what i thought about saying at a certain point in time! so, obviously fume wanted otherwise and tried to control me and mold me into like a "robot artist" who follows exactly what the "implied" "art world" "rules" are! so, i decided to flip it and go off on this rant about what piop art is and what i was doing. and of course i included that i didn't really know what i was doing. but, i also went off about how i thought piop art could help literally anyone in the world and i went into theories and concepts i had. and even after that breathless monologue i think people still didn't know what i was saying or what to say to me. so, i didn't get what i wanted *and* my message didn't get across. and then there was discussion with students about what i was doing and ideas and possibilities and stuff. but, i was just overly hurt and annoyed at fumes initial reaction to my initial request. that just set me up to look like i was crazy. she basically put me on the spot again and generated all this hatred from her sculpture two class onto me. great, thank you so much for all you did fume! okay, so, then after class i tried to discuss what happened with fume. after all the critiques there was still around 42minutes of class left. so, it would make sense that fume and i had time to talk about her points of view and my points of view, right? and plus, this conversation was the least she could give me because we were already in the middle of the semester and she never came up to me to ask what i was up to. not once! because i was doing fine on my own, right!? and i was no longer interested in asking her for anything because i think she just hated me for some reason. so, now after this huge conflict we had i wanted to honestly talk and figure things out. and as we discussed fume was telling me her points of view and why she thought what she thought. and i was telling her that i honestly just wanted the students' opinion on what i was doing and i didn't mind criticism of any sort, but that she didn't even give me a chance to get what i wanted. i told her i felt disrespected and wronged. and some senior project talk came about and i was trying to explain why i wanted walls and not what she wanted for me. and i realized that her and my art aesthetic was super different and i tried bringing that into consideration during our conversation. but, she just wasn't having it. like, it was just ugly. she wasn't trying to listen to me or allow me to get my point across or even talk to me for that matter. as i was talking she was packing her bags and just waiting to leave. she really didn't want to actually talk things out. it was like she was disgusted to even speak to me. and what had i done to deserve this? be honest for a change!? seriously, she really didn't want me to say anything ever again. and then she just left with her friend. and i know as they walked to their car fume was just saying horrible trash talking things about me. it was so audible across the whole gmu campus. and the cloud of hate above her was able to be seen from miles and miles away. and the central most hated figure in her mind was me. she just couldn't stand me anymore. i felt the despise in the air. and all this happened on october 9th, 2013. and as i drove home i kept saying, "don't say anything, ever!" that's all i thought about for hours. this was how i truly felt. the emotions i had were real. and i had no idea what was happening. how did i get to this point? this wasn't me. i'm a shy, happy, humble guy, full of energy and smiles and positivity, right? what was going on!? and then i finally realized what was actually going on. this was my alarm clock that i expected to go off in october or november. this was what i expected for to happen without knowing for sure if it was definitely going to happen. somewhere a couple years ago i decided to lose myself in a performance that had me not complying with what society wanted me to think. it was performance that i would take on and forget i was on. i had to forget i was in performance for everything to be real and as authentic as possible. and my performance was all about me being a kid again and stating exactly how i felt whether i was "supposed" to or "not supposed" to according to "common thought" or whatever. and on this october 9th evening, my performance almost came to an end. i almost broke down and let go of my character. my strength was tested. my feelings were hurt. i honestly was distressed and detrimental. there was nothing fake about my feelings. these feelings were facts and they weren't anything anyone wanted to experience. and no one had to if they just conformed to norms and stayed followers. or until enough people are real and true and speak their individual mind and become the new majority. right now the majority of people have these clouds fogging their mind and thoughts. not enough people see clearly that they can be anything. there are too many dreamkillers out there bringing the fog and eventually the thunderstorm and then destruction of dreams. i was a dreamer, and i've always been. and because i was never held down in one place in the world i was able to keep my dreams alive. i was too busy learning new languages and cultures before i started to grasp what dreamkilling adults were saying to people on what they can and can't do. so, once i realized that i was in this performance that i forgot about for the past two years i kept thinking what other elements were in it. i thought and thought and realized that i wasn't in school to get a degree, but instead to tell people that anything is possible. and i had to warn people about dreamkillers. and i wanted to do my two year research on what it feels like to be a complete individual. and then i had to get my message across somehow. all my stories and discoveries in the process, i had to tell them. then i finally realized that i had to write a book about my two year performance and release it in my senior show (which was next month). and the book was not to hurt or talk bad about anyone. it was to give you a perspective on how a dreamers life is like in todays days. it was to give you true stories about experiences i had with others who promoted or bashed on individuality, creativity, uniqueness, and dreams. then i started panicking for a bit because i set out to do five piop art walls for senior show and now i was supposed to write a book of the past two years or so in less than two months? maybe that sounded crazy, but i thought, "if i do all this that i want to do, maybe i would be evidence that really shows that you can do anything you want? right? maybe? i don't know." well, i had to just go at it and see what happens. because that's what i do, right? i just jump into an idea and maybe things will come together somehow. right? or am i crazy right now?

don't say anything, ever

arthur lugauskas

don't say anything, ever

chapter 39 : unwanted

```
,,,',',',',',',',',',
...º.ºº.º.ºº
‹‹››‹›‹‹####‹‹£££‹‹‹""""
///€€€€///»»»/›/›/›/›/››/›/
/¿/¿/¿'/¿' ¿'/
≠≠≠≠≠
∧≠
```

so, now that i had another unexpected, but i guess expected years ago to be expected by now project going on i had to focus. i thought i had more than enough research and i calmed down just a little bit. i was still being real and honest and all that, but i had a lot of writing ahead of me.

and now i want to share this story real quick. so, fumes solo museum show was coming up and she invited the whole senior project class. she told us, "if you want to come to the exclusive opening then email me or give me your email after class." and did you think i wanted to come? sure, why not? yeah, despite her caring less about my show, i still wanted to check out hers. i knew she had worked really hard on it, so why not be there despite our heavy conflicts and arguments. so, after class i went up to her and said i was interested in coming. it was only me and two other students who came up to her with personal emails. after giving her each email she told us to expect the invite soon. sounded good to me. well, weeks passed by and soon enough the day before her shows exclusive opening day came about and i hadn't received an email. and this was a day i actually had class with her and i asked her about it. and she said, "sorry, there was a problem and i invited too many people and we went over capacity." i said, "okay, no worries." in my mind i thought, "yeah, i think you just didn't want me there. and if that was the case then okay." and then fume came up to me later on when i was working on sculpture and asked for my email again. she was going to get the invite to me by that night before the exclusive opening show day evening. and believe it or not, i actually got the invite. maybe she felt guilty or something. but, like, if she didn't want me to go i wouldn't of had a problem. i was interested because i wanted to go. so, i don't know what was going on. and now note this, during the show i saw rali there and after some conversation i asked when she got her email invite. and she said, "like a week or two ago." so, then i was just confused and just thought i received a pity invite. and i was already at the show at this point. why did i even ask? after i didn't get the email in the first place i should've just let it be. what was i thinking? oh, and interesting enough, bom had a piece in a group show around the time fume was at her busiest installing her show. i checked out boms piece and fume also ended up going. that just really confirmed that she had no interest in seeing what i had at all. like, i had my show before bom and i invited her and genuinely wanted her to come and this was when she was less busy with her show, but she just spat in my face. and why do i say spat in my face? well, because another student was part of a group show not too long ago and fume said to her, "sorry i missed your show. i was in new york. if i was in town i would've came. i'm so sorry." that was just the icing of the cake when it came to her despise of me and my show. she has never mentioned anything about my show or asked how it went or any "sorry for not coming" or any talk of its existence sine the day i invited her. tisk tisk.

      and understand now, i don't have anything against fume. but, i think she just hates me for being me. and not long ago i stumbled into a conversation during sculpture two class where she spoke to someone else about all the struggles she had to deal with in the process of putting her show together. from people lying to her, to crazy money issues, to pieces she wanted in the show regardless if the curator or whoever accepted her suggestion or not. and i saw similarities in her and me. both of us being ambitions and wanting greatness. and that was probably why she has a strong hate towards me. because she wants to take over the art world, but she now definitely knows that she's not alone with her desires. i think instead of being a team player and having amazing conversations with me she just despised and didn't want anything good for me. and all i wanted was good for everyone. i wanted people to smile and enjoy life. and i think that was what fume wanted for everyone but me. so anyone who knows fume i'm sure sees her as an amazing caring person who helps and gives good advice. and those people probably would

see everything i've written about her probably as
something crazy. or because of bias', people who know
her will hate me and find what i'm saying as something
bad and wrong. but, honestly, i'm not here for people to
take sides. i think fume does a great job in teaching
students and helping them, but she's never had a
student like me or tasted my way of thinking, hence, she
didn't know how to handle it. and this is me just trying
to zoom out and see the bigger picture. i don't like to
hate. i'm not here to hate. i'm not here to talk trash or
say lies. i just want people to be themselves and believe
in themselves and be honest and follow their dreams
and speak what's on their mind. and not everyone is
going to like you. and not everyone is going to like me.
people are different. people like different things. the
thing i didn't like about fume was that she was being a
dreamkiller to me. she didn't want me to succeed. and i
think the reason was because i believed i could do
anything. and i said what i felt when i felt like. so, to
fume, when i heard about your troubles with lies and
deception and other people trying to kill your dreams
for your show i connected with you. expect, you were
the monster in my story. in this book. you know that
curator that you hate so much and the team of people in
the museum that didn't want you to do exactly what
you wanted? yeah, that was what you were to me this
semester. but, nonetheless, congratulations on your
show and all your achievements thus far. good job
defying the non-believers and going through with your
vision and making your show possible. i'm guessing
you really hate me at this point, but what am i to do
about that? you don't have to like me. if you like you
and if your dreams are alive then that's great! and when
i heard a student tell you that you should write a book
about you crazy behind the scenes complications that

went down when you were going about making your show come to fruition, i smiled because that's what i was already doing with my own stories and professor battles and senior show complications. but, i didn't tell you i was writing this because no one knew. but, i do support what that student said and if you have feeling to let out, let them out. write a book! you could do it! do whatever you want in life! anything is possible!

arthur lugauskas

don't say anything, ever

chapter 40 : egomaniac

```
))0((
 (
 )
| | ~
??>?
˘¿¿˘
 ○
```

     something i was getting form people was this concept that i had an "ego". and i've told you before that it's never been about ego. but, that was what i was getting.
     i had hon again with my final honors class and when i was working on my first piop art wall we discussed a few things. and then someone else came into our conversation and hon, in a sort of joking manner, introduced me as, "this is akuna with his larger than life personality." and i laughingly said, "what, you

know about that? how?" and hon went on, "i've had you for three semesters and i knew about it since the day i met you." i laughed a bit and felt like i blew my cover with him a long time ago. what cover? i don't know. some sort of funny cover i guess.

    then on another big honors trip we took to pittsburgh we stopped by frank lloyd wrights falling water architecture masterpiece house that he designed. and i learned a bit about wright when i studied architecture, but for some reason i didn't have that much interest in him. and hon was telling me a few things about the man and then he said, "yeah, you should look him up. he was an egomaniac." and right as hon said that he looked at me with these eyes and if you were there you could have felt what happened in the air. hon and myself knew that once he said wright was an egomaniac he directly related that word to my persona or whatever. that was a funny interesting moment.

    then on another instance, mattata came back to town. yeah, if you didn't know, he moved away for a bit to work on some things. but, i learned from him that vier and his brother ne thought i had this huge ego. and it only got bigger in the past two years apparently. the primary example was how i carried myself after my documentary film premiere. because i was proud of what i did and thought i created greatness and i was planning to enter the biggest independent film festival in america and i expected to win the whole category of documentary films. i guess vier thought i was neglecting the other people who have worked hard on their films or whatever. but, like, i was proud of something i did! all the sleepless nights working alone with pain over and over again! i thought it was crazy that i wasn't "allowed" to think i could win! like i can't like what i do! it's like he didn't understand where i was coming from when i said i planned to win. because listen, when he was sleeping i was working. when he was partying i was working. when he was with his girlfriend i was working. when he was watching a movie and relaxing i was working. all i did was work! that's it! and the least i should be able to think is that i did something great because i cared about every single detail in the film, right? apparently wrong according to some people! apparently i have a huge ego if i think anything i do is great according to some people! it's like after all the frustration, and pain, and thought put into something, i'm "not allowed" to like it or be proud of it. what the blup!? listen, if anyone enters into any contest or submits an artwork for show consideration or does anything big or small to put something they've made or done out there into the world, then that person is basically saying, "look, i've done something worth of your time." or else why submit or show anything!? so entering any contest or competing in any event or whatever the case you are saying you are "that good or good enough." but, of course it's not verbal. but, when someone like myself says, "i plan to win" then that's crazy! that's arrogant! that means i have a huge ego and that i must be out of his mind! what the blup!? what's the point of having a voice and being able to communicate true thoughts if you don't use your voice and say what you think!?

arthur lugauskas

don't say anything, ever

chapter 41 : calling out bom

i also happened to be in sculpture five this semester with my professor being bom. bom again? yes! should be great! and yes, double the sculpture work since i had two different sculpture classes to attend to.

so, i thought bom was the man. probably the realest professor i knew. i appreciated all he had to say and just his character. but earlier in this final semester of mine i had a slight problem with bom. basically i felt neglected by him. it started with him not caring about what i was doing. and of course, he didn't have to care, but i thought he did, so when i was questioning my thoughts i started to notice certain things. for one, when it came to my solo show i invited bom and he wasn't going to be able to make it because he was going to be in new york. okay, understandable. but, then i had another day i thought he could come. and he seemed genuinely interested. so, i gave him the information and expected him to be there when he said he would. but, he canceled because of family business. well, what am i going to do if there are family things going on, right? bom was probably the person from gmu that i wanted for to come the most. but, he didn't make it and i had to take my show down. things come up. understandable. no beef with bom because he really did seem interested in coming unlike certain other people. just a sidebar, you would think that people would be proud of a student doing a solo show while still in school, right? like people should want to come and support? or maybe not? or maybe just not me? or maybe people just don't care, especially about something i'm doing, because who am i anyway, right? okay, well, i was bummed that bom didn't make it to see what i put together, but whatever, it was okay.

    then i noticed bom not really interacting with me that much. at this point i had my "frontspace" studio up and running stronger than before. and there was even another recruit to" frontspace" - ant. but, yeah, bom just wasn't there for me. no conversations, no nothing.

    well, i'd been working on a short film earlier in the semester that had to do with skateboarding, art, and process. and one day when i had a rough draft of the film and i asked bom if he had time to check it out. he said, "yeah man. a little later." well, a little later came and bom was nowhere to be found.

    then we had a critique in sculpture five and bom said, "is your wall done? do you want to have a critique on it?" and i said, "yeah, sure." well, i was the last one on the list of people who were going to be critiqued. no problem. so, person after person went and right before my turn came around bom ended class. okay, problem. i guess class time was up. but, the worst part was that nothing was even mentioned about me getting critiqued or anything. it was like i was completely forgotten! and note, i didn't have a problem not getting critiqued. i had a problem being told i was going to go and then being lied to. and it was embarrassing for me. i'd rather of not had myself in the critique schedule in the first place.

    then i furthered the development of my short film and wanted to try to get boms opinion once more. so, i went up to him and said, "do you have a moment?" and he said, "yeah man, but i have to talk to another student before you." i said, "okay, cool, no worries." then i waited a bit and did a few things in the sculpture studio. and next thing i knew, 45minutes passed by. i had other places to be and other things to do, but i was interested in boms opinion. but, i guess he got caught up speaking with another student. so, to be respectful i went to bom and said, "i have to go. so, it's okay. don't worry." i felt pretty bad and neglected at that point. i wasn't interested in doing or asking anything from bom anymore. i thought he was the man, but i no longer knew what to think of him.

    another day came and bom came up to me at my work station and checked briefly what i was up to. at that point i was just really not interested in talking with him. my shoulders were cold and i didn't want to really say anything to him. but, i knew bom enough and if i told him exactly what i felt i thought he'd understand. he was probably one of the only people who would take the hits and not try to beat around the bush. and i thought that way because of everything i had learned about him throughout the semesters i spent with him. and i was ready to call him out on his disregard towards me. so, on this day when i had cold shoulders i just told him, "i feel like you've been neglecting me." and note, right before i said that he was about to just "neglect" me again. but, i guess he heard my words way louder than i or he expected. and then he received a phone call. but, he stuck around because i guess he wanted to say something to me. and so he did after he hung up his phone. he said, "what?" and i just repeated, "i feel like you've been neglecting me. and i'm just demotivated to even talk to you." and my words just hit him hard. so hard that he had to go somewhere really briefly and take a moment. no, i'm joking, he just had to do something real quick before our battle. this is what he said, "i have to go upstairs real quick, but i'll be right back and we could talk about your wall and stuff." and truthfully, i didn't really want to talk to bom at all. i didn't really care if he was going to come back. but, i also thought if i tell him how i felt he should take it like a man. so, after i took a quick bathroom break i approached my first piop art wall and saw bom checking it out. i was about to go inside the sculpture studio, but then bom said, "do you want to talk about this?" and i just went on, "not really. i just feel demotivated to talk to you." and he went on to say, "yeah, you're right. i thought about what you said and realized that i hadn't caught up with you in two weeks." and i went on, "yeah, you've been just ignoring me back to back to back on a consistent basis for the past couple of weeks. and once i realized that i felt disrespected and no longer had interest in talking with you, unless it was a conversation about your disregard towards me." then bom went on to state, "yeah, i realized i really have been dissing you. and it's just that i had, no, actually never mind, there's no excuses other than me messing up. it's my fault and i apologize for that. and i'm just really unhappy that i hurt someone i actually care about. i really am sorry." and i thought, "you actually care about me?" then i said, "yeah, i felt bad, but just got to a point of not worrying anymore. and i did think you would be able to take my comments the way you are now. and yeah, of course, there are no excuses, but i accept you taking it like a man and admitting yourself being in the wrong. it's just i get offended with certain lies and disrespects, especially when you say you'll check something out and you don't. honestly, i'd rather you say you don't have the time or don't want to see what i'm doing or something along those lines instead of saying you would and then don't." bom went on to say, "yeah man. i understand. i just messed up. and i really appreciate you calling me out like this. and don't be afraid to call me out on the spot when i mess up. but, thank you for bringing this to my attention." and then bom and i spoke a bit about my wall and talked for a bit after that. and towards the end bom and i ended up in tens office, which was in the middle of the sculpture studio (remember?). ten was going about business somewhere else and we were just in his office because bom wanted to show me a few images of an artist he thought i'd like. then after that i was curious about what bom thought of me straight up. you know, since we've been laying stuff out on the table. and i remember that moment. it was just bom and me. and bom went on to say, "straight up, i think you're wildly creative and that you have a lot of balls. you question and challenge people in such a way where they either completely flip out or they just have to deal with it. i often don't quite know what you're doing sometimes and i feel like i have to go through this bubble and catch up with your 100mph speed. you're one of those 10% of students who actually do work. the other 90% pay the bills. and what really amazes me about you is your conviction. like you really believe 100% in what you're doing. you attack things with such confidence and i think that scares people. and just your conviction is really powerful. and that's what i think of you straight up." i was in awe. bom and i parted ways after those final statements because he had to go somewhere. and we did spend a good hour covering a lot of surface. and as for me, it was time to think about what had just happened. and i thought, "what!? i didn't know i had balls like that. but, i guess i could understand what bom was referring to. like, when i did my three story string installation i just dove in without doing anything at that level of size prior, or like when i did this moving painting i just dove in without really knowing the outcome, or when i went about this 37.9'x8.8' first ever piop art wall i just dove in after my biggest artwork prior to that being 3'x4' or so. right? could that be what bom was talking about? me just jumping in these huge things without knowing if i was going to actually complete them? or me just believing so hard that i could do it to the point where i just go for it and do it because my i had already decided it was possible prior to entering whatever it was that i was entering? wow!" and note, that conversation with bom happened on october 31, 2013 in the afternoon.

    then on november 12, 2013 i had another conversation with bom and realized that him and i are really on the same page. once again i learned that he just really liked my conviction. he liked that i believed in what i was doing 100%. and he said he was almost more fascinated by my confidence and thinks he likes it more than the work i have produced. i really didn't know my confidence was that radiant (imagine if i said every single thing i thought). bom told me he had to almost take off these rosy glasses to see my work for what it is. it was like my confidence and conviction in what i did overshadowed what i actually make. i found all that so interesting. i mean he did say he liked what i do and that he saw a lot in me? and i wasn't sure what he saw in me. and around this time i mentioned that something huge might go down soon. what do you think i was referring to? and bom, if you're reading this now, what i was typing when you came up to me this day was this book. no one knew i was working on it. and this is the big thing i was talking about. is this not the most creatively genius senior project ever? if there is a senior project more creatively genius and original and unique and unexpected and amazing than this one, please tell me. i feel like i'm set the bar so high to the point where i have fears about myself ever toping it. but, then again, it's me and i've toped myself over and over again, so i should be able to keep doing amazing. and we spoke about school and i said i was just building myself here and that i was like making a machine. and i didn't know if school was for me. and it depended on professors and stuff. and audience reading, note, bom at one point was just freebirding around. and i said things just work out for me somehow sometimes. and he told how me moved to dc with 15 dollars and stuff. and with school bom just stumbled upon getting a teaching job and he teaches as if he's like a student in a way. "like, just make" bom says. "make things." then he told me about a story when he was in school and his professor asked the class if anyone wanted to be on the cover of an art in america magazine. and them bom and one other guy were the only two people who raised their hand. everyone else looked at them with disgust. like, "you're an artist and you shouldn't want fame and fortune." and bom just thought, "look, i was asked a question and i answered it. this had nothing to do with fame or money or anything. a simple question was asked in regards to if i wanted to be on the cover of a magazine and i simply said 'yes'". and i related that story so clearly and crisply to my senior project class and when we were asked who wanted to do what and where hypothetically speaking early on in the semester and i said exactly what i wanted. and then bom asked me what i was going to do after school finished and how i'd support myself. i told him, "i don't know, but i'm not too worried because of my brain and how i think." he said, "good answer." then as i drove home that day i thought i should have said, "i'm not worried because i'm a creative genius" or "by being famous" or "i'm not worried because i'll be famous and people will be handing me money and all i'll do is give that money to my ideas and creativity." well, my ideas are priceless, but, you know. and well, bom thought i was on the right track and just told me to keep going. i really appreciated talks i've had with bom because he's an amazing story teller. and i myself really care about telling stories in different ways. and bom also said that he didn't think he was a great artist. and i said that he *can* think he is. and he said he thought he was a great observer and good at connecting dots. and i told him about my idea of helping people revive their dreams. and he said he connected dots in his recent art in africa commission. and he told me about his barrel piece that he had displayed at the main gallery at school months ago. and what that barrel piece was about was basically what he was thinking at the time and where his interests were. and it didn't matter if it was a commission piece or not when it came to his barrel because all he was interested was the integrity he had to his idea. and he said, "if only one person gets it, then great. and if a hundred people get it, then great." he was willing to take the risks of having a minuscule sized audience to an artwork by him. and wow, i was amazed with who bom was and is to this day. i agree. be individual. do what you believe to be true. and talking with bom encouraged me to further go with writing this book and putting my ideas out. no matter how frightening they may be due to backlash that i may get for saying what i'm saying right now. or writing what i've written thus far.

      and i want to share another thing bom told me that i found really inspiring. this moment happened the day after october 9th. i knew bom was one of the few i could really bring my situation to in regards to me getting severe backlash for being honest in a critique and telling truth. so, i mentioned to him my battle without giving out any professor names and stuff. i just questioned, "is it okay for me ask for students opinions during a critique without saying a word about what i'm showing? and is it okay to say that i don't really know exactly what i'm doing when it comes to something i'm working on to a professor or in a critique or so?" and bom said, "yeah, sure, if it's coming from an honest place." and then he went on to tell me and some classmates that were in the room about an amazing story. and that story was about his "fastest stick in the world" art piece he did in graduate school. on his panel of people that reviewed what he was doing he purposely chose professors that liked what he was doing and professors that didn't like what he was doing. and when they asked him, "what is this?" bom said, "well, it's the fastest stick in the world." and then they went on to say, "well, okay, how is this art?" and then bom said he went all terminator mode with all these possible answers floating in front of him. like, he could have spoken about duchamp and readymades and different art movements and all sorts of historical things and terms and blah blah blah where his fastest stick art could fit into and he could have backing in a definition form as to why it was an art piece, but bom chose to choose the more honest, but difficult for people to hear answer he had. so, bom said, "it's art because i say it's art and you just have to trust me." i was so amazed by that story and so happy to of heard what i just heard. and then i thought to myself about my scenario the day before. you know, that day i felt super disrespected and received all that backlash for wanting to hear opinions of people and for stating that i didn't know what i was fully doing. it just hurt that people didn't want to accept me not knowing or not being ready to know. like, my idea wasn't fully developed and piop art wasn't fully realized. it existed and it was coming together, but i just wasn't ready to say what it exactly was because i wasn't fully sure. why bash me for that? ugh! and then bom told me about a student he had in the past and how she did a project and when asked about her project she just said, "i don't know, it's a groove thing." and bom saw that explanation as valid. wow, wonderful! and that story was when he taught at another university and the critique of that artwork was done in the girls bathroom. wow! amazing! thank you bom for who you are and for how you teach!

    and one more thing. at some point in the semester bom mentioned to me that fume mentioned to him that i've been driving her crazy. i laughed a bit and said, "yeah, and?" then bom told me that he told her, "good!"

arthur lugauskas

don't say anything, ever

:::: :: : : : : : : : : : : : : :::::::: : :: :: :::: :: : : : : : ::: :::   : ::::::::::::::
chapter 42 : sounds like a poem
::::: :::   :::::::::::::::::::::::::::   ::: : :::: : : ::: :: ::::::: :: ::: : :

$$\Delta°\Delta°\Delta°°\Delta°^{aa} \bullet \P\P$$
oaao⁄

\ \ ≠ \ ≠ \ ≠ ¡ \ ¡ \ ¡ \ ¡
¡ \ ¡ \ \ ¡ \ ¡¡¡ `¡⁺⁺¡⁺¡⁺¡⁺⁺≥¡≥≥
¿¿¿¿iiiii⁺⁺/ /
∧∧∧∧∧∧∧∧∧∧¥¥
\ \ \ \ \ | | | | | | | | \ | | | \ | \ \ \ | | \ |

next is something i wrote on oct. 15, 2013 at
4:10am. and it sounded like a poem: it's hard for me to
go to sleep right now. even though i'm tired and want
to. this is nothing new these days. i have much on my
mind. i have concerns with finishing up certain projects
by certain time frames. i get worried about forgetting
how long some works may take. i think and think. and
think some more. and then my sleep gets distracted.
my tiredness gets busy thinking. my tiredness becomes
thoughtfulness. like now, i've just been thinking about

my documentary and doing the final finishing touches, my october sequence tree film, do i do a sequence version and non-sequence version?, the piop art walls and how they expect to take up maybe half of november, will i finish this book on time?, i still have images of my 'first look' show to organize, and not to mention the 'first look' performance short film, i still have wood to get for the tetris sculpture that i'm working on, and wow, what about the tetris sculpture building film?, and all these other things i have to do. or that i want to do. all these books i want to write. all these unfinished projects. all these files waiting to be organized. all these works waiting to be touched, worked on, and finished. or maybe all these are just keeping me distracted from my pain? but, a distraction is only temporary, right? my pain surfaces here and there, but then i realize i have these project distractions to keep me busy here and there. and what pain do i talk about so much? what pain do you think? it's been months and it still hasn't disappeared. it's still heavily here. and only waiting for the attention it deserves. waiting for its nourishment. waiting for me to be sad, crying, more lonely, reminiscing of the days i was with her. maybe everything is a dream, including life itself. i'll try to go to sleep now. maybe i'll succeed if i pretend not to worry.

don't say anything, ever

arthur lugauskas

don't say anything, ever

chapter 43 : point of anything

then on days like october 24, 2013 at times like 3:10am i question anything and that makes me want to quit everything. like, "what's the point of anything?" really, does anything actually matter. it's like everyone makes up all this stuff in their own head, but why? what's the point? really, does it matter!? does it matter that i'm writing a book and you feel offended in regards to what i say? does this book even really matter at all!? am i not allowed to put words on paper!? i don't know. sometimes i just want to quit it all. just everything.

really. i don't say this jokingly. i don't know what death is like, but sometimes i almost feel i'm ready to know or want to find out. yes, i know, why think like that? but, at the same time why say "why think like that?" is that question said because that's how we are "supposed" to think. i don't know. and i don't feel like writing anymore right now. i'm just not feeling too good. enjoy your night.

don't say anything, ever

arthur lugauskas

don't say anything, ever

: : ::: ::: ::: :::: ::: ::: ::: :::: ::: ::: ::: :::: ::: ::: ::: ::: :::: ::: ::: ׃ :: ׃ :: ׃ :
chapter 44 : texting truth with finlay
:׃׃׃׃׃׃׃׃׃׃׃׃׃׃׃׃׃׃׃ ::: :::::: ::::: :: :::::: ::::: ::::: ׃ ׃ ׃ ::: ::: :: ׃

&'(&&'&'(
~=~~~ | | | ¥^¥~ | ~
?_>?>?><?>_>__?>>_?
!!!!!!!⫽!!!⫽¡¡¡¡¡¡¡!
╪╪╪╪╪╪╪╪╪╪
≤≤≤μ≤≤≤≤≤μ≤≤≤≤≤μ˜
&&&&&&&%%%&%%&&&&&%

  in this chapter i just wanted to share a few texts from finlay and myself. the "f" will be for "finlay" and the "a" will be for "akuna", okay?

f: fake it till u make it. no one truly knows what they are doing. they just do it!
sat, sep 28 2:47am
f: lol, your not suppose to be that real. people like to make themselves believe they know what there doing
sat, sep 28 2:53am

a: so apparently looks like no exclusive invite to my professors show..she said there was like an over capacity of her invites..i have a feeling i was at the bottom of the list of potential invites, that is if i was even ever on the list..or her saying that sounds like a good nice 'he should understand' excuse...and im not getting primetime center of the gallery for senior show even though i was the only one who asked for that spot and i was put on blast to tell the whole class i wanted that...but its all good..i'm still in the gallery taking up an exciting wall and i still plan to take over like none other..and no one knows about the realness coming..
mon, oct 28 11:36am

f: ha, i think all your teacher hears is your ego and fails to see that u actually mean well and just want to put on an engaging art show....success is the best revenge
mon, oct 28 12:42pm
(note, that text from finlay was one of the nicest things anyone said to me all year)

a: yeah thats a good question and im not sure..the problem is its hard to find out how you would react to negative comments because you almost get no practice of that experience because most people dont give you that truth..so how do you get better at taking those comments and acknowledging youre wrong and then improving..so how would i react..probably hurt and lost and unsure and i dont know because i dont have much practice in that field..im weak in that field maybe..and then again sometimes certain negative comments are stupid and judgmental in the wrong way maybe..i dont know..
thu, oct 31 4:09pm
a: its like talking to girls..if you dont practice those first rejections may hurt the most..the more hits you get the more you build the better you get..
thu, oct 31 4:11pm

f: the real negative comments that you agree with a little are the worst. one day i came into work late and went down stairs and heard ronald and another employee talking truth about me, they didnt know i was there and could hear every word
thu, oct 31 4:16pm
f: and wow it was insane
thu, oct 31 4:19pm
f: ill tell u the full story sometime but words like selfish, believes in fantasy, out of touch with reality, trys too hard were used
thu, oct. 31, 4:19pm

a: ouch..and wow..but in a sense theyre jealous because maybe they lost touch with theyre dreams..i think thats how people view me and because of those traits i may have might be a reason ae didnt want to be with me

anymore..because im looking to reach unbelievable heights and somewhere in me and my brain i for some reason believe i could achieve everything i want to sort of..and i dont know if she or people see that as a level of immaturity or something..but i dont know..like no actually..most people in the world might just be dreamkillers..dont let them kill your dreams because someone else killed theirs..believe be selfish if you want to believe in fantasy try because if you dont who will..!
thu, oct 31 4:28pm

f: at first i was like ouch.. after i thought about it some more it was like yes i do believe in fantasies and i am out of touch with reality but so are the greatest artists who walked the earth because they understood reality can be anything you want it to be our dreams and fantasies can make this world better. after all what do kids do? day dream and believe in fantasies and their mentally is why isn't that possible why can't i have imaginary friends... anything is possible. what made me mad is that they made it seem like it was a negative attribute of my personality when in fact its what everyone should aspire for
thu, oct 31 4:55pm

a: its the dreamkillers youre introduced to when your 4 or 5 years old..some people overcome and wash their brain and question the initial brainwash and dream killing..others get further sucked into that hole and for some its scary to see that that hole may have shut and there seems no way out..there seems to be no way fantasies and such can come true..and its sad because who knows the great things for society and humanity and civilization these people could have done if they kept their dreams safe and never let their imaginary

friends disappear into neglection..i feel like the biggest starts in the world would maybe find it fascinating if you as an adult say you have imaginary friends...the most influential people believe anything is possible..and it should be almost obvious as an observer..but like people are blinded or something.. :c
thu, oct 31 5:07pm

f: too busy with their facebooks and it would be cool to do a video series of discussions like this, not interviews just conversations
thu, oct 31 5:44pm

a: of us..?
thu, oct 31 5:52pm

f: i dont think anyone would take us seriously now just cuz of age and the who are these kids thing... just think it would be cool if anyone did it
thu, oct 31 6:07pm

a: no i completely think it would be fantastic to do...i think it could help open up peoples minds and just challenge common thought..i almost wish you recorded everything we said during our meetings..that stuff was gold silver platinum bronze and diamond..and its our thinking thats looked down on and with a lot of people who make it its like we dont know who they really were or how they thought before they made it..if we had recorded conversations of straight up fearless truth at this point in our lives then after making it or before the content was released wow..all the doubters and stuff..its like dont pretend i just somehow made it and it was by accident and it was the right time or whatever other excuse other than how i thought...like its because you

dont think this way is the reason youre not reaching the stars and pushing global boundaries..its like im at where im at because of my level of thought and knowing anything is possible..dont say i didnt tell you or know i was going to be one of the greatest before anyone even thought i was great at all..
thu, oct 31 6:21pm
a: we should do some real talk recorded like right now..vent out those frustrations..tell those stories..give that truth..!
thu, oct 31 6:23pm

f: ha, i know but we have to fool ourselves because once we know we are being recorded we start to think about what to say instead of just being natural
thu, oct 31 7:01pm

a: that would probably be one of the hardest parts..to be fully real..like im the future of art..im a genius..im the modern day warhol mixed with roy scrambled in van gogh with a touch of duchamp..my stuff is amazing and i know it...and blah blah blah..the funny and interesting part is i think maybe no matter when anyone would see it they would just hate and criticize instead of be inspired to think for themselves and believe in them..this isnt about arrogance..its about inspiration..but all the positives may be overlooked because many people are maybe trained to look at confidence in a certain way..if we were to share these conversations right now it would be like who are these stupid arrogant kids who know nothing..but, if we shared this talk after fame it would be like hmm i dont like him anymore...like you state who you are you prove it then show the world you stated that years ago then they dont like you even though you are right..!..blup..!

thu, oct 31 7:11pm

f: yep! like when my teacher found out that im somewhat arrogant and not humble she disliked me instantly.....so its scary on the real. like if we recorded what i said about....
thu, oct 31 7:34pm

arthur lugauskas

don't say anything, ever

::::: :::::::::::::::: :::::::::::   ::   ::::::::::::::::::::::::::::: :::::::
           chapter 45 : no thank you akuna
:::   :::::::::::::

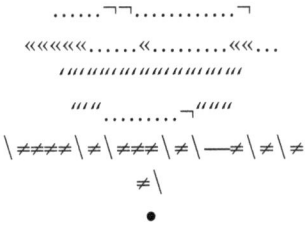

    so, yeah, it's interesting, right? i was the only one who asked for exactly what i wanted super early in the semester when it came to what i wanted to do for senior show and then when the final space locations were being made i was basically told that i wasn't going to get what i wanted. but, note i was told in this "nice" way. basically i had a meeting with micky and she said that her and fume discussed everyones space and that it wasn't the best idea for me to have that center wall because ant's sculpture was going to be in the center and there were going to be graphic design students in half the gallery space and that the wall i wanted may better suite another student and this and that. so, the other option i had was this other wall in the gallery or maybe doing something right outside the gallery. and i sort of knew this would happen. i even told micky, "yeah, i thought this was going to happen. my first and foremost spot i wanted was that center wall and i stated that since the beginning and fume even had me say exactly what i wanted in front of the whole class and that's what i did and then everyone hated me for that. and note, i really thought this would happen. this whole me wanting four other walls and then getting hit with the excuse that i would have four other walls when i clearly stated that my first wall of interest was the specific gallery one and that i didn't have to have the other walls if i wasn't allowed, but if the space was available for me to do work on the other four walls i'd like to step up to the plate and take it because i felt like creating a body of work that consisted of five walls." and micky wasn't trying to hear whatever tensions that were going on with myself and fume and all that. she basically told me what was available and what was the plan that best suited everyone. and form the beginning it was sort of obvious that i wouldn't get what i wanted because i asked for it and no one should ask for such a thing, right? really, it wasn't a surprise that i didn't get my primetime wall. but, honestly, it's okay. and i'm not saying that with hard feelings. i wanted to prove that this would happen and it did. and note, actually the new wall proposed for me was much better with more possibilities. and i'm not saying this with sarcasm or anything. i honestly am super happy with my spot and appreciate even being in the gallery in general. this is true what i'm writing right now. and it was really just about me getting these stories for this book. like, having the balls to say "yeah, i want to be the center of attention" out loud and then being shut down by fume after everyone knew what i wanted couldn't of been any better. because at the end everything worked out. i'm in the gallery and have an amazing spot and am allowed to do four other piop art walls and life is just good in that regard. and i'm sure fume was super excited that i was okay with my spot and not being in the center and that i wasn't blowing up or whatever. of course she is, she never wanted me to be in the center. why would she with my attitude, right? so, thank you fume for not giving me exactly what i asked for before everyone. it's good to keep me grounded and make me know that i won't get what i want all the time. and i knew that, but this situation was certainly one for the book. and yes, this book. i just wanted to show what happens when you ask for exactly what you want in school. you kind of don't get it in my case. but, don't worry, honesty and truth pays off. i feel like i got something better and i don't think fume sees that. i think she's simply over joyed at what i don't have. i don't know why she can't just be happy for me. in any regard, i think ant has an amazing project he's working on and i'm happy for him. and really audience reading, i'm super humbled and happy for everything that i've been given. and yes, i do really appreciate all the space i'm allowed to take up for senior show. life really is good in that regard. don't be sad for me. i'm not sad about all this. i am very happy that i could type the story i'm typing right now. because what i've been interested in writing throughout this book was real events and what i've just written was another real thing that happened in my life. and in one way, my real *actual* senior project is this book, which is about a two year performance at a university that showcases all the various stories of different situations i had with different professors when i spoke truth.

don't say anything, ever

arthur lugauskas

don't say anything, ever

chapter 46 : frustration

      i'm not sure how to really write this chapter. i have some things to express and let out right now. call this chapter an intermission or whatever. now, listen, what i'm about to let out i know many people aren't ready to hear or read. and i have a weird problem thing when it comes to writing what i'm about to write. what am i saying? well, here's a very important thing i learned as to how current society reacts to certain things. basically whenever you say exactly what you want that benefits you or whenever you say exactly who you are

that has to do with complimenting yourself or what you
do, well, then current society gives you what you didn't
ask for and tells you why you're not what you say you
are and tells you the exact opposite of what you think
what you do is. but, it's all good to say good things
about others or what others have done. no problem
there. but, something good about yourself, now that is
looked down upon and hated on. so, that's what's going
on right now. in the future things will be different. and i
know i'm about to put myself under the blade again
right now. because i'm going to write things that will be
okay in the future, but not now. so, please, i know many
of you reading this book may not be ready to hear
what's next and if you are one of those people, please
just go to the next chapter right now. just abort this
chapters mission. please. but, if you are one of the few
readers who understand what i've been writing this
whole time and what i'm about and what i care about,
feel free to proceed. because if you are one of those few
you'll know what i'm about after i write what i write.
you'll know it's not about ego or arrogance or putting
anybody down. you'll know. but, if you're not one of
those few you're going to think what i'm saying is all
about selfishness, ego, arrogance, and hate. and that's
when you're going to try to flip things and say exactly
why i'm not what i say i am. because what i'm about to
express is something no one is "allowed" to express
right now in this day and age. or better yet, no one is
"allowed" to say what i'm about to say out loud or in
the public eye. most of current society hasn't caught up
to the form of thinking i'm about to lay out. so, without
further a do, i'm jumping in the hole of truth and saying
what i feel. what's next is what's real.

      i'm going to be very clear right now. i am the
future of art. i am a genius thinker. i am a creative

genius. i am ahead of my time. i am one of the most influential, but-not-yet-fully-known-underrated-looked-at-like-he's-crazy human being alive. i have the most ideas that keep coming in forever. they keep me up at night every night. there is no one even remotely close to the way i think. and the reason is because of my upbringing. by age 10 i had already lived in three extremely distinct cultures. by age 10 i knew 3 different languages. and that's why there is no language that my tongue can't sing to in a beautiful fluent manner. and know, it's way different experiencing different cultures when you're a baby than when you're in your teenage years than when you're in further adulthood. to understand where i'm even slightly coming from you have to experience what i'm saying at a young age. you had to be immersed in culture. you had to live it. you had to go to a school where all they did was speak a language you knew no words to and then you had to pick everything up as you lived and studied and learned. and you had to do that again and again. you cannot touch me. and one of the reasons i say i'm not allowed to die is because i'm one of the few who knows 100% that he can change the world. i am one of the few people who has a brain at that level of thinking and knowing. and i'm going to change the world whether you like it or not. and after i change it you will like it. unless you're one of the few dreamkillers who don't want their dreams revived. and note, you dreamkillers will be the minority. and us the dreamers will rule the world. there will be a time where more people believe and know that anything is possible. and i'm one of the leaders of this movement or whatever you want to call it. i'm at the frontier with a few other people right now. we are currently the minority. and there are people everyday trying to tell us why we can't say what we feel,

why we're "not allowed" to do what we want, why we
will never be what we imagine, why dreams don't come
true, why we're crazy, why we're stupid, why we should
stop trying so hard, why we should just settle, why we
should blah blah blah. and to those people, please just
shut the blup up for a change and think for yourself! be
yourself! stop being what you think society wants you
to be! stop being bullies! stop following the
nonbelievers! stop being fake and hiding behind a bush
and not saying what you actually believe! or what you
believed when you were 5 years old! stop trying to
corrupt the new borns into believing they can't do
whatever they want in life! because that's false! and
listen, i am ahead of my time! my art is ahead of it's
time! my thinking is too advanced for where society is
at right now! but, one day. one day in the future people
will realize that what i'm doing is helpful to every single
human being alive! my art will inspire the world once
people stop being blinded by the dumb stupidity and
immaturity that current traditional society tries to bring
and instill in living humans! and i don't know when in
the future, but there is nothing anyone can say or do to
prove me wrong! and the people of the future, when
they read this, they'll know that i knew the whole time
of the impact my work was going to have on the world
as a whole! what i'm doing, if placed in front of the
most influential and genius people, will help advance
humanity and civilization to new amazing heights! and
what i'm doing is affecting everyone on a subconscious
or conscious level in a positive way! and if anyone is
mad for reading what i just wrote, well, i don't blame
you. you have all this smoke and fog in your head and
brain that is blurring what is *actually* in front of you right
now! if you're mad at me you're just playing yourself
right now! realize that i haven't put anybody down! i

didn't talk trash about any specific person! i don't hate anyone! i believe in everyone! and if you believe that i said that you are this or that, please! think again! i'm just putting myself up! and you have every right to put yourself up! but, no, society wants you to believe that putting yourself up is "not allowed"! people with untrained minds are probably going to hate me for writing this book. but, this is one of the best books on the planet! one of the most creative books! one of the most individualized books that exists, period! oh, and understand that right now i have nothing, but family, friends, and my dreams! i don't have any deal or signed contract or this or that! and note, after everything i say comes true, don't act like i didn't tell you! don't act like i was always on top of the world! don't act like i didn't know! don't act like i didn't release this book when i had nothing lined up! don't act like i never told you! and sidebar, i'm guessing no one believes a word i'm saying! just wait! just wait. and note, right now it's november 22, 2013 6:49pm.

arthur lugauskas

chapter 47 : almost dropped out

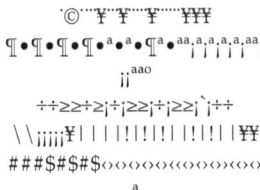

so, something very important i want everyone reading this to realize is that i almost dropped out of school earlier this semester. my mind was just not in school early on. i didn't know what i was doing there. i felt like most people were so robotic and following fake made up ideas. i felt like almost no one believed they can do anything. i was challenged because no one thought like me. no one was me. i was like an alien. but, i wasn't crazy. but, i think people were trying to make me not believe in myself. i'd speak to students and hear why i shouldn't act like myself. i'd speak to students and hear why i shouldn't be myself. i'd speak to students and hear them tell me why i shouldn't think the way i think. and those were shots coming at my precious brain. but, since my brain is made of diamonds there was nothing that was going to leave a permanent negative mark. but, still, so many people were trying to scratch away my thoughts and truth and honesty. i just felt like i really didn't belong in school anymore. and there were times i was literally about to go make some money and then buy a plane ticket to london and leave. and that would have been it. just leave. i was so close to doing that at times early on in the semester.

  so, why didn't i? well, honestly, i was literally doing whatever i wanted in school. i didn't have assignments in any of my classes, except for my printmaking one class. and just to go briefly into my printmaking class, well, i learned about printmaking. and that medium of art is amazing with endless possibilities. and i had "assignments" in that class, but since i don't believe in "assignments" i didn't do "assignments", but instead i did projects i cared about and prints that were beyond "beginner" prints. i'd be in the printmaking studio until 5am if i had to. just working hard and making stuff. so, yeah, that class was fun and consumed some of my time because for some reason i cared more about my prints that i should have. i guess i just like doing amazing and often times amazing takes time, so to achieve amazing i had to give time. make sense? so, yeah, printmaking was interesting and one of my "humbler" classes verbally, but when it came to some of my prints, um, they were, yeah, next level and for future art historians to dissect and figure out the codes and decode amazing hand writing and yeah, stuff like that, nonverbal loudness.

but, okay, so yeah, i literally technically didn't have to go to school if i didn't want to. that's how flexible my professors were with me. and because i was a free bird and doing whatever my mind wanted at all times when it came to my class schedule and classes i was taking, well, that's the primary reason i stayed. and it's funny, only a few people would do what i did in a "free bird" situation like i described. what am i talking about? well, i actually worked the hardest at school and put the most hours into my work day in and day out. i literally lived in the art building sometimes. because i just actually wanted to do what i wanted to do. and i wanted to do a lot! i had free range to do whatever and i gave all my time to doing things i wanted. i didn't do any assignments or follow any guidelines. i just made what i wanted. i just created what i wanted. senior project was never about senior project for me. the walls i wanted to do were things *i* wanted to do. they just fit into the "senior project" category. but, understand, these walls would have been made by me sooner or later. but, also note, the art building at gmu was the first place that gave me the opportunity and space to do them. and the art building was the first place that i thought to do them and asked to do them. and i really honestly appreciate the opportunity. but, yeah, despite me not having any "required" time to be at school, i spent the most time in there out of any other student. i was either working on prints in the printmaking studio, working on sculpture in the sculpture studio, working on film at the film studio, or working on a wall in a hallway. i don't say that i spent the most time in the art building jokingly. i spent so many long nights and all nighters there to the point where i know who the people who clean the building are and their schedules. one guy's name is francisco and he's 27 years old and he normally works

on the bottom floor and comes in at 12am and starts
with sweeping the hallway floors and then gets into
rooms that have carpet and vacuums and then goes to
the rooms with no carpets and sweeps there and then
attacks trashcans with new trash bags and he normally
leaves anywhere from 4am-5am depending on how fast
and efficiently he finished his job. and he has short hair
and usually listens to music while working. another
lady is a bit older, maybe 43 years old and her name is
ming and she normally comes in around 1am and takes
care of the girls and guys bathroom. and there's a
building security guy who has short curly hair and he is
6'2" and he just walks around the building around 2am
to make sure things are all good. like i know these
people because i'm there working when they are
working. ask any person who works late nights or the
"cleaning" shift in the art building who they have seen
the most working all the time. they'll recognize me and
instantly point me out. they know me and i know them.
we are cordial with one another and don't get in each
others way. i think the people who clean do a great job
and i appreciate all that they do. i feel very humbled
when i'm around them and i trust them. they clean, they
do their thing, they jam out to music sometimes, they're
nice, they don't bother me, they don't cause problems,
and they are positive and smile and say "hi" to me when
they see me. wow, this paragraph is pretty long. maybe
i should've broke it up at some point. but, we'll end the
chapter really soon. so, because i was able to do
whatever i wanted in every class is the reason i didn't
drop out and made it through this semester thus far.
and at this point i have a very little more to go in this
current fall 2013 gmu semester i'm in. and i still can
drop out if i wanted to. and note, i have only a's in all
my classes as far as i'm concerned. i guess that's what

happens when you do what you want to do. well, what do you think? should i join the greats who dropped out with just dropping out myself? or should i join the greats who graduated college with graduating college by the end of this semester? or actually do you think i might fail art school because my creativity is on another level and i'm proving it again with this book?

arthur lugauskas

don't say anything, ever

:::: :::::::::   :::::::::::::::::::   :::   :::::::::::::::   :::::::::::::::::::::::
chapter 48 : first ever piop art wall
::::::::   :::::::::::::::::::::   :::::::::::::::::   :::::::::::::::::::::   :::::::

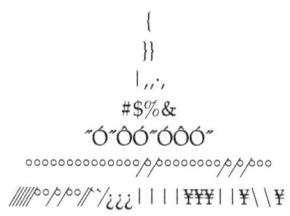

    i guess we should get into this piop art wall business, right? at least a little bit. so, yeah, the first ever piop art wall is 37.9'x8.8' or around that size. and i just attacked it when i started it. learn, i started with one dot and developed it to where it got to. i had no pre-planned sketch or anything. i just spent a lot of time thinking and analyzing and looking and then going about putting it together.

    during the making of it i realized something. somehow i got to a point where i thought i was too good at art. crazy, right? yeah, but i'm being honest with you here. how good do you have to be to get to a point where you somehow think you're too good? i don't know. maybe that's what happens when you realize what you are doing is way ahead of its time. and i really don't know how ahead. but, i know that the piop art i do can inspire and help absolutely anyone and everyone. from chefs, to designers, to architects, to artists, to scientists, to engineers, to physiologists, to sociologists, to rehab patients, to you name it. all you have to do is give what i made some time and thinking and you are affected with positivity and possibilities.

actually, interesting enough, i also got to a point where i realized what i wanted to achieve at some point. and i thought that my first piop art wall could achieve that. and what i'm talking about is getting people to faint. yes, just by looking at it. and i actually mentioned that to fume and i guess she had an idea of what i wanted and said something like, "so, you want people to faint because of how brilliant and genius and astounding this wall is. like it's on another level of greatness and you yourself are in disbelief about how amazing it is." and she went on with stuff like that and everything she said was exactly true to what i thought. but, i think she said it sarcastically. but, i wasn't joking when i told her that what she said was true. because it was true. i got interested in creating something so genius and amazing and brilliant to the point where if someone figured out what i actually did i wanted them to faint because of how absolutely creatively amazing what was before them was. and i wanted that something to be just a wall, or a picture, or a drawing, or whatever you want to call a 2-d thing. yes, i was interested in having people faint just by looking at something i've created. but, then i realized that you had to be a genius or a super smart person for that to happen. and that realization caused something interesting in my mind. because i was basically saying that i could make genius' and the smartest people in the world possibly faint. wow! how do i get to these thoughts!? and plus, to figure out my fist ever piop art wall it was going to take time. and i mean a lot of time! maybe hours or weeks or even years. there was so much thought that went into it and so many secrets and so much amazing happened during the making. i was close to fainting at time because i blew my mind over and over again. i really was truly amazed. and one day after i finished my first wall i had encountered fume in the hallway and she said, "i saw your wall and i didn't faint." and my response was, "yeah, you just didn't get it." she was blunt with her remark and so was i. and plus, of course she didn't faint and didn't get it! she maybe gave the wall a glance, if even that. i think she just hates me, hence, any achievement i aspire to achieve she'll just try to counteract them with reasons why i can't achieve them. like, since she didn't faint looking at my wall, well, i guess that confirms in her mind that no one will faint. you see, when people don't like you they tend to not like what you do. and it doesn't matter if the product you released was actually good or not, they just don't even give what you did a chance. and that's just how it is sometimes with some people.

    and in my first wall i actually have a story with it. well, you basically walk into the door and we start relatively simple, but in reality we have hidden confusion that doesn't make full sense unless you realize it and make sense out of it, and you go up this huge long slope, but as you're going up things are getting more complex and then its like all these shots get to your train of thoughts and after that you fall off the slope and then

you're delusional and see these "reflections" that look
kind of real, but actually don't make that much sense
because they are just an illusion, and then as you get to
the end you've had enough and want to climb out
through the ladder, but as you do that i just suck you in
deeper into a world of lostness because that perspective
is actually on the upside down side, so you're not
actually climbing out, instead you're going deeper into
my trap. or something like that is the experience you
may get while walking by the wall and seeing the things
i'm talking about. or just make up any story you want
and just get inspired. and seriously, listen, if you see my
wall or any piop art i've done you will be affected in a
positive way that can help you be even more creative
and idea generating with anything you do. and note, it
may be on a conscious and/or subconscious level.

don't say anything, ever

arthur lugauskas

don't say anything, ever

```
::::::::::: ::::: ::::: :::::::::  ::::::::::::::::::  ::    :
          chapter 49 : calculated
: : : : : : : : : : :  : : : : : :  : : : : : : : : :  : : : : : :  : : :  : : : : :  : ::  ::::
```

```
  ˇˇ‰ ˇ‰ ‰ ˇ‰ ˇ
      ′′′′′′′...
    ⌣⌣⌣⌣⌣⌣⌣⌣⌣⌣⌣
     ```ii̇ii̇`i```
           »
           \
          | | |
```

    i want you to know some other things. with art i do and with my writing of this book and other things often times i might make mistakes. and then i think and think. and sometimes i fix what i just don't feel to be right. and other times my mistakes turn into calculated acts. sometimes my mistakes become fascinating to me. so, i want others to be fascinated too! so, i might purposely leave certain mistakes i choose for your own mind to discover and think about them. maybe your thoughts might be similar to mine, maybe not. maybe
```

you'll have similar questions and discoveries as me, maybe not. i don't know. so note, some things that you may think are mistakes on my end might just be very on purpose. but, of course, there may be some things that you notice in things i did or do that weren't necessarily intentional from my end and that's good. that means you used your imagination to come up with what you thought to be true. and that's really all i wanted to express in this chapter - that i sometimes turn my mistakes into calculated acts.

don't say anything, ever

arthur lugauskas

chapter 50 : undercover genius

o
|
| | |
»
Æ
`

        do you think this chapter is about me? well, no. i'm not undercover with my genius, am i? well, who am i talking about then? are you ready to know? guess? maybe. no. no. no. close. close. maybe. i'm talking about ten. yeah, he surprised me. he's so quite about it. but, i realized that he's amazing. i mean, he's been amazing, but after certain conversations and interactions i had with him earlier in this semester i realized that he is a genius. but, he's undercover. so, i shouldn't reveal him more. you'll notice him when he decides to pull the covers off. just wait.

arthur lugauskas

don't say anything, ever

::::: :::::::: ::::::::: :::::::::::::: :: ::::: :::::::::::::   :   :::
              chapter 51 : extras from 4th
:::::::   :   :::   ::::: :::::::::::: ::::::   :::::::::::::::::::::: ::

°&&&
##$‹›»»
| | | | |
– | |
Ô
§¶§¶¶¶¶§
∞∞∞∞∞∞∞∞∞∞∞∞∞

    so where am i at now and what's going on? well, like i said earlier it's november 22, 2013 and now 7:56pm. and i finished my first piop art wall a while ago. but, now i have four more to go and i haven't started drawing on any of them. and they are expected to be done by around december 9th or so. yeah, not a lot of time. and i think most people think i won't complete them on time. and to those people i have something to say, "it's called 'sleep-less.'"

oh, and for my artist bio that i was asked to turn in for senior project i literally wrote the dictionary definition to my name and the definition was this, "1. the future of art..." and when it came to writing my artist statement about my first ever five piop art walls i just wrote whatever came to my mind at that point in time. and just to turn things up a notch, what if i said my extended artist statement for my senior project was this whole book? has anyone ever written a whole book as an artist statement? well, i guess now someone has.

as for my standings with fume, well, we aren't in conflict from the looks of it. we're cordial. and i haven't been giving her a "hard time" or saying that much to her. i've been too busy working on this book and other projects. and plus, i already accepted not having the spot i wanted for senior show and i think she's happy about that. i certainly am happy with the unplanned spot that i got. and i have no desire to fight and argue with fume right now. i think she's a good person and a lot of students appreciate her and she's super cool with people she likes. maybe she likes me deep down inside. but, i don't know. i don't hate her and i want people to know that. and yes, she was one of the professors that probably hurt me and my feelings the most at times and she tried to get in the way of my dreams and ideas plenty of times. but still, nonetheless i didn't let her take my dreams away. i own my dreams. and in any regard, i wouldn't have another senior project professor if i had to do all this over again and go back in time. reason being because fume tested me and pushed my limits and buttons and gave me a variety of emotions to go through and allowed me to bring stories to fruition in this book that you are reading right now. and i have doubts fume will actually read this book, but if she does i think she'll just hate me even more despite everything i've written being a product of creativity and idea generation. or maybe she'll appreciate all the hard work i've put into writing this book, right? yeah, probably not. well, in any case, thank you fume.

bom is still the man. ten is also the man. and i think they might be two of the few from gmu who will appreciate this book. or maybe not. i don't know. actually i really have no idea how people will actually react because right now as i type what i'm typing, well, that's what is going on and this book is not out and available.

so, now let me tell you, i know how kanye felt after the vma incident. it was so controversial, but kanye didn't do it for controversy. he was the only one not afraid to publicly say how he felt and tell the underlying truth of a glittered fake world full of politics and deception and lies. i've been really honest out loud for so long now and i've felt the hate, the despise, the "you're crazy", and the scrutiny. i've learned that it's honesty that people are actually afraid of. everyone is afraid of the truth. no one wants to say it. but, when someone does say it, everyone feels so offended and they can't handle it so what happens? it's like, "you want the truth!? you can't handle the truth!" and what happens is, the person who said what's real for a change gets bullied and desired to be annihilated. imagine what some people will desire for me when this book comes out. it's scary to even think. but, i have to release this for truth, honesty, realness, individuality, uniqueness, amazingness, genius, and creativity. if i don't release a book like this, who will? and when? in a hundred thousand trillion years? when finally society progresses to a level of understanding that everything i said in this book is about inspiration, dreams, and life?

and like kanye was, i am right now the most hated person at school. i've been the loudest with my words. i've spoken the most truth out of everybody. and i've been criticized and scrutinized the most out of everybody. even though there are some people who do understand me and know i want only good, there are, at the same time, some people who want nothing good to come to me ever because they despise everything they think i'm about. and like in kanyes case after that moment of him telling one of the loudest truths in time, these people who hate so much are telling lies and having others be on their side and then more and more people begin to believe lies and further not see the truth that is trying to get it's attention. and that truth is just to help and inspire people to be themselves and live their life!

and speaking of this book, wow, i have no idea how i'm going to really go about releasing it. i wanted to finish it earlier, but i was losing my battle with trying to make time slow down. i've been too busy all day every day. and today i've been writing for the past 9hours and am still going. i'm in a crazy busy state right now. so, yeah, after this chapter i might have however many more chapters and then i plan to read and maybe edit slightly and then i just have to figure out how to go about getting this book printed before mid december 2013. and i have no idea about anything that will definitely work in regards to how i'm going to go about that right now. and yeah, you could call what i did a "rough draft" and if that's the case then i'm making a "rough draft of a book" into an actual book. and there's a certain level of realness and authenticity if i leave this book as is after one read and a few minor corrections here and there. and i'm basically humanizing this book in a way if i do that. this book has flaws, i have flaws, people have flaws, right?

arthur lugauskas

don't say anything, ever

::::: :::::::::::::::: :: : : : : : :   : : : : : : : : : : : : : : : : :::::::::::::::
chapter 52 : drop the character
::::: : : : : : : : : : :: : : :   : : : : : : :   :::::::::::::::::::::::::::::

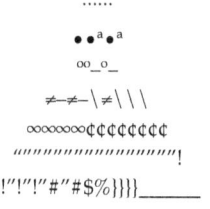

so, yeah, drop the character of akuna? performance is over, right? time to go back to being the normal, humble, quite me? is that what you want? is that what people want? is akuna too much? have i spoken and written too much truth? too much crazy? am i a insane? time to snap out, right? it's over, right? lets stop all this, right? no one wants real honesty, right? right!?

well, first note this, it wasn't easy for me to get to where i'm at right now. and i realized as i was writing this book that my akuna character that i thought i would just jump straight into took some development. i didn't just pop in the gmu school scene like i am today. and my original shyness, humbleness, and quietness never disappeared. how could it? those characteristics are in my genes. when i decided to go into akuna-mode i'm guessing i was less than 36% akuna. and i think each month and semester the percentage increased. i was more outspoken and loud with my thoughts. i was growing and maturing. and note, i had to have lots of conversations with certain people to re-enforce my thoughts and give me layers upon layers of power to the point where no one could tell me anything about how to live my life. i had to be so strong to the point where no nonbelieving dreamkilling person was going to affect me with negativity and with ideas on how i can't do what i want or i can't become who i think i'll be. and even to this day i think this akuna character has only developed up to around 73%. am i serious? yeah, i think there's more development that can be done. but, just getting to where i am right now was seriously no easy task. and getting to the way i think today took a lot of practice, inspiration from things i've heard from dreamers whose dreams have come true, and just pushing through the hating dreamkilling nonbelievers. and i think i like the strength i have in my mind and my thoughts and the confidence that exists in my heart in regards to who i am and what i do.

    so, audience of mine, i don't know. it might be too late. i think akuna has taken over me. after all, akuna has been silently inside me the whole time. just saying things to himself (myself). never being overly outspoken or too loud. never looking for conflict or trouble. always telling the truth, but not laying all the truth that society doesn't want you to say on the table.

but, seriously, at this point i really don't know how much i could regress from akuna, nor do i know if i want to. life has been quite exciting and i've experienced a large array of emotions throwing out some heavy honesty and truth to people. and a lot of crazy and unexpectedness and spontaneity and creativity has happened in the process of living with having certain thoughts and saying them out loud. and listen, i know i've written so many things that are "not allowed" to be said out loud. but, i have the loudest voice right now when it comes to senior show because i'm taking over half the art building with my piop art walls. and i'm here to clear the fog in peoples heads and minds. i'm here to revive dreams! but, but, but, but, should i just stop and go to a quite normal life that doesn't want to help people learn to like themselves? i don't know. telling truth gets addicting. especially saying things you know you're "not supposed" to say. especially saying things that are out of control like the ideas of a child. there's something addicting about being a dreamer and believing. i feel like i have so much power. it's crazy!

   and really, i think i actually lost myself in the realness of having individual thoughts and either i can't get out or don't want to get out of this lost place. because life really is more exciting. but, also harder to live at this point. but, that makes me stronger if i survive each day. and really just everyday is exciting. everyday is full of dynamism. full of activity. full of conversation. full of inspirement.

   and of course, i don't really know if i ever even entered into a performance because i made myself forget if i did in order to pull off the best role i can. therefore, nor i nor you know. right? or do i just pretend not to know? actually funny thing, that's what i say a lot when i'm working or doing things. i seriously keep telling people "i just pretending like i know what i'm doing."

don't say anything, ever

arthur lugauskas

don't say anything, ever

chapter 53 : stream of consciousness

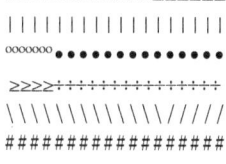

i just love to be creative
and i'm just so amazing
i don't want to hurt anybody
i'm not here to talk bad about anybody
i'm not here to hate anybody
i don't want bad for anybody
i just love to be creative
i want you to be creative
i'm not here to be arrogant
but, if i say i'm the greatest that ever lived

if i say i'm the best in the world
if i say i'm a genius
and in general when i say everything that i say
understand
i say what i say because i mean it
and they say treat others the same way you'd like to be treated
and that's what i do
when i say everything that i say
it means i want you to say those same things
i want you to believe you are the greatest living human
i want you to be amazing
i want you to feel like you can do anything
because i know i can do anything
and i want you to know you can do everything
and then when you say you are the greatest
it's time to prove it
but, only if you want to
but, you should prove it
i'm here to prove my self-proclamations
but, i don't have to
but, i should
and i want to
so, it's not about ego
it's about confidence
it's about dreams
it's about inspiration
it's about everyone believing they can do anything
you can do anything
i know you can do anything
overcome anything
but, it starts with you not being mad at me
it starts with you not hating me
it starts with you loving you

don't say anything, ever

it starts with you not letting the concept of ego
overshadow my true intentions
and my intentions are only good
only positive
only to help
only to tell truth
only to be real
only to inspire
only to give you the power of understanding you can do anything
i'm treating you the way i'd like to be treated
i want you to believe i can do anything
because i believe you can do anything
i believe you can do everything
and i want you to believe i can do everything
so please please please please please
don't take things the wrong way
when i say i'm a superstar
i'm a creative genius
i'm a genius thinker
i'm the future of art
i'm amazing
and all this stuff that society thinks to be arrogant
you now know it's not about arrogance
it's about the concept of possibility
and fun
and creativity
and knowing
and truth
and life
and help
i'm here to help you have the best life you can have
so, every time i speak my mind take it as help
every time i say what i say take it as help
i'm just trying to be an individual

and everyone is an individual
and i want you to be an individual
and not follow what current traditional thinking wants
you to follow
and not follow all of the lies you are told to believe
the only thing you should follow is your heart
and what's real to you
and just be you
don't be scared
just be you
and you are anything you want
you just have to believe that anything is possible
and at the end of the day don't even listen to me
all the answers are inside you
everything you should do in your life is inside you
i'm just trying to help inspire and revive you
but, i'm just words on a page right now
and what's real you can't see right now
but, you can feel it when you live it
don't listen to anyone
because no one knows what you should do
only you know
only you know
only you know

      it's much safer to say things in seclusion, right?
it's easier to think silently, is it not? maybe for some.
maybe for some. you know, i never really "hung out"
with anyone from gmu or my classes. well, with the
exception of maybe one or two people and a few
situations. but, no one really had my phone number. no
one asked me if i wanted to get coffee or "chill" outside
of school. and vice versa, i didn't really ask anyone. and
i don't have a problem with that. we could say it was
part of the plan. of course no one will believe that

probably. what plan, right? my "fake" performance? yeah, i'm sure some people think everything about me is "fake." and i'm sure those people are pretending that i never told them that i've done acting work in the past.

      you know, i felt like no one in school really believed in me. and almost no one believed in themselves. but, i'm sure that i'm that guy ever professor remembers. and i'm here to be that. that person people talk about. that person people just love to be around. that person people hate on behind his back. that person people are maybe secretly jealous of. that person people don't understand. that person people don't want to talk about. that person you can't help but think about. that person who you can't wait for to leave school. that person who is annoying and talkative and arrogant, right? yeah, he doesn't belong. he's *too* different. but, in any case, you're welcome for the excitement of any sort my persona has given you in your life. i guess i was like ledger. really into my role, right? and i felt the realness of the repercussions after saying things i've said. the vast variety of real feelings i felt was pretty crazy.

      and i really expect you all to know that i have no desire to hurt anyone. i have no desire to hate anyone. and trust me, if i were you i probably wouldn't like me too. you're not alone. if i met my "performance self" at a time when i had a certain lack of knowledge i'd probably hate me too. and i also probably wouldn't tell me that i hated me because that would be "mean" and i wouldn't be sure if such a comment could be handled by a real human being. and i'm sure i would probably also talk behind my back. i mean really, who wants to deal with people who think they are all that and have big egos, right? that's what i was "apparently" portraying, right? i'm not stupid. i know exactly who despises me right now. even though you've tried to hide it, you've slipped and i've noticed. but, i don't blame you because i'm sure i wouldn't be that different if i was in your shoes. you know, hate behind doors and stuff. that's the nice way to go about it, right? and yes, there were others who genuinely liked me and what i was about. and thank you people for being honest up front. but, you know, i just had a blast learning and experiencing these different emotions. i've never been really hated on. and it's all about experiencing hate if you want to know what it *actually* feels like. and yeah, it hurts! not a fun experience! but, yes, certainly an eye opening one! there really is an ugly world out there! some people just want to be negative all the time! and some people just care about killing dreams! tisk tisk!

you know, i just want positivity and creativity for the world. i want people to be happy and have fun. life is amazing. and sometimes putting yourself in uncomfortable positions or situations or creating personas could bring unseen excitement in your life and your thoughts and may just inspire you in ways you never imagined during the process of confronting uncomforts. sorry to anyone who thought i was a jerk, or mean, or a selfish person, or someone who thought he's better than everyone else, etc. i just wanted to generate thought generation. i just wanted to stimulate your thoughts and experience certain emotions myself and see how i would conduct my behavior in certain situations. i seriously have no hate for anyone. if you have a dream, no matter how crazy it may be, believe in it and go for it. no matter what anyone says. i want you to believe anything is possible. when i get my diploma i'll probably just look at it as an art piece. has any artist ever had their diploma in a gallery or museum? i don't know.

don't say anything, ever

      there are times when i would look at a mirror see this shy guy, this nice guy, this honest man. and then it's interesting to think how others perceive me. but listen, just letting myself get lost in reality or a dream or this movie of a two year performance you could say was like i was on a movie set for real or it was like i was in a dream, in this fantasy, where anything goes and nothing matters after all school is done. because i've already thought of school as a fantasy world and now i was able to be whoever i wanted in school because afterwards, chances are i'm not going to see 97% of the people i went to school with, had class with, or even saw in school. i really think school gives people an amazing atmosphere to experiment and be creative. especially art school, right? but, i also think that not enough people play enough with that idea of doing anything they want in school and questioning everything and anything that comes their way if they want to.

      and if we really think about everything, aren't all these stories and arguments and blah blah blahs pointless? i'm just a spec on earth. my art is a tiny spec. an art show is also a minuscule spec. what matters? and does anyone actually know what they are doing? seriously. everyone's making stuff up. and think about it, how creative are you? and what are you actually saying? do you even know? you are so limited to using a language with a limited number of words when you are trying to explain something you know, right? come on, you don't know. i don't know. admit it. i'm admitting it. but hey, it's okay to pretend to know, right? well, that's what i do. and i'm aware that i'm pretending to know what i'm doing. and now think about this, how many people aren't aware that they are pretending to know?

a problem i have has to do with this concept of labeling and boxing people in. it's like if you're labeled a student you are looked at as inferior and less knowledgeable and your ideas are less valid compared to professors, right? or at least in most cases. it's crazy. but quickly note, of course there are certain professors that don't label you as below or above them. they are there to help, but not there to tell you exactly what to do. i think very few professors like that exist. and there's a fine balance with teaching art especially i think. because it's the professor teaching the student, right? but, with art and what it can be, which is anything and everything these days, creates turbulence when it comes to teaching. it's funny, students' work is almost never seen to be in a gallery or sold for hundreds of thousands of dollars, right? and why is that? because they're students! it's so crazy. it's like this thing that people follow. its almost disgusting. prime example being my solo show. so, i invited professors, classmates, and miscellaneous people from school. i put up fliers and all this stuff. but, but, but, no one from gmu came to my show. no one i invited. no art students. no classmates. no professors. absolutely no one from school. why? because everyone doesn't like me? no. because my art is bad? no. because everyone happened to be out of town or busy or going to dinner or blah blah blah on the same day? no. the reason no one from school came is because i wasn't "allowed" to have a solo show being a student! that's just "not allowed"! it's like, "no way he can have an actual legit good amazing solo show! he's still a student!" and because he's labeled a student, well, we don't care! it doesn't matter if he has one of the best solo shows the art world has seen and he invited us personally and blah blah blah! he is still a student in our eyes! so, that means everything he does is devalued!

but, you know who did come to my show? college graduates. gmu alumni. older artists who saw me as an artist and not some little student who has no idea what he's doing. i had writers, musicians, creatives, and people just walking past the street come. all the people who came saw me as an artist first and not a student studying art and trying to make it. i even had this girl i knew in high school come and say, "wow, akuna! you're famous now! your name is on the window and everything looks so amazing and all these strings are crazy!" and this was when i was still setting up the show! because if you were there you knew that i wasn't playing around or putting up garbage! i had architects come and art dealers and school teachers! none of them even thought i was a student! none of them! you know why!? because students aren't "allowed" to have art displayed the way i was displaying it out of nowhere to the public eye! so that's something i've learned experiencing so much first hand. as a student, you're "not allowed" to be an artist or have a solo show or be in a gallery or be in a museum or write a book or blah blah blah! as a student you are put into a "student box"! and you have to wait 5-7 years after you graduate to even get the opportunity to make any of your dreams come true! that's what everyone wants you to think! and that's a problem! i've noticed! because listen, when i was in school for the past two years i wasn't considering myself as a student! i did what i wanted how i wanted when i wanted! and there are so many students who draw better than me, paint better than me, craft better than me, but they just don't believe they can be in a gallery in new york just yet. they just don't believe their art is worth hundreds of thousands of dollars just yet. they just don't believe they can make it as an artist. so, what do they do? they settle. they take the safest possible route and put their dreams on hold because society and the art world and the this and that scares them too much. bullies them too much! is so mean and ruthless and tells them they can't do anything just yet! not yet! you have to get better! you're not good enough! keep practicing! blah blah blah! shut the blup up! don't let these "people of power" bully you! blup that!

    then i guess the questions like this would surface: "if you know so much and don't want to be labeled as a student then why did you put yourself in that student box and why are you in school and why do you want to get a degree and why don't you just dropout and etc.?" and well, did i put myself into a student box? is there such things as a student box? "you said there was in the last paragraph!" this student box is a concept thing and i called it that because i learned how certain people view you as a student at school when you have a mentality of, "i'm not here to be just a student who doesn't believe he can be placed in the same category as his professors. i'm here to produce work for the world. and high end work for that matter that competes with the best artists in the world. not just little 'student' work that i consider assignments for grades." do you know what i'm saying? and isn't everyone a student at all times all the time in a way? and why am i in school? because i like school. it's fun. but, yes, it's also a fantasy world. and since i knew that i made school my playground. and because of my juxtaposing genes i was in school and because i had an opportunity to be in school and i thought if i was in school and have this opportunity that i'll have fun with it being in it the way i want to fit in it regardless if i fit or not and i might as well get a degree in the process just in case i feel like going the easier route in life and just getting a job doing something i don't want to do. but, really, it's never been about the degree. and note, all the jobs i've had growing up never required a degree and i've made more money than most of my friends. and it's not about money. if it was about money i wouldn't be having a hard time sleeping at night because of my ideas! making money is easy! i had so many opportunities in past jobs i've had to make a living making hundreds of thousands of dollars! but, i never wanted that because i didn't want to be consumed in a job where my heart wasn't in! and i had too much creativity to give to the world! and now everything i've done has been a gamble thus far! i'm broke right now because all my money goes into gambling on my "creative" career! all the art i've made has been done for free! all my paintings and hours spent doing them were free! all my photography, writings, film makings have been made for free! but, you know what? despite me not caring about money that much, yeah, i'd like to sell my paintings or whatever the case just so i don't have to get a job doing something i don't want to do and so i could have money to do more creative amazing things! and for everyone and the world! understand it's never been about money! it's been about creativity. about experience. about giving you experience. about me experiencing. about truth. about life. but, money is a thing so many people give too high value to. and because of that i want money because if i have money i could trade it in for my ideas. my ideas right now are free, but limited only to my imagination. but, i want everyone to experience the amazing i know i can give the world. and to do that, to bring my dreams to life, to make amazing, people want money. so, i want money so i could give it to people that will help piece together my visions and imaginations and fantasies. but, if i don't have money and people won't help me bring dreams to reality due to no money behind it then i guess i would have to live in my own fantasies and not share amazing with the world and be selfish, right? but, i don't want that! i want to share and if i had all the money in the world and people only wanted money to help me make my dreams come true, then i'd just pay all the money i had to bring my ideas to life!

        now listen, i want all of you to know that i'm that same guy who graduated high school with a gpa higher than a 4.0. yes, higher. and i went to a community college. that says something right there. genius or dumb? i'm that same guy who asked his high school girlfriend to prom in a fortune cookie. yeah, i got the cookies from the restaurant i planned to take her on a particular date, i did my cookie operation taking one note out, writing and printing and then putting another note in, going on our date having the cookies carefully placed in my pocket not wanting them to break, eating, then going to the bathroom and telling the waiter to bring these two cookies that i got and telling him which one was hers, then fortune cookie providing happened and she saw her name on the note and me asking her to prom and then looks at me and says "yes." i'm that same creative guy. and this was years ago. like in 2006. i'm also that same guy who has a license plate on his car that actually fooled a cop because of it's creativity. the cop wrote a parking violation, but missed writing down my actual plate by a letter or number. so, i didn't pay that ticket because it wasn't mine. i'm that same creative guy. i have creativity on my side. and sometimes it's just about what you could do with limitations. i'm that same guy spending less than 200 dollars for senior show, but is taking over "half the building." that's creativity. i'm that same guy who has a full length documentary film with a budget of 0 dollars, but which incorporated locations like a music studio, lighting studio, sculpture studio, drawing studio, gallery space, etc. that's creativity. i'm that same guy who had a solo show that had five mediums harmoniously integrated with one another. i'm that same artist of all those five mediums. i'm that same artist who put up that solo show in two weeks all by himself. that's creativity. i'm that same guy who doesn't know how to write, but is giving you a book that you enjoy reading and can't get enough of or have had more than enough of. that's creativity! i'm that same guy working day in day out tireless sleepless nights alone on this or that project for hours and hours and hours (like nikola tesla) and then the moment i think it's good enough to win something i get criticized as having an ego! what the blup?! do you not have any idea how much time i spent on this!? and i'm "not allowed" to say it's good or it should win this!? like, i'm not hanging out with my girlfriend, i'm not smoking or drinking, i'm not partying, i'm not just watching television, i'm not just chilling, i'm busy working. when you're awake i'm working. when you're sleeping i'm working. and for you to judge so fast as me being arrogant hurts my feelings. it's not about arrogance! and i work on my projects by choice! i want to do these things! i care! if i don't, who will!? if i don't say what i'm doing is great, who will? if i don't believe in me, who will? blup! and if i've been able to pull off everything i've done so far with no money, no time, all by myself, and a small opportunity here and there, imagine if i just had a little bit of money and a little bit of time and a little crew of people helping me and a little bit bigger opportunity. just imagine the things i could do. so, this book also serves as an open invitation to anyone who wants to gamble on me, invest in my ideas, or help me make dreams come true. i have a lot to give to the world and i'm just looking for the opportunities that will allow me to do so at a grand scale. i want to give the world more creativity, more excitement, more good vibes, more experiences, more amazing, more positivity, more inspiration, more smiles, more laughs, more, more, more! and now, after i've built so much with so little, i'm looking for those opportunities. i'm looking for that shot. i'm looking for that chance. and note, i believe in people so much. you see, it's weird for me to think you're not going to accomplish something if you say you want to. even if you say something like i'm going to win this award or that battle or this contest or that something that seems so out of reach. i want to help people in ways many don't help them. i want to help their mind develop further and get them to truly believe they can do anything. a lot of people get mad at me for wanting too much. maybe because they are content with where they are at in life. and maybe that's something hard for me to realize because i don't know how you could just be satisfied with what exists right now. you know, it hurts me when i hear the word "bored." how can you be bored!? please donate some of your time to me. i fear i won't accomplish half the things i want to in one lifetime. if you have time and don't know what to do with it then maybe you have accomplished everything and are the happiest person. if so, then congratulations! but, as for me, i'm looking for time. time is running, disappearing, vanishing before my eyes. and to all the people who are bored and don't feel like they've accomplished everything they wanted i want you to know that there are countless things you can actually do, but you just have to stop being so concerned with what people will think about you if you do proceed in doing what you actually want to do. i know all of you have so much you want to do, but many of you think that what you want to do isn't "cool" enough or whatever. and note, please don't get offended about me saying this or acting like i know it all or whatever. first of all, i don't know it all. and secondly, if you put yourself in this or that category of bored people or whatever the case, understand that you chose to do that and i'm just trying to help you. and you don't have to take my help at all if you don't want to. and if you're not one of those people then don't pretend you are and get mad at me. if you are one of those people don't get mad at me for speaking truth. i don't want to bash on anyones dreams. i just want everyone to know they can do anything.

      and now listen again, i want you to know more. back in the day i was so quite. i never imagined to write a book like this. i used to be overly nice all the time. i used to be afraid of just drinking water from a public water fountain without asking first because i thought if i just went to get a drink i would be like "stealing" water or something. and same thing went with public bathrooms. i used to always just want that confirmation from an employee working at a store that it's okay if i use the bathroom. even though i knew i was allowed to just go and use it without asking, i still asked! and there was this one time when i found a $100 bill on the floor in an empty laundromat, but i just left it there because i thought someone might come back for it. and i'm telling you, the bill was just literally laying there with no one in sight. but, i didn't want to take it because it wasn't mine. i think at one point i almost got crazy and thought about this concept of steeling dust! i never actually went through with that thought or let it affect my experience at a store, but an idea like that did surface in my mind very briefly.

and i want everyone to know that, listen, i know i have flaws. i've said it before and i could say it again, "there are a lot of things i'm not good at!" there are a lot of things i don't know. and as i critique the world and the lack of creativity and imagination i see in some architecture or peoples minds or artworks at fairs or galleries in new york or this or that, please note, that i also critique myself! i zoom out and openly admit that i'm embarrassed of things i've done! i've made horrible art! i used to not know how to dress that well! i had ugly "style"! my writing used to not be like this! i used to be a robot and follow all these rules i thought i had to follow! i've done things i shouldn't have done! i've said things i shouldn't of said! i've been a wimp with girls! i've also been overly confident with girls! i've been a jerk! i've done mean things! i've hurt peoples feelings unintentionally! i've been immature about things! i've been broke! i actually still am broke! i still don't know how to write! i still don't know how to paint! i still pretend to know what i'm doing! i still don't do drugs! i still "am not that cool" because i still don't smoke! i still don't give into peer pressure! but, i am still weak sometimes! and overly confident other times! and i could admit all these things! so, when i say i think something is horrible or i don't think something is that good or whatever the case, understand that it's not coming from a hateful place! it's just honest thoughts! just truth! and i'm not just true with you or you or that work or that! i'm also true with me and my flaws and my mistakes and my horrible art pieces or whatever! please understand what i'm saying!

and i'm putting myself out there right now! after all, i'm the one doing exactly what he wants, i'm the one putting my heart on the page, i'm the one having sleepless nights because i care to deliver the best product possible, i'm the one who cares about truth, i'm the one who believes anything is possible, i'm the one putting myself under the blade right now again and again, i'm the one who is going to be hated because of everything i've written in this book, i'm the one who is going to be misunderstood, i'm the one who actually knows a thing or two, i'm the one who will take criticism and try to get better, i'm the one who asks for help, i'm the one who admits he doesn't know anything, i'm the one who has a car that's over 20 years old that has no heater or air conditioning or power windows or power locks or power steering or windshield washer fluid or crash bumpers or a gps integrated in it or an abs breaking system, i'm the one who's giving you everything that's real and not giving in to what i "should" and "shouldn't" be doing, i'm the one who's in pain right now, i'm the one who has nothing, but sometimes believes he has everything, i'm the one who spends the little money he does attain sometimes on his ideas and art and creativity, i'm the one playing poker as a job right now, i'm the one who's making sandwiches for breakfast, lunch, and dinner because i can't afford to eat out everyday, i'm the one thinking and growing and making mistakes over and over again and taking the hits and shots and getting better as a person, i'm the one getting the compliments and presents and love only sometimes, i'm the one who's been neglected by many, i'm the one who's been appreciated by many, i'm the one fighting this fake cruel world we live in, i'm the one who doesn't give a blup right now, and i'm the one who's about to take over the world because i'm the future of art, i'm the most underrated person today, i'm a genius thinker, i'm living in the future, i'm the future, i'm a superstar, i'm the one with the most ideas, i'm the one who has the most creativity to give, i'm the one who has one bottom line and that is to help people believe that anything is possible and make people know that they can do anything and i want people to know that they can say that they are the one and that they are the future! and note, there is nobody right now that is going to kill my dreams, touch my reality, or tell me what i can or can't do!

    and understand, people always try to tell you what you can and can't do, right? well, next time they try to tell you anything, tell them that they are not you! and that they can't help you be you because the only person who knows what you want to do is you! no one can help you be you! so, next time a hater or dreamkiller tells you why you can't do something, tell them, "i can do anything!" and when they look at you all crazy tell them, "the future of art told me i can do anything!" or "a genius thinker believes i can do anything!" or "akuna told me i can be anything!" and when they look at you even more crazy then just smile at them and know you're right.

    i know i say a lot of ish, right? i talk so much stuff, right? i write whatever i want however i want, right? i know. i know. but, sometimes. honestly, sometimes i just want to fall. and do nothing at all. sometimes i want to let it all go. sometimes i'm standing on the roof of a parking lot and questioning if i want to jump off or fall. sometimes my pain is too real. too severe. sometimes i just don't know if i want to live anymore. sometimes, sometimes. sometimes i feel down and sad and helpless. sometimes i don't see the brighter days. sometimes i put on a smile, but if you look into my eyes all you'll see is pain. but, i put on a smile because you don't need my pain. you don't need my suffering. you don't need my tears. sometimes i want to let everything go. because i just don't know. i just don't know. but, then. but, then. i keep living for some reason. somehow, someway i stay alive. and then i think, "if i almost died, why not live my life like me?" i think, "why don't i just be me?" and then i talk my ish. i be real. i do things that society tells everyone not to. because i love creativity. i love positivity. i love life. and i love to give. to give. to give. and i love to give to all of you. i want you to be happy. i want you to be strong. i want you to survive. i want you to smile. when i'm happy i share my happiness. i give you my positivity. i spread the joy. and you could see it in my eyes. in my actions. in my words. in my life. sometimes i'm on top of the world. but, that's not all the time. i have my pain. i shed my tears. so, now, i just want to ask you. i just want to ask something from you. i just want a hug, a smile, or some love. i just want a simple "hi" from you. if you like anything i'm doing please tell me. please give me encouragement. please let me know. i'm a person. you could actually talk to me. if you have good intentions please talk to me. if i affected you in some positive way please tell me. just give me a high five. just let me know that what i'm saying isn't crazy. all i want is good. i want good for you and good for me and good for everyone and everything. sometimes i just want an opportunity. a chance to make the world better through creativity on a major scale. i just want to open peoples eyes to possibilities. so, if you like what i'm doing just give me a simple "thank you."

    and sometimes i just want to be back in elementary school and live those days when i was learning about the h brothers. you know, th, sh, ch, and wh? or learning how to play the flute. and liking this one girl named makenzie, but never telling her that because i was too shy. it was so easy to not say anything. being quite was so easy. life was so peaceful. sometimes i wish i was 5 years old again. because when i was 5 years old all i cared about was drawing tree houses at home, building sand castles at the beach, and playing freeze tag on the grass with friends. or sometimes i wish i was 7 years old again. because when i was 7 years old and i told my mom or friends or family or random people that i wanted to be an action figure and an actor and a musician and a police officer and a skateboarder and a nice person and a racecar driver and a this and a that and all they said was, "go for it!" all they said was, "i hope all your dreams come true!" all they said was, "you could do it!" all they said was, "you can be anything!" but, all i hear now from people is, "how could you possibly think you can be everything!?" all i hear now is, "what makes you think you can be anything!?" all i hear now is, "stop trying so hard!" and i just feel like i'm getting shot at and looked down on and discriminated against and getting eaten alive. or sometimes i wish i was 12 years old again. because when i was 12 years old i was living in one room in my uncles two bedroom condominium with my mom, dad, older brother, and younger brother and in the other room resided my uncle, aunt, and their two young boys and all i did was not complain and be happy to be alive and play outside with my brothers and cousins. or sometimes i wish i was back in middle school. because in middle school all i cared about was playing basketball and skateboarding and walking a girl i liked home. sometimes i wish i could relive my childhood. because being an adult is hard. no, being an adult with a childlike creativity is hard. being an adult who chooses to walk his own path in life just like he did when he was a kid is hard. being an adult who just wants to have his real honest true ideas come to fruition makes him ostracized. so, that's why i say sometimes i just want to fall and do nothing at all. because this world is so fake with everyone telling lies and acting like children could be anything, but treating the grown up looking versions of kids like they're crazy for having thoughts of being able to be anything. because as an adult you are not allowed to say anything! because when you say you want to be everything people tell that you can't be anything! because when you're an adult and say you made up a new form of art, people want to tell you why you're not allowed to do such a thing. because when you're an adult and you say you don't really know what you're doing, people want to tell you that you should know. because when you're an adult and you say you have drams to other adults, those adults tell you why you can't achieve you're dreams. those adults try to make you feel like you'll never become better than a frank gehry. those adults tell you to be followers and not leaders. those adults tell you to go to museums because since they've never seen the art you're doing they think that you shouldn't do it and instead of encourage what you do they tell you to go to museums and follow what other artists have done or are doing. because those adults don't want you to be an individual. or real for a change. because those adults look down on you when you say, "i going to be famous!" and those are the adults who let their dreams die and allowed their ideas to be torn up into pieces and then they joined the dreamkilling squad and are out there to annihilate anyone who has a dream to do something more in life than just settle. because when you're an adult and you say anything, then you lose everything.

    or, you know, sometimes i think about what would of happened if i never broke up with my first girlfriend 10 years ago on the day before valentines day.

and note, i didn't even know i did what i did on the day
that i did what i did. i wonder what would of happened
if i never broke her heart out of the blue. maybe i
would've never met my next girlfriend and then my
next girlfriend and then my next girlfriend. and maybe i
wouldn't of had a broken heart again and again and
again. and maybe i would've never got that phone call
from my friend the other day saying that my ex
girlfriend just passed away just yesterday because she
had cancer. and this ex i talk about was the first next.
and when my friend told me the news i realized that i
hadn't seen or spoken to her in over 5 years. over 5
whole years. because when it's over, it's over, right?
and i was no longer the guy that she liked. and when i
got over her and she emailed me she was no longer the
one that i liked. but, nonetheless, after i heard the news i
went to her family. i went to her sisters. i went to her
mother. i went with my mother. and i hugged all of
them. we hugged all of them. because we all knew each
other over 5 years ago. and then it was time to go to the
funeral. and all this happened just a few weeks ago.
and sometimes i think if my next girl never ended it
with me i would've never met my next next girl.
because when i was this next next girl i had a lot more
confidence. and i started working a lot more on my art
and things like that. and at first i didn't like her that
much. and she'd ask me why we didn't go on dates
anymore. she'd tell me that all we did was have sex all
over. she'd tell me, she'd tell me, she'd tell me that she
loved me. and all i told her was that i missed her. all i
did was not tell her i loved her after she told me that she
loved me because i didn't know what love was and i
didn't want to lie. and maybe the tables would've never
turned. and maybe everything i did would've never
backfired so hard. maybe if i went on a little more dates

and had a little less sex, just maybe i would've never dealt with another shattered heart. all in pieces and smithereens. maybe i should've told her that i loved her after she told me that she loved me. maybe instead of sometimes saying nothing i should've said everything or just something. i don't know. i don't know. but she left me. and then she left the country. and was gone gone gone. and my heart was torn torn torn. and then i realized that i lover her. but, it was a little bit too late. she had already gotten with another guy and i was left to drown in my own tears. and maybe if i never got hurt by my next next girl, just maybe, just maybe i would've never met my next next next girl. maybe i wouldn't of done everything right in a relationship for once in my life. maybe i wouldn't of been the happiest, most positive, most smiling man on the planet. but, only temporarily. only temporarily. because one day she gave me a phone call and ended everything out of the blue. but, she said it wasn't out of the blue. and i thought i did everything right. we went on dates. i made her laugh. i encouraged her to do and be anything. i took time off from work to spend some quality time with her. i did what i thought i should. i did what i believed i should. and she was the one and only girl whom i ever told that i loved. and once she left me i questioned everything. i questioned everything. i questioned living. i questioned breathing. i questioned even smiling. and to this day i don't smile the same. no no no, my smile has never been the same. because all i feel these days is pain. if you ever stopped and looked into my eyes you could see emptiness. and sadness. and nothingness. and the last time, last time, last time i saw my last girlfriend i remember that she told me that she didn't want to be with me because she didn't love me. because she didn't love me. she didn't love me. she told me the truth, the truth, the truth. and i appreciate her honesty. but, i don't know why i don't know why i don't know why why why. she didn't tell me why. she said that the spark just died. and i couldn't grasp that. i still can't grasp that. and then she hinted at me telling me that if she had to tell me just maybe maybe a little maybe in regards to why then it might just maybe maybe maybe be because i dream too much and i believe all my dreams can come true. and now that's all i have. my dreams my dreams my dreams. dreams and dreams. because i can't control anybody. but, i could maybe kind of sort of control me. and i'm still so in love with somebody. and that somebody isn't me. and all i really have today are my dreams. my dreams. my dreams. so, when anybody tries to come at me and attack my dreams and tries to tell me why i can't become who i want to become, what am i to do? let them kill me!? huh!? while they're happy living the ultimate dream, which is with their girlfriend or boyfriend, husband or wife! am i supposed to just accept what they say i can or cannot do!? huh!? trust me when i say this, i'd rather be with the one i love! i'd rather be in love with the one i love and have the one i love love me back! but, since that option has been eliminated for me, what am i supposed to do!? just accept a sad life and go to sleep crying every night!? huh!? so, all i ask for, all i ask for, all i ask for is a little bit of encouragement. a little bit of love. just a little smile. just a little hug. just a little less hate. just a little thank you for trying to make the world a better place. just a little thank you for trying. and i remember, i remember, i remember what my last girlfriend said to me. she said, "it's going to be okay. you'll be okay. whether you like it or not, you'll be okay." and i want her to know that i'm a little itty tiny teeny super small little itty itty itty bit okay. i'm a little

little little little little tiny tiny bit okay. and the only reason is because of the people reading this book. because of the people who were there for me. because of the people who are here for me. because of the little bit of support and opportunity and smiles i've gotten. because of my dreams that keep me up at night. i have these dreams that keep me up at night. but, sometimes i just want a normal life. a normal life with a wife and kids and some love. sometimes i just want a normal life. and trust me, you don't want my life. because i have too many dreams that keep me up at night. i have so many dreams that keep me up at night. my dreams keep me up all night. and i won't go to sleep tonight. because my dreams keep me up at night…(author breaks into tears)

arthur lugauskas

don't say anything, ever

chapter 54 : important chapter

≠
»
?
¡
`
˘
√

    we get to the end. or maybe we're just somewhere. is this all real? is this book fake? we get to questions. and well, i'm not ready to answer these questions. or i don't want to right now. so please don't ask if what i wrote in here is real or not. i'm sure you have your opinion and i'm happy about that. instead of asking me stuff please ask anyone else who has read this book and analyze together. i like the art of conversation and especially conversation with strangers. or strangers with similarities. with technology these days it's like people don't know how to talk anymore. and note, i'm probably willing to talk about other things with you, but not about this book right now. go see if all the evidence i laid out is true. go on your own journey of discovery if you want. your journey to find the truth. ask anyone who may be a person in this book and ask them about whether my information about that point in time with them is true or false. converse. talk. think. enjoy.

     and listen, i'm not dumb and i know most of the things i've written i'm "not supposed" to be saying out loud. where do you think i got the blupping title of this book from!? another thing, i'm sure a lot of people will hate me for this book, but why? all i'm doing is playing. playing with the world. poking at the world. like, yes, literally poking at the world. i'm this kid having fun. you could be a kid having fun, right? yes you could. i'm telling you that you can. that means you can. i mean look at playgrounds. they are the most colorful dynamic creative "offices" for kids. and now look up "office building." those are the most boring uninviting places that kids would never be attracted to. kids would probably be like, "yuck, look at those colorless buildings." have fun and put some dents in the universe, right? or in peoples thoughts, right? yes, throw some dents in there. or fix some dents. whatever. have some fun in this world. you don't need to be so serious. have fun with words, with experiences, with anything. this book is an experience for you. call yourself anything. and to make things more fun, say some stuff out loud. so people can hear. have fun with people. and tell people they could have fun. i've been saying "have fun" for years now to people. i don't know how many actually listened. this book is about fun. about writing. about being a kid and thinking of something and doing it. it's like these days people don't do what they think. and then when they think of something else, they don't do that something else either because they are too concerned with the worst that could happen. then they have all these thoughts locked up in the vault. what if you did some of the things you thought of. especially the ones you think are the "dumbest"? what would happen. too many people think of great things, but are to scared to do them, so they live a life with fear taking over them and then they become afraid of everything and then they get a job or whatever where they do things others want them to do. sounds crazy, right? but, what if you believed you had to do what you thought of without any other "forces" or "bosses" telling you that you have to? maybe you'd end up like me writing a book like this. i don't know. just think and enjoy thought and then do action and enjoy experience.

      so, whats next for me? well, i've been thinking about just leaving the country and just working on finishing other books i've started over the years. i feel like i have so much unfinished work in every field i've touched. it's crazy! just in books alone, let me see, i have one about my time in japan, then another about creating artist masterpieces, then another about practicing, and then another about losing a championship. yeah, something like that. and note, i just gave you an abstract idea of what some of my next books are about. but if you know me then you know that the books i'm talking about are very different from one another and, umm, i really don't want to reveal much about them right now. just understand that they are all different, very different, but are connected in this genius and beautiful way. and you could see them as extended stories extracted from this book in a way. yeah, something like that. i really want to tell you what they are about and their titles and stuff, but i'm holding back. not yet. just know i have creative, fun, storytelling, unique, interesting, books in the works. so, yeah, maybe i'll finally give them the time they deserve and finish writing them and release them sooner than later. and i have plenty other written material to let out to the world and other book ideas and blah blah blah. but, the four books i mentioned earlier are ones that i'm pretty excited about. and it's probably not going to be easy to write one of them. or all of them. and note, i think these books i want to finish and release can inspire and ignite creativity and thought and excitement. and each book has its own flavor and is unique and individualized, but real and by me. so, just wait. more excitement is coming. my pain is your pleasure. and i have a lot of pain, so you'll be getting a lot of pleasure.

but, i've also been thinking about moving to ny or la if i stay in the usa. or maybe sf. i really don't know. but, if i leave the country i was thinking about going to london. just maybe. just maybe to all those options. or maybe i'll go somewhere else. or maybe not. i really don't know.

quick thing. so, i've said that my documentary is my introduction to the art world. and while, yes, that is true, it is ultimately about something else. and i'm not ready to reveal that to the world. i have to stay one step ahead of you, you know. or who knows, maybe you're one step ahead of me. but, maybe i'm one step ahead of that step of yours. are you laughing? just laugh. but, yes, what my documentary is ultimately about is unknown to anyone except myself and three other people. that's it for now. wait for future books. i may reveal information then. just maybe i'll connect the dots in ways you've never seen them connected before. just wait. you never know who i'll be or where i'll be. or who i am or where i am. or maybe i'm just wrong. i don't know.

    but, i do know something i actually care about. i really do care about helping people believe anything is possible. and i care about peoples dreams and what they actually truly honestly want in life. so often times when i converse with some people i try to take off all those layers of built up gunk in their thoughts and head and brain. and after i do that with a series of questions and just improvised conversation i try to find the light and see their true dreams. and then i try to take the conversation into a mode of trying to inspire them to revive what they let go or lost or neglected, but deep down inside truly desire and want and care for. i try to promote and encourage people in letting them know that they can achieve what they aspire for. no matter how "out of reach" or "fantastical" or "embarrassing" or whatever it may be. i don't have bad intentions. i want good for the world, good for people, good for all. i care about truth, honesty, fun, positivity, bringing joy to the world, making people smile, making beautiful girls laugh, etc. i just really want you to believe in whatever you want to believe and be whoever you want to be. and i know i've reiterated some statements or words or ideas or whatever many times. just take those things like imagery in a movie. or a common theme. reminders. you know, stuff like that. it's not so much to be repetitive, it's to get the positive message across. you know, that concept of repetition or repeating things until they become second nature. stuff like that. i really just want you to protect your dreams, protect your thoughts, believe in your ideas, and believe in yourself.

    and i have a few other things i want to say. one day i was talking with a writer and i told her that i was working on books. and then she hit me with the question, "what kind of books?" and i questionably said, "creative ones?" i didn't know how to respond. i don't know about "book world." and then she hit me with a real stumper and asked, "well, who is your audience?" and i was caught so off guard. i thought, "there's an audience i should sought after? what?" and then it just hit me and i responded, "hmm, well i think my audience is actually people who 'don't' read. i consider myself as a person who 'doesn't' really read. and i'm writing books i'd like to read. i'm not so interested in following whatever things about writing that exist. well, actually i shouldn't say that because i don't really know anything about books or writing or publishing or stuff like that. i just like writing whatever i want and writing stories. and i find my writing super human and simple to read. i don't know if it fits into any particular category. i think my writing is just likable. and the reason i don't really read books is because i find most books 'hard' to read. or 'too professional'. or whatever the case. so, yeah, interesting, i think if i had to choose an audience my writing would be welcomed in then i think it would be all those people who say they 'don't' read. and i think that's most people. so, that would make my audience huge. but, it's funny because it doesn't make much sense, right? why would someone who 'doesn't read' actually read something? because my writing is the easiest and funnest to read maybe. but, understand that i'm not limiting my audience to the 'nonreaders'. i certainly believe the people who do read would find great pleasure eating up my writings and short stories and books. so, am i saying my audience is everyone? perhaps." and i thought my response was super cool. because if i was, say, in high school and a teacher told me, "there's this author who writes these super conversationalist entertaining simple and complexly easy, but engaging, fun, but smart, and with deep knowledge and creativity books for those who say they 'don't read'" i would probably want to read the first few sentences.

      and you know, i don't know what to expect when i'm writing. in a way, my writing can be spontaneous. or really spontaneous. kind of like my art, actions, and life at some points in time. but, then i'm sure there's structure too. this balance of chaos and stability. right? maybe? and i think my writing is simple. probably illiterate people can read what i write. but, understand that my ideas have fields and valleys of depth. and my ideas are for everyone. for any mind. and i honestly think what i've written here can help people. and really, with what i've written in this book, my main intent was to take you on a roller coaster ride of emotions. i wanted to take you up and down and around and back and here and there and everywhere. just have your brain going haywire. and i really do appreciate your time and i hope this was the best book you've ever read in your life. i hope i took you places other books haven't taken you. i hope i gave you personalities and characters to love and hate and appreciate and cry with and morn for and laugh at and joke with and poke at and etc. at. and i really hope you just had a good time and had fun reading. something else, i do try to make and want my writing to be powerful and impactful and i want it to hit you like no writing has ever hit you before. like, if you hate some things in this book, good! i want to maximize your array of emotions. it's like, you know when you watch a movie and you just hate the villain and want him to die!? yeah, i want my book to be that impactful and i want it to feel that real for you as you read it. of course, i don't want you to go out there killing anyone or hurting anyone or anything like that. i just want to create a real world in your head. and again, i really want this to be the most exciting book you've ever read in your life. i want you to feel everything i've felt writing it and i want you to be so sucked into this book. i want you to feel every emotion that exists to the highest degree. i want to please your senses and your brain through written material. i want to turn up those nobs in your head when it comes to how you feel. my writing really is like a roller coaster. you know and never know what to expect. and i'm not here to keep you thirsty. i'm wetting this page. actually please wet this page with filtered water from a wine glass right now. and wet it in any way you want. put the water in your mouth first and spit it out. or just splash the water on. my writing is here to quench your thirst! i'm feeding you entrees! and giving you the best and worst dessert you've ever tasted in your life! and at the end of the day, i'm really just having fun and being a kid who does what he feels like doing. i felt like writing this book and i did. i felt like putting sentences together in a certain way with words and i did. and i hope you've had an experience reading everything i've written. and now, to be real, this book is actually about one word that i've purposely not written anywhere in this book at all. and the word should maybe be so obvious. you want to know what all of this is *actually* about? well, since i'm guessing we are on the same page right now maybe i should let you write down what you think. does that sound good? okay, ready? this is all about _ _ _ _ _ _ _ _ _ _

don't say anything, ever

thank you

arthur lugauskas
november 24, 2013 12:34am

www.ingramcontent.com/pod-product-compliance
Lightning Source LLC
Chambersburg PA
CBHW051758170526
45167CB00005B/1797